The Yankee Way

PLAYING, COACHING, AND
MY LIFE IN BASEBALL

WILLIE RANDOLPH

Willie Randolph

The Yankee Way

The Yankee Way

PLAYING, COACHING, AND MY LIFE IN BASEBALL

WILLIE RANDOLPH

*it***books**

AN IMPRINT OF HARPERCOLLINS PUBLISHERS

THE YANKEE WAY. Copyright © 2014 by Willie Randolph. All rights reserved. Printed in the United States of America. No part of this book may be used or reproduced in any manner whatsoever without written permission except in the case of brief quotations embodied in critical articles and reviews. For information address HarperCollins Publishers, 10 East 53rd Street, New York, NY 10022.

HarperCollins books may be purchased for educational, business, or sales promotional use. For information please e-mail the Special Markets Department at SPsales@harpercollins.com.

FIRST EDITION

Designed by Renato Stanisic

Library of Congress Cataloging-in-Publication Data has been applied for.

ISBN 978-0-06-145077-8

14 15 16 17 18 OV/RRD 10 9 8 7 6 5 4 3 2 1

For my wife, Gretchen,
your love and support made this all possible

For my mom and dad, whose work ethic and
determination taught me to be a better ballplayer

Contents

For the Love of the Game

I n one way or another, I've been involved in the game of professional baseball since I was first drafted in 1972. That's more than forty years. In that time I've seen a lot of changes in the game, everything from stadiums to salaries, from equipment to egos.

One thing has remained constant.

I've always loved the game of baseball.

Still do.

And that doesn't mean that I loved the game only when I was participating in one of the eleven World Series championships I was blessed to take part in. I loved it when I was an eighteen-year-old warm-weather city kid freezing my butt off and enduring one of the worst slumps of my life in what seemed the frozen tundra of Thetford Mines, Ontario. I loved it when I was a twenty-two-year-old kid watching Chris Chambliss lead off the bottom of the ninth in game 5 of the American League Championship Series (ALCS) against the Royals with the loudest 372-foot home run ever hit. That ball carried the Yankees back into the Series for the first time in a dozen years and triggered the wildest celebration I have ever seen. I even loved the game when the dreaded Boston Red Sox did the unthinkable and climbed up off the mat and won four straight against us in the 2004 ALCS. Fifteen days later, I was still in love with the game when, at the age of fifty, I became the first black manager in New York baseball history.

And yes, even in the early morning hours of June 18, 2008, when Omar Minaya was too upset to say the words "You're fired," I still loved the game and still wanted to be a part of it.

I would have loved the game and the city of New York even if I'd never advanced to play anywhere beyond the sandlots of Prospect Park in Brooklyn. The taste of a cold Champagne Cola drunk outside of Jimmy's Grocery Store to celebrate the first victory with the Bullets (my first youth league team) might not be as memorable to some as a champagne shower in the bowels of old Yankee Stadium, but for me the memory is just as fresh.

The saying goes that the heart knows what it wants. From the first time I saw and heard Mets games on the radio and television, I knew exactly what I wanted to do—play that game and have my name called. I can still hear the voices of Ralph Kiner and Lindsey Nelson, still feel the powdery tang and the stale snap of baseball card chewing gum, and still hear the echoes of me and my buddies haggling over trades as I coveted my Donn Clendenon, Tommie Agee, Roy McMillan, and Jerry Koosman cards. No day was better than the ones I spent at Shea Stadium as a kid. Money was always tight around the Randolph house, so we had to do some turnstile jumping and take advantage of some of the charity programs that offered neighborhood kids free tickets. Regardless of how I got in there, looking down on that green diamond was like looking down on the carpet of some Taj Mahal compared to the dust and clumps I was used to playing on.

You've got to love a game and a city a whole lot to forsake one of the blessings that your parents bestow on you. I was mostly a well-behaved child—and my parents wouldn't have tolerated anything but—yet I told everybody that my name was Mickey.

I have old friends who still call me Mickey. When I'm in Houston, I'll often leave tickets for my dear old friend Lou Rodriguez, who lives in Texas now. As soon as I heard a voice calling, "Mick," from behind home plate in Minute Maid, I knew Lou was in the house. When I was at Tilden High School, I even signed myself "Mickey Randolph" on forms I had to fill out. I wouldn't be surprised if I signed my name as Mickey on my first driver's license.

"That's what we thought your name was for years," said Joe Laboy, who I played ball with from age thirteen, and who is now an appliance salesman.

I thought Mickey was a cool name. I was a Mets fan, sure, but you have to be flexible in life, and Mickey Mantle was a New York baseball icon. Like the real Mick, I was a switch-hitting shortstop back in the day, until I went all-righty when I was about thirteen. Even though he was a white man from Commerce, Oklahoma, and I was a black kid from Brooklyn, New York, even though he learned to hit against a battered tin shed and I learned to hit against a graffiti-covered project wall, in my mind we were practically blood brothers, bound together by our stances and our speed and my overactive imagination.

I first met the real Mickey in the spring of 1976 when I came over to the Yankees in the Pirates trade. He walked in the clubhouse, blond and brawny as ever, with the blacksmith forearms and the big smile. What are you supposed to say when you meet a baseball god? I don't know how I greeted him, but I'm sure I stammered a lot. I definitely didn't tell him that I imitated his stances or that I claimed his name for my own. It would've been way too embarrassing. Now that I think about it, Mickey must have loved the game as much as I did, and I think he would have understood why I claimed his name off the waiver wire.

My teachers and my family didn't call me Mickey, but around Betsy Head Playground it was all I heard. Betsy Head was my home away from home as a kid. Set in the heart of Brownsville, the ten-acre park was built in 1915 with money from a British philanthropist named— guess what?—Betsy Head. The park won awards when it opened, but Betsy wouldn't have been too pleased to see it fifty years later. The place was full of broken bottles and garbage, and when you dove for a ball you needed to make sure you didn't land on a syringe. It takes a lot of love to stretch your body out on such a potentially dangerous surface, but a base hit is a base hit and it was my job to prevent them.

The park had a Little League field at one end and a full-size field at the other, with intersecting outfields. The infields made Thetford Mines look pristine. There were enough rocks to start a quarry, and there was no such thing as a true bounce. If you could catch ground balls at Betsy Head, you could catch ground balls anywhere. I took bad hops in the face, head, you name it, but it made my hands good and it made them quick. Back then we didn't even pay any mind to the conditions of the field. Betsy Head was where my teams played. It's not as if we had a lot of options. Besides, being on the Betsy Head infield beat almost every alternative. As my friend Phil Davis said, "Sports was the way we got away from the real devils in life. Between that and church and school, we didn't have time to get into the devils that were out there."

I also played a lot of football when I was a kid. The surface was usually asphalt, and my position was always quarterback. Our neighborhood team was called the 19ers. The name made perfect sense. We got our shirts at a place called John's Bargain Store—the local five-and-dime. We bought every football shirt John had on his shelves. The only problem was that they were all the same number: 19 (drove those fledgling defensive coordinators nuts). We used to barnstorm around Brownsville, challenging other teams to games, and though you can't look it up, the 19ers did not lose very often.

I liked basketball too, but baseball had a hold on me all its own. The first book I read was *The Jackie Robinson Story,* and before I was even on chapter 2 I think I knew I wanted to be like Jackie, wanted to play in the big leagues. (Who knew I would wind up playing his position?) I'd watch every Mets game on TV and do batting stances in front of a full-length mirror in between innings and after the game. If I didn't have a real bat—and I usually didn't—the curtain rod would work just fine. Henry Aaron, Willie Mays, Stan Musial, Roberto Clemente, I did them all, and Rod Gaspar too. Years later my wife, Gretchen, told me that when we were younger she would often sit on a bench in the projects at night and look up at my apartment and see the silhouette of me doing Donn Clendenon and Jerry Grote and all my other stances in the window. She was completely loyal even then.

And I was loyal to the game despite all the pressures to stray from it and my idealized version of what an athlete should be. My stance show started early and went late, except if I had a game the next day. If I had a game, I was in bed early. I knew nothing then about big league ballplayers' carousing or after-hours exploits. To me, if you wanted to be an athlete, you didn't drink, smoke, mess around with drugs, or hang out in the projects. You went to bed, got your rest. You made sure you were ready to play the next day.

And I was.

My friends would call up to my window ("Yo, Mickey, c'mon out with us") and apply every wrestling hold of peer pressure they could, but I never weakened. I just went to bed.

For the love of the game, I traveled all over Brooklyn and the city playing ball, on too many teams to count, from Our Lady of Mercy to Funelaria Cruz. The coach I remember most was the late Galileo "Gally" Gonzalez. Gally reinforced my love of baseball through close contact with his. He didn't want to have anyone on his team who didn't think the same way he did—that baseball was a great gift we should all cherish. He was a stocky man with a gravelly voice, graying hair and a mustache, and the leathery, sunbaked skin that so many baseball lifers have. He wanted to win every game. Bad. He yelled at us all the time and cursed in two languages. His practices were nasty. He'd make us play in close on the Betsy Head infield and then would smash grounders at us. You got smacked in the head, you shook it off, kept going. There was no other choice, really. Gally brought a football mentality to coaching baseball. He didn't believe in softies.

There was a kid on our team once—I don't remember his name—who didn't take to Gally's hard-driving ways, and after getting reamed out by Gally one day, he stood out in right field, crying. No one said a word as Gally strode slowly out toward second base, then into the outfield. The poor kid must've been petrified. I tensed up as I watched Gally walk out there like a sandlot sheriff. I wondered how rough on the kid Gally was going to be. I hoped he might sympathize with him or at least cut him a break. Hoped that Gally would finally back off a little.

Gally arrived in front of the kid. Backing off, apparently, was not in his mind-set.

"If you are going to cry, you better leave right now, because I don't want no crybabies on my team," Gally said.

Gally wanted to make you a man. He wanted to make you tough. I was almost always the youngest guy on the team, and one of the smallest. He cut me no slack, made me painfully aware that my love of the game could bring me joy or pain and sometimes a bit of both at the same time. Looking back at it now, I think Gally sensed how much I loved playing ball, thought I had potential, and was determined to be harder on me than anyone.

When I'd go off to play ball on a Saturday morning, there were times I wouldn't be back until the end of the day, so my mom would make a sandwich for me. She packed it up nicely and put it in a brown paper bag. I was very protective of my sandwich. It made me feel good knowing it was there, that my mom made it for me. One day Gally walked down the bench, reached down, and snatched the lunch bag out of my hands.

"Hey, what are you doing?" I shouted. "That's my sandwich!" This was way out of character for me to speak to an adult this way. But I was shocked by Gally's actions and reacted accordingly.

"I'm giving it to somebody else," Gally said.

"You can't do that. That's mine. My mother made it for me."

Gally looked at me with a half-sneer. He paused a minute, my sense of violation building by the second.

" 'Oh, my mother made it for me,' " he said, mocking my voice. "The little momma's boy wants his sandwich."

He still had my bag in his hands. He showed no sign of giving it back and, in truth, seemed to be enjoying this. I didn't know what to do or say. I started to cry, and that was all Gally needed to see, because as we know, he had no use for crybabies. So then he made fun of me for crying, in front of the whole team. I felt completely humiliated. He was wrong to be doing this to me. The contents of that bag were much more important to me than the nutritional value of the bologna and two pieces of bread. I didn't care how much Galileo wanted to get into my head or toughen me up. This wasn't fair. He was stealing my lunch, not to give to another kid who was hungry—that would've been different—but just because he knew how important it was to me and somehow saw that as a sign of softness. Part of me wanted to storm off and never come back and play for him.

That day, it turned out, would come soon enough.

I will say this for Gally: there definitely was a method to his madness. He wanted me to be able to handle anything. He wanted me to go out there with a full suit of emotional armor so that nobody, no turn of events, could touch me. In his mind, love of the game could have been a weakness, could have made me too soft. Loving the game was one thing, but loving to win was another. The two often go together, but not always. I didn't have to be taught either kind of love, and in time the two became nearly inseparable.

Gally didn't want to win two out of three, or three of four. He wanted to win every game, and he'd be all over our butts if we didn't comply. Gally was a Billy Martin of the barrio, hypercompetitive and feisty to the core. He believed that winning was a habit, same as losing. He never let up. For that reason, I'm not sure he ever forgave me for what I did when I was fifteen years old.

I knew a guy from the Tilden Houses named Frank Tepedino, who was the groundskeeper, the man who tended to the flowers and mowed the grass and kept it looking really nice. We had our share of run-ins with him, because we were forever hopping his chain-link fence to get onto a little patch of grass to play ball. Mr. Tepedino, the uncle of a Yankee first baseman by the same name, got tired of chasing us off, and one day he called a few of us over. I thought we were really in for it this time.

"I coach an American Legion team called Cummings Brothers Post," he said. "If you guys love to play so much, why don't you bring your bats and gloves and come down for tryouts this Saturday? We have a good team, and we play a good level of competition. I don't know if you know the Parade Grounds, but that's where we play our games."

The Parade Grounds was a complex of ball fields in Brooklyn's Prospect Park. It was where Sandy Koufax and Frank and Joe Torre and all the Brooklyn greats played. I didn't know much more about it, except that I would be there that next Saturday. I got up early, took a subway and a bus, and went to the tryout. When I stepped into the complex, I felt as though I had come upon a whole new baseball world. The fields were smooth and manicured. They had lines and dugouts. They had on-deck circles! Compared to what I was used to, this was Shea Stadium. Hell, this was Shangri-La.

From that moment, I knew that I wanted to play there.

The tryout went well, and soon I had a new team and Cummings Brothers Post, a fraternal organization established in honor of two young brothers who died in World War I, had a new shortstop and leadoff man. It wasn't just the field I liked. It was that the competition was better, and more than anything, it was a place where big-league scouts were known to come by and watch you play and, if they liked you, maybe even give you one of their little calling cards.

It was a great opportunity, the only trouble being that now I would have to deal with the wrath of Galileo Gonzalez. He had nurtured me and toughened me—he had stolen my sandwiches. Now somebody else was going to benefit from that. I knew Gally was going to like this about as much as losing a doubleheader. But I had to talk to him. I found him in Betsy Head Park. Like a guy about to break up with one girl because he had fallen for another, I was really nervous as I walked up to him.

"Gally, can I talk to you for a minute?" I began.

"What's going on?"

"Well," I said, "I tried out for a team in the Parade Grounds. They want me to play for them, and I think I'm going to do it." Gally's face went blank at first. He took in what I said for a few seconds, and then his face quickly turned flush with anger. He didn't want to hear anything more.

"Why you going there?" he said. "Why? They don't want you. They don't want no kid from the projects. They've never wanted no kids from here. Why you wasting your time? Why would you leave our team to go play for strangers?"

He didn't call me Benedict Arnold. But he might as well have. I knew I wasn't going to be able to soften the blow. I just tried to speak from the heart.

"I'm sorry, Gally," I said. "I don't want to leave my friends. I don't want to leave you and my team. But the Parade Grounds is where the best players from Brooklyn have always played. You know that. You know it's the place to play and where the competition is the best. I'm sorry. I am really sorry, but I just think I have to do this."

He mumbled something and then turned and walked away. It was the last conversation I ever had with Galileo Gonzalez.

Now, understand that loyalty is huge to me. Was then and is now. The idea of being disloyal to Gally and my teammates weighed heavily on me, but when it got down to it, I knew I had to go. My dream was to make the big leagues. Cummings Brothers was going to give me more games on better fields against better players. It was going to get me out there in front of the scouts—the white men with their sun visors and clipboards and beach chairs who could make my dream happen. For years I'd seen guys who were great players—better players than me— who didn't want to leave the neighborhood and never wound up going anywhere. These were guys I admired and looked up to. They stayed in the neighborhood, and then their baseball careers stayed in the neighborhood too. As terrible as I felt about leaving, my gut was telling me that this was something I had to do.

And you know what? I never regretted it.

All these years later, it's very humbling to think about that time of my life and to think about my good fortune, to wonder why I was the lucky one, why I was the one who made it to the big leagues when guys like Joe Laboy and Blackie Ortiz and Georgie Cruz—my baseball brothers—did not. These were friends I played alongside for years, guys I learned from, guys who could really play the game. Georgie Cruz could pick it better than me at shortstop, better than just about anybody I ever saw. Joe Laboy could do it all, and Blackie Ortiz, well, he may have been the best of all. Blackie was an undersized first baseman, maybe five-foot-seven or -eight, but he had the quick and powerful wrists that all great hitters have, and he could hit the ball out of anywhere. Blackie was a hell of a ballplayer. The Mets invited him to a tryout at Shea Stadium, and he did really well, even had a scout tell him he was definitely pro material. The Mets asked for his schedule, then found out almost all of his games were at Betsy Head.

Scouts didn't go to Brownsville. It was too dangerous. Blackie never got drafted. He's been a motorman for the New York City subway system for twenty-five years.

I'm not discounting the work I put in to make it to the majors, because I put in a ton of it. I was as dedicated to the sport as a kid could be. But there's more to it than that. I believe God had a plan for me, and I believe I have been incredibly blessed to be able to follow that plan. I believe I had the good fortune to stay healthy, to stay clear of trouble, to be able to make good decisions. But the most important blessing of all was to have a loving family who gave me the rock-solid grounding I needed to get ahead. When you have parents who tell you that you can do whatever you set your mind to, and who really believe that, well, it makes all the difference.

Even though I was like most professional players and eventually had to deal with salary issues, free agency and collusion, the demands of media and ownership, and all the rest that goes into the business side of the game, I never lost my childlike enthusiasm for the simple (or not so simple, really) act of fielding a ground ball, feeling the bite of the seams as a ball left my hand, the almost no-sensation feel of a well-struck line drive, and the sound of my spikes as I dug around first base and headed toward second. That's why I wanted to coach and eventually manage. I wanted to teach the fundamentals, the finer points of the game, share my experiences, and help mold the next generation of players, but mostly I couldn't give up the thing I loved.

I believe I will get another shot to manage in the big leagues. I really do believe it will happen, and when it does I will take everything I learned from my first go-round with the Mets and be the better for it. Whatever happens, whatever I do, I will keep going to work and getting after it, the way my parents did in the fields.

They did what they had to because they loved us. If it weren't for them, I never would have had the amazing opportunities and experiences I've had in the game.

For me, dignity and respect don't come merely by winning. They come by doing your best, always, no matter the circumstances. They come by persevering and by paying more attention to the process of life than the box score of it. Dr. Martin Luther King, one of my heroes, expressed it quite succinctly when he wrote this:

"If a man is called to be a street sweeper, he should sweep streets even as Michelangelo painted, or Beethoven composed music, or Shakespeare wrote poetry. He should sweep streets so well that all the hosts of heaven and earth will pause to say, 'Here lived a great street sweeper who did his job well.'"

I DON'T SWEEP STREETS. I work with ballplayers. I do it with everything I have and all the passion I have. Before every game I managed with the Mets, during the national anthem, I would close my eyes and recite a special Bible verse of my mother's: "I can do all things through Him who strengthens me." Those ten words have a remarkable ability to center me and fortify me. Moments later, the pitcher would be looking in and the leadoff batter would be in the box, and it would absolutely be the best time of the day. A baseball game was about to begin, and more lessons were about to be learned. What could be better than that?

I don't know if it is possible to love something too much, and maybe some people could say that my intensity and passion were responsible for both the highs and lows I experienced in each of my roles in the game. I will say this: I'd rather be hanged for my errors of commission than my errors of omission. Put another way, I'd rather lose because I cared too much than because I didn't care enough.

I've also heard people talk about spreading the love. Well, I'm blessed in that regard also. My wife, Gretchen, who I literally fell for in the sixth grade when I tried to impress her by leaping a fence and wound up flat on the ground and needing seven stitches to boot, has been my most loyal supporter. She's seen countless games, and I'm not exaggerating when I tell you that she knows nearly as much about the game's tactics and history as just about anyone else I know inside and outside of the game. My son Andre played the game and spent a few years in the Yankees' organization. My daughters Taniesha, Chantre, and Ciara were all good athletes and put up with having an absentee father for much of the summer. We all are grateful for what baseball has meant to our lives. Andre and I still go to a few games, and most recently, we attended Mariano Rivera's moving and well-deserved retirement ceremony. Though the new Yankee Stadium is a far different place from the old Shea Stadium I first attended, I felt that same thrill rising up from my stomach when I caught sight of the ball field. Green is the color of hope, I'm told, and every time I see a field I'm filled with the sense that all things are possible.

The pages that follow detail many of the things I love about the game of baseball—the people, the places, and the events that I recall. Some of them are painful, but that's one way to measure how much you care.

I also know this beyond a doubt. I am many, many times blessed. My career has spanned the explosive growth of baseball, and I have made a living and provided a life for my family far beyond what my mother and father, sharecroppers in the 1950s in South Carolina, could have ever imagined for playing a boy's game. My mother was working the field picking cotton for fourteen to fifteen hours a day while carrying me inside her. She did what it took. For a long time, even after I was a major league All-Star, my father worked his regular day job and then climbed into his gypsy cab to troll for fares.

I paid attention to my parents' work ethic and commitment, and I learned. And I think that more than anything is what got me through that rough year in Thetford Mines. I ended up hitting only .254, but I led the league in walks (110) and runs (103) and stole 38 bases and wound up being an All-Star second baseman for a team that won the Eastern League championship. And then things—good things—started happening very fast. I hit .339 in a half-year in AAA ball. I was a midseason call-up by the Pittsburgh Pirates, and in that organization I found the big brother I'd never had, Willie Stargell, and got my first taste of postseason baseball. A few months after that I was traded to the New York Yankees.

And so began a baseball journey that continues to this day, my years carved out in 162-game installments. My years with the Yankees' organization spanned several generations of players whose names both longtime and new fans could easily recite along with me. The roster includes names like Berra, Jeter, Rivera, Piniella, Martin, Rodriguez, Lyle, Gossage, Brosius, Dent, Nettles, Martinez, Williams, O'Neill, and the list goes on and on. Whether I'm recounting the thirty-six different shortstops I was paired with, the heaviness of my heart at the loss of Thurman Munson, or the inspired wackiness of Mickey Rivers and the other residents of the Bronx Zoo, I want you to feel the passionate intensity that I brought to the game and my role, however small, in the Yankees' success story. I know that my scoring three times in an ALCS game pales in comparison to the three home runs Reggie Jackson hit in a World Series game, but that was my role.

I'm a table setter and proud of it. I'd like you to sit down and enjoy the spread I've prepared for you. It's going to be a lot of fun.

CHAPTER 2

A Winning Start

On the evening of July 29, 1975, the night I became a big-league ballplayer, I was so excited, I probably couldn't have remembered the lyrics to "Happy Birthday." I had to keep it simple, and these were my thoughts: I had just turned twenty-one. It was a Tuesday. Life was good.

Very good.

Unless you've spent a lot of time in what passes for a clubhouse in a minor league ballpark, you can't appreciate how different it is to set foot in a major league clubhouse. That's especially true of one that has been done up by a successful franchise. The '75 Pirates were defending National League East champions. They played in what today we think of as baseball's version of the housing projects—an Astroturfed, multi-use doughnut of a stadium known as Three Rivers—but their clubhouse was like a penthouse suite in the Waldorf-Astoria Hotel in comparison to what I was used to.

Staying in a hotel was also a far cry from the accommodations Gretchen and I had found in Triple A. With the exception of one trip to Puerto Rico when I was a youngster, I'd spent almost all of my time in New York City. Adjusting to life away from home wasn't always easy. Still, I was able to perform pretty well in my first season of pro baseball, hitting .317 in the Rookie League and dealing with my new second base position without much trouble. I moved up to A ball the following year, at Charleston back in my home state of South Carolina, not even fifty miles from my birthplace of Holly Hill. I hit with much more pop (8 homers, 6 triples, and 25 doubles) and stole 43 bases, earning the promotion to Thetford Mines. By the time I escaped the cold and the ruts and the asbestos, I was mentally stronger and ready to take on the challenge of Triple A ball. I was also a married man.

I proposed to Gretchen in the middle of the 1974 season, during a road trip to West Haven, Connecticut. She came up from Brooklyn. I snuck out to a jewelry store and bought a ring, then went back to the hotel. I didn't get on one knee or anything dramatic like that, but I popped the question to the girl I'd loved from the first time I saw her. The way my season was going, I was a little surprised she didn't say no. We got married just before spring training, and then I headed down to Bradenton. I had a good spring, and when camp broke Gretchen and I headed north for Charleston, West Virginia, home of the Charlies, the Pirates' AAA affiliate. The Charlies were famous for their logo—a smiling baseball with a derby hat and a cigar. In the local paper, the *Charleston Gazette,* the ball would be smiling if the Charlies won and frowning if the Charlies lost.

I was in town long enough to be amused by Charlie, but not much longer. My stay lasted ninety-one games and taught me a couple of valuable life lessons:

1. Do not live in a redneck trailer park if you are an African American.
2. Be careful where you get caught speeding.

I'm not sure what Gretchen and I were thinking, but when the Pirates broke camp and we ventured north to set up our first home together, we wound up settling on a mobile home in a tiny town outside Charleston called Rand, West Virginia. It's not far from the Kanawha River, a place that has since gained fame for being the hometown of NFL star Randy Moss. With a small salary and our first child on the way (we worked fast), we wanted to live as economically as possible.

We accomplished that. And we got what we paid for. Maybe less. Our first clue that we hadn't selected wisely, housing-wise, was finding out that our next-door neighbor slept with his shotgun.

The second clue was that not only was there no welcome wagon to greet us, but almost nobody would even speak to us. The newlyweds from Brooklyn might as well have been completely invisible.

Trouble wasn't long in coming. While I was off on an early-season road trip, Gretchen was resting in the trailer when she looked outside and saw a mangy and suspicious-looking man with a white German shepherd prowling around not far from the window. She lowered the blinds and quickly called me, managing to reach me in the clubhouse. I heard the panic in her voice. I told her to stay calm and said whatever I could think of to help that process. Gretchen wasn't calm at all. How could she be? She was pregnant and all alone in a trailer park with a prowler outside her door.

What words were going to fix that?

As she lay there, she heard the door knob begin to rattle, first lightly, then much more vigorously. Now the prowler was trying to force his way in. Now he was one flimsy lock away from who knows what?

Gretchen was terrified. All she could think of to do was scream, and that's what she did, as long and as loud as she could. Our neighbor with the shotgun—he actually was the one person who was very nice to us—heard her screaming and burst out of his trailer, shotgun cocked and loaded.

"Hey, get away from there!" he bellowed, and with that the prowler and his white German shepherd were off into the woods.

In the morning, I called the club's general manager and told him what happened. He asked where we were living.

"You are living in that redneck trailer park?" he said, alarm rising as he spoke. "We've got to get you out of there. That's no place to live." Somebody from the team came right over and drove Gretchen to a hotel. When I got back, we packed up and said good-bye to the trailer park forever, making sure we stopped to thank our guardian-angel neighbor with the shotgun.

Gretchen and I and the baby on the way settled into a nice routine off the field. On it, I was having my best year yet, hitting close to .340, leading the league in hitting for most of the first half of the season, playing a good second base, stealing bases without being caught even one time. One notch from the majors now, I began to think for the first time about getting the call, about what that would feel like. The Pirates were in a pennant race, so I figured that at the end of the year, when rosters were expanded, they might bring me up to give me a little taste of the majors.

One day late in July we were on a road trip in Rochester, New York, when Steve Demeter, our manager, asked me to come to the ballpark early. I was apprehensive. I didn't know what the issue was. I rifled my brain for possibilities. I was still rifling when Steve sat me down in the little square visiting manager's office.

"Willie," he said, "you are going to the big leagues. The Pirates want you on the big club. You've got to get to Pittsburgh as soon as you can."

I all but froze at the sound of his words. I thought he was joking. I really did. Never did I think I'd be called up in the middle of the season. Steve had been a career minor leaguer; his cup of coffee in the major leagues was not even half full, consisting of fifteen games in 1959 and 1960. He extended his hand and wished me the best.

As soon as I left the office I found a pay phone and called Gretchen.

"Hey, Gretch, it's me. Guess what?"

"What?" she asked.

"You better start packing, because we're going to the big leagues," I said. The next sounds I heard were shrieks of joy.

It was time to move again, for the best reason of all. I took a bus back to Charleston, we loaded up my Ford LTD, and we took off in the wee hours of the morning. We headed north on Interstate 79, bound for Pennsylvania, a 169-mile trip to the big time. My head was dizzy with excitement and anticipation.

The excitement stopped when I saw a blue blinking light in my rearview mirror.

I looked quickly at the speedometer. I was going eight or ten miles over the speed limit on a dry, empty road at two in the morning. I was hoping this was just a routine stop. My heart was pounding. I pulled over.

A big, jug-eared policeman appeared at my window, shining a flashlight into my face and into the car. He had a big hat and a jowly, no-nonsense face.

"License and registration," he said.

"Right here, Officer," I said, quickly producing them. I felt like I was in a movie. A bad one.

"Where you goin' so fast this time of night?"

"I'm a ballplayer for the Charleston Charlies, Officer. I was just called up to the major leagues and have to get up to join the Pittsburgh Pirates as soon as I can."

He wasn't impressed. Even a little bit. Maybe the guy was a Phillies fan. I don't know. My father used to call cops like this in the South "High Pockets." The cop seemed to be in love with his authority and with the fact that we were scared.

Mr. High Pockets told me he was going to give me a speeding ticket and that I had to follow him to the station house to pay the ticket.

I couldn't believe what I was hearing.

"Officer, if you want to give me a ticket, I'll be happy to pay it, but if you don't mind, we have to get to Pittsburgh. My wife is pregnant and tired. I have a game tomorrow. Can't you just give me the ticket and I'll mail in the payment?"

He glared back at me. Uh-oh. He looked ticked off that I had the gall to even make the suggestion.

"That's not how we do it around here, son. You follow me to the station. Now let's go."

He got back in his car, and we followed him to the next exit, onto a windy side road, then onto a dirt road that had more craters than the moon and was not much wider than a base path. I mean, the trees and bushes were practically sticking into our car. It felt as though we were on that road for a hundred miles. With every mile, my feeling grew stronger and stronger that we would never be coming back. It felt like *Deliverance*, except we were in a car, not a canoe.

At one point I was a split-second away from slamming on the brakes, throwing the car into reverse, and hightailing it out of there as fast as my LTD could go. I'll admit it: as a young black man in that situation, I couldn't help thinking about lynchings and back-alley beatings and all the atrocities perpetrated on black people in previous eras. I half-expected a big old sheriff to come out of the woods and say, "You in a heap of trouble now, boy."

I turned to Gretchen.

"Why do I have the feeling he wants to kill us?" I laughed nervously. Gretchen didn't laugh. At all.

After half an eternity, we finally got to the station. I had no idea what town we were in, and still don't. The car was caked in mud. In front of us was a dilapidated brick station house, not much bigger than a one-car garage. There was a chubby officer seated at a skinny desk in the front and two small holding cells in the back. A drunken old man was in one of them. The other one was ominously empty.

Maybe they're saving it for us, I thought.

The jug-eared officer handed me the speeding ticket.

"Cash only," he said. I wasn't going to do any more debating. I just wanted us out of there. I pulled out $30 and handed it to him. I had a feeling the two officers would be dividing it up and going to a saloon. At that point I didn't care. We got back in the Ford and somehow found our way back to the interstate. Every mile that we put between ourselves and the station house brought another wave of relief.

Gretchen and I arrived in Pittsburgh just before dawn. The Phillies were in town, and there was a ball game later that night. I never saw a trailer park or the inside of a station house in the boondocks again. I was in the major leagues now.

BACK IN '75, I had no real thoughts about how off-the-field factors would play into winning. I was too excited to think about much else besides how I'd realize my dream. I looked around and saw the uniforms hanging in the lockers: Willie Stargell's number 8, Richie

Hebner's number 3, Dave Parker's number 39. Finally I arrived at the locker that belonged to me. There was a uniform waiting on a hanger, number 18, sparkling white double-knits with black and yellow trim. My name was across the top of the back. I ran my fingers over the letters. I wasn't beyond the "R" when a shiver ran down my spine.

The only thing that made my first day in the big leagues less than perfect was that the greatest Pirate of them all, number 21, Roberto Clemente, was not a part of it.

The first Latin superstar, Clemente was a hero to me and a lot of the kids I played with growing up. He had a game all his own, with a great arm and that slashing swing and the way he'd slide into bases, almost as if he were flying into them. He had so much passion for the game, and I loved that about him too. I loved it when the Pirates came into Shea because chances were, you were going to see number 21 do something spectacular. I was drafted six months before Roberto died in that New Year's Eve plane crash while making a relief mission to victims of an earthquake in Nicaragua. It would've been an incredible honor just to meet him, never mind wear the same uniform.

A couple of hours before game time, I found out that I would not have to wait long to make my debut. Rennie Stennett, the regular second baseman, had sprained his ankle. Danny Murtaugh, the manager, posted the lineup, and my name was at the top of the order. That's how I found out I was playing. Danny was a sour, rotund man who was much more into chewing tobacco than being the welcome wagon. He wasn't big on motivational speeches or niceties, or talking to rookies for that matter. Call me into his office and give me a pep talk, tell me he was glad to have me with the big club? Ask me how I liked playing for his son in Triple A? Forget it. My name was in the lineup and that was all I needed to know, and all he wanted me to know.

Besides, he had bigger fish to fry than a pan fish like me. We were in the middle of a pennant race, and that first game was against the Phillies, who trailed us in the division. I felt like the new kid at school, anxious but not nervous, knowing that if the Pirates thought enough of me to bring me up, I belonged on the field. Becoming one of the guys wasn't even on my mind. If I did have any nerves, they were put to rest immediately by getting involved in the action early. I was in the middle of a 6-4-3 double play in the first inning, off the bat of the hard-hitting but lead-footed Greg "The Bull" Luzinski. I came up to the plate for the first time a minute or two later. As I heard myself introduced and walked toward the box, everything seemed big and bright, as if a million megawatts of power were bathing the stadium in light. Three Rivers looked like the Roman Colosseum to me, and I felt like a gladiator. I was surprised I wasn't more nervous. I just felt completely alive and tuned in to the moment. All my senses were on overdrive, soaking up every bit of the experience.

The pitcher for the Phillies was a left-hander, Tom Underwood. He was a smallish guy like me who was drafted the same year as I was, a good pitcher, though not overpowering. I got a good pitch to hit and drove it to center, but Garry Maddox caught it on the fly.

Two innings later, in the bottom of the third, I came up with two on and nobody out. I settled into the box, got into my crouch. When Underwood wound and delivered, I was right on it. I swung and made solid contact, rapping a single to center field. As I ran to first, the Colosseum looked even bigger and brighter than before. I turned the bag, then retreated to first and found myself face-to-face with the muscled physique of Dick Allen, the Phillies' first baseman. He was looking straight at me.

"Nice going, kid," he said.

"Thank you, Mr. Allen," I said. Dick Allen looked like a black Paul Bunyan to me. I was not just in awe of him, I was mesmerized by him. I kept looking at the rippling muscles in his arms and forearms. If I'd had a pen and paper, I might've asked for an autograph right there at first base. Also, this was a guy who could have very easily dismissed me as a nobody and here he was *talking* to me.

Dick Allen had a borderline Hall of Fame career. In his fifteen seasons, he would hit 351 home runs and drive in 1,119, while hitting .292. He was back with the Phillies at the tail end of his career, a guy who'd been the National League's Rookie of the Year in 1964, a seven-time All-Star, and winner of the American League's Most Valuable Player Award with the White Sox in 1972.

"Never let anyone play your position," Allen said. "It's your position. Treat it like that. Play every day, kid. Don't ever take a day off."

"Thanks, Mr. Allen," I said.

I took those words to heart, and for the bulk of my career I owned the second base position, particularly with the Yankees. In spring training, we call it winning a spot on the ball club, winning the battle for a particular position. That's the first kind of winning that you have to do when you're a major leaguer. Yes, you want to win games, but you also want to contribute as much as you can to the team's success, and that means being out there on the field playing. Sure, you have to understand your role on the team, but I'm not sure too many guys really accept that they are backups or reserves. You have to believe that you belong out there, that you own that spot in the lineup. Just because you own it doesn't mean that it can't be taken from you, just like Gally took my sandwiches. You shouldn't ever take it for granted that your name's going to be on that lineup posted in the dugout.

The other thing about winning that I took from Dick Allen's statement was this: have some respect for your elders in the game. The flip side of that is that veterans can, and I think should, feel the responsibility to pass on to younger players some of the values that are important to how you play the game and how you go about winning. Call it old-school schooling, but I was raised in the game and deeply influenced by older guys, many though not all of them African American, who felt it was their duty to help a young guy out.

On that Pirates team, Willie Stargell, who in 1976 was thirty-six years old but had been in the big leagues for fourteen years already, took on that role for me of big brother. And he was a big brother, but with an even bigger heart. Like a big brother, Willie taught me some good and painful lessons. The painful stuff wasn't so bad, really, but Willie thought it was fun to beat on me—punch me in the biceps, put me in a stranglehold—all those big brother–like kinds of moves. The man was strong, and my arms were little pipe-cleaner kinds of things in comparison. Even though I was from the big city, which earned me one of the nicknames that Willie anointed me with—"Slick"—I still had to learn how to conduct myself like a major leaguer off the field.

"Pops" schooled me in how to dress, where to eat, what wines to order with meals. It wasn't exactly like I was attending the Willie Stargell Finishing School, but it was close. And you have to remember, this was the mid-1970s: disco was in full swing, and the clothes we wore—well, the less said the better. Fortunately, I wasn't too much of a trendsetter on my rookie salary of $16,000, so no jumpsuits, crocheted suits, or anything else too Superfly. I did like hats, or "brims," as we sometimes called them. I remember one time I was in downtown Pittsburgh, eyeing an applejack hat, when I caught sight of Larry Demery, a young pitcher, in the window's reflection. He stepped out of a turquoise green Lincoln Mark IV, complete with opera windows, a vinyl landau roof, and the Continental spare tire hump. You would have thought he was a pimp, given his platform shoes, knee-length suit coat, and fedora. Demery wasn't alone in his fashion statement. I can remember Pops wearing a fur coat, Dave Parker and a few others with their man-purses, and the outrageous Dock Ellis looking like he stepped out of a clothing ad in *Ebony* magazine.

What I remember about that Pirates team and those first experiences in the major leagues was how the guys seemed to have an on-off switch. In the clubhouse, Harold Melvin and the Blue Notes, Gloria Gaynor, the O'Jays, and other groups were playing on the boom boxes and guys were dancing around. Guys made regular visits to the clubhouse bulletin board to see what Willie Stargell and his camera were up to. Willie loved photography, and he would take pictures of guys at weird angles and then post them on the board so that others could enjoy the laugh and post a funny caption. That was our early form of social media, I guess. Willie caught me from below once and took a photo that earned me another nickname—"Goose Neck." Seeing myself on that bulletin board, a midseason call-up, did make me feel like I belonged—even though a distorted, skinny-necked image of me was hardly flattering.

Come game time, though, while we weren't deadly serious and expressionless, we had a more focused kind of fun. That team was loose and fun-loving, but we also knew how to win. One win in particular stands out. In late September, we beat the Cubs, 22–0, at Wrigley. Fewer than 5,000 fans sat in the stands, and not nearly that many at the end, when Stennett finished off the best hitting day of any player in the twentieth century with an eighth-inning triple.

That made him 7-for-7, at which point Murtaugh told me to go in and pinch-run for him.

Talk about being a caddy. But I didn't mind. It was cool to have a front-row seat for history. I celebrated later in downtown Chicago, with my version of a night of debauchery: I went to a liquor store and, despite Willie's tutoring, bought a bottle of Mogen David wine. I guess I hadn't made the connection between ordering good wine in a restaurant and buying it in a store.

I went back to my hotel room, watched TV, and drank the bottle. I got a buzz on, and the next morning I had the first hangover of my life. That was it for me and Mogen David wine. I went back to my choirboy lifestyle.

On the last day of the season Murtaugh stopped by my locker. He was typically expansive.

"Ever play third base?" he asked.

"No, sir," I said.

"Well, you're playing it today," he said.

"Yes, sir," I said.

Half the regulars were out, resting for the playoffs, nursing their own hangovers from the final Saturday night of the season. Soon enough I had a sour stomach myself to deal with.

I handled my first chance okay, but the rest of the day . . . well, let's just say I wasn't asked to star in any how-to-play-the-hot-corner instructional videos. I caught the ball well enough. But the first basemen standing across the diamond—Willie Stargell in the first half of the game, Ed Kirkpatrick in the second half—looked like they were on the other side of the country. I airmailed the ball over their heads twice, then compensated by throwing a grounder to them on my next chance. We finished the day with seven errors. Three of them were by the rookie third baseman.

Raise your hand if you are surprised that I never made another big-league appearance at third base.

As much as that hurt my pride, I wasn't too down about it. After all, we'd won the division and were heading to Cincinnati to take on the Big Red Machine in the playoffs. If you're not old enough to remember the Reds of that era—and that year in particular—let me tell you this. They won 108 regular-season games. They won their division by 20 games. They were led by a Hall of Fame manager named Sparky Anderson. With the Yankees, we had the Core Four—Derek Jeter, Andy Pettitte, Jorge Posada, and Mariano Rivera—who all have a shot at making the Hall of Fame. The Big Red Machine's eight players most frequently thought of as members of the Big Red Machine included baseball's all-time hit leader Pete Rose; three Hall of Fame players in Johnny Bench, Tony Pérez, and Joe Morgan (and Rose, whose on-field achievements are Hall of Fame–worthy); six National League MVP selections; four National League home run leading seasons; three NL batting champions; twenty-five Gold Glove winning seasons; and sixty-three collective All-Star Game appearances. The starting lineup of Bench, Rose, Morgan, Pérez, Concepción, Foster, Griffey, and Gerónimo (collectively referred to as "the Great Eight") played eighty-eight games together during the 1975 and 1976 seasons and lost only nineteen.

Talk about winners.

And talk about exciting. Even though I knew that I wasn't going to get a start in any of the games, I still had that kid's night-before-Christmas feeling going through me. Stepping out onto the turf at Riverfront Stadium, with bunting draped all around the stands, the crisp October air, and early fall coloring everything with a special light, I'd arrived in one form of baseball heaven.

Still, I don't want to idealize things too much. Yes, we all wanted to win because winning was important to us, but we had other motivations as well. In 1975 the minimum salary for a major league baseball player was $16,000 per year, with an average salary of just under $45,000. If you won it all that year and your team voted you a full share of the winner's proceeds, you'd get just over an additional $19,000. If you lost in the World Series, you'd earn an additional $13,000 or so. I'm no math whiz, but with the help of a calculator, that $19,000 winner's share was 42 percent of the average salary. If you were a guy earning the major league minimum, winning the World Series and getting a full share would mean you could double your yearly salary. Now, I'm a New York guy, and I know about bonuses and salaries and Wall Street and all that, but getting that kind of money on top of your salary is pretty strong motivation for winning. Pride is one thing. Being able to feed your family is another. To be fair, allowing for inflation, that $16,000 was equal to nearly $70,000 today, and $45,000 translates into the buying power of approximately $165,000. But the percentages remain the same whether you're talking about 1975 or 2013 dollars.

As much as I loved the game, baseball was how I made my living, like every other major leaguer. I was thrilled to be in the playoffs, as were my teammates, but I heard something said with greater frequency as the season wound down: "Don't be messing with my money." That's a polite rephrasing, but you get the point. I need this playoff check. I might have to get a job in the off-season (which a lot of guys did) if I don't get that check. I want Christmas money to buy toys for the kids. I might want to take a vacation. I'll have to make some adjustments in the house and maybe do some renovating. That postseason money was huge for us.

The positive side of what some might think of as greed is this: guys back then held each other accountable. If a guy wasn't giving his all, or he was making too many errors of aggression that were contributing to losses, the veterans would get on him with a not so subtle and not so gentle reminder. Putting this in context helps you to better under-stand that old cliché about a lot being at stake in the playoffs. I didn't want to get a job in the off-season to make ends meet. I was a young player, newly married, and I took my responsibilities as a husband

and provider seriously. Like any regular wage earner concerned about who's getting overtime and who isn't, we had a deeply vested interest in getting to the playoffs and succeeding once we were there.

Of course, reality set in pretty quickly. We got swept in three games by the Big Red Machine, being outscored 19–7 in the process. As I mentioned, there are a lot of formulas for winning, and one of them says that pitching matchups are crucial to success—the righty/lefty matchup being one of the most highly touted of them. For that reason, Danny Murtaugh decided to go with three left-handed starters—Jerry Reuss, Jim Rooker, and John Candelaria—hoping to slow down left-handed-hitting Joe Morgan and Tony Pérez. Playing the so-called percentages didn't work, obviously, but I already knew that playing by the book didn't guarantee results.

What I didn't know was that I was going to learn another lesson. Not everybody expresses their competitive desires in the same ways. Put another way, being a winner sometimes means being selfish. Like Dick Allen pointed out to me, you've got to want to keep your spot. That means sometimes playing when you aren't at your best. That might be considered selfish, but there's a fine line between self-interest, self-sacrifice, and the desire to win.

Maybe it isn't fair to cite Dock Ellis as an example of how self-interest can come across in the wrong way. After all, today Dock is probably as well known for his claim that he threw a no-hitter—one in which he walked eight men but still gave up no hits—under the influence of LSD. Dock was his own man and went his own way both off and, apparently, on the field. The truth, though, is that he was a hell of a good pitcher too. You don't go 19-9 and 15-7 in consecutive years like Dock did in '71–'72 unless you've got some good stuff. In '75, after a couple of mediocre years, Dock was slowed by injury a bit and only went 8-9. Still, he wanted to pitch in that series and made no bones about the fact that he wasn't happy with Danny Murtaugh's strategy.

Dock had a fit, and if he had proven anything in his big-league career, it was that you could never predict what he would do next, especially when he was angry. About three weeks after I was called up, Dock directed a clubhouse tirade at Murtaugh and was suspended without pay. During the 1971 playoffs against the San Francisco Giants, Dock was incensed because the bed in his hotel room was too small, so he went and found another room. That was nothing compared with the time Dock pitched such a fit with a Riverfront Stadium security guard in Cincinnati that he had to be subdued with Mace.

Dock was so enraged at Murtaugh about not getting a start that he protested by sitting in the dugout with curlers on, refusing to report to the bullpen. It reminded me of the stories I'd heard about the 1971 All-Star Game, when Dock was named to start for the NL against Vida Blue and said he wouldn't do it, because there was no way baseball would let "two soul brothers" start in the All-Star Game. Baseball did indeed let two brothers start, and Dock wound up being the losing pitcher in the only All-Star Game the National League lost between 1963 and 1982.

He finally backed off in game 1 against the Reds and pitched two innings in relief in an 8–3 loss. Murtaugh called him in the next day and told Dock he had to apologize to the team.

Dock said okay, and Murtaugh called a meeting.

"I talked to Dock," Murtaugh told us, standing in the center of the clubhouse. "We're a team. We stay together no matter what. Now Dock's got something he wants to say to you guys. Dock."

With that, Murtaugh took a step back and Dock took a step forward. The curlers were gone. Everyone's eyes were on him. I was ready for contrition.

We got something else entirely.

"You all look like a scared bunch of mother[bleep]ers," Dock began. "That's what I see in here. Guys who are scared. Guys who won't play or don't want to play because they're candy-asses who don't want to play against no Big Red Machine." I looked at Murtaugh's face, and he looked as red as Pete Rose's hat. His body was almost quivering. I was afraid he might choke on his chaw of tobacco.

Dock continued. "Al Oliver is playing his heart out, and the rest of you look like you want to be hiding in the bathroom. What a bunch of pussies."

Murtaugh had heard quite enough of Dock's "apology." He stepped up next to him, his squatty body pushing right up into Dock's.

"All right, goddammit, that's enough, Dock. You haven't shown me a friggin' thing. Nothing at all. You bail out on the team and sit on the bench in goddamn curlers, and now you are saying guys don't want to play? You got no right to talk to anyone that way, you son of a bitch." And then the five-foot-nine, fifty-seven-year-old Murtaugh called out the six-foot-three, thirty-year-old Ellis:

"C'mon, Dock, it's you and me. Just give me three minutes." Murtaugh put up his fists.

"Sit your little ass down, mother[bleep]er," Dock said.

With that, Don Lefferts, one of Danny's coaches, charged Ellis and, I'm not kidding, had to be restrained by five guys. Murtaugh tried to get at him too. Dock was screaming and cursing—almost everybody was it seemed.

I stood by my locker, shell-shocked. All I could think was, *Oh my God. I can't believe stuff like this goes on in the big leagues.*

I had no idea then, but Dock's display would serve me well in the coming years after I joined the Yankees and played through the "Bronx Zoo" years. At the time Dock went off, I was pretty surprised, but I later saw it in another light. Dock didn't go about it the right way, but he was trying to say that he wanted the ball badly because, as a starting pitcher, that's your job. He wanted to pitch, and I wanted to play. He bitched about it, but I didn't.

Which of us was more eager to win? Did his more dramatic performance mean that he cared more than I did? If I didn't throw my helmet down in disgust when I thought I was a victim of a bad call, or if I failed to come through in the clutch, did that mean I cared less than Dock did? Or later, as a manager, if I didn't get run from a game, did that mean I didn't have my players' backs or care enough about them to protect them when they went off? Questions like these would stick with me throughout my career; I still struggle with them today.

I was very fortunate that my first experience in the major leagues was with a winning team, a playoff team. But little in this game, or in life, is black and white. I wasn't in the Reds' clubhouse, so I have no idea if they had the same kinds of internal tensions and blowups that the Pirates had in that series. From the outside, they looked like a cohesive group of All-American-type guys. Pete Rose was lovably pugnacious, Johnny Bench the quintessential boy next door, Tony Pérez the cool, laidback Hispanic guy. But who knew what boiled and bubbled beneath that surface appearance? Teams weren't subjected to the kind of media and social media scrutiny that they are today, and the money wasn't as great as it is now, so fans seemed less interested in the kind of dirt that doesn't cover an infield.

All I know is that when I was a fan and a player in the '70s before I got to the big leagues, the Reds and Athletics were the dominant teams in major league baseball. The Oakland A's of that era seemed to be the complete opposite of the squeaky clean Reds. That's all been talked about and documented before, so I'm not going to go into a whole lot of detail here, except to say that the spectrum with "creative tension" at one end and the "united clubhouse" at the other is often held up as an ideal. Both ends of this spectrum, though, may be myths. All I know is that talent can overcome a whole lot and winning on the field can cure a lot of what ails an organization off of it.

And I also know for certain that being on a championship-caliber ball club as a young player had an impact on me as a player, coach, and manager down the line. At the time, though, I was too busy enjoying the winning feeling, and then too eager to rid myself of the hateful feeling of having failed to win it all, to really give it much thought. Now that I've put some distance between myself and my playing days, some larger patterns emerge. I've moved beyond the simple "winning is good, losing is bad" duality, though I've got to say—there are times when I wish it could still be that simple.

I'm a big sports fan, so I hear things like this all the time. Best golfer to never win a major championship. Greatest player to never win a Super Bowl, an NBA Championship, a World Series ring, the Stanley Cup. As much as I love the game, I think my relationship with it would have been different—maybe not terrible, but definitely not as good—if I hadn't been fortunate enough to be involved in so many championships in my professional career. As you'll recall, Gally Gonzalez helped to fire the newly formed clay of my desire to win into a hardened vessel—kind of like a trophy with a figure of Mickey Mantle at bat atop a wooden base. Things weren't like they are today with the "everybody's a winner, everybody deserves a trophy" mentality. I coveted prizes for victory both then and now.

What fascinates me about winning is that as much as there are certain formulas for winning in baseball—and here I'm talking about how to build a championship-caliber ball club, not just how to win an individual game—not everyone agrees completely about how to build a winner. Sure, most would agree that being strong up the middle of the diamond is important, but exceptions come to mind—not every winning team has that combination of skills. Some teams stress pitching and defense. Others want to mash and bash. I can be really simple about all this and say that you have to score more runs far more often than your opponent does, but we also know that there's more than one way to skin that cat.

Every player who fields the ball has to make the transition of getting the ball out of the glove and into his throwing hand. You do that ever since you first picked up a ball and glove, repeating that simple act thousands and thousands of times, and it becomes second nature. As a middle infielder, the longer you play the game the higher you climb up baseball's ladder and the more quickly you're expected to be able to make that move. A strong arm can make up for some of the bobbles that inevitably result when you move from fielding a ball to throwing a ball, but a lot of those bang-bang plays that don't go your way might be a result of a fractionally too slow transition.

As ballplayers, we have to make all kinds of other transitions, just as everyone has to do in their lives. Besides being exposed to winning organizations early in my career, I believe that another reason why I succeeded in the game was that from the very beginning of my career I made transitions. Good fielders have soft hands, which means that they give in to the force of a batted ball and don't fight it with force. I know that the idea of a player being "soft" usually has a negative association, but I use the word in a different way in this context. Knowing how to make transitions and developing a temperament that balances giving in to the ball with going after it are important skills to achieve success.

If Willie Stargell had me enrolled in his finishing school, then my trade to the Yankees was like going off to college and making that pivotal transition from something known and comfortable to something unknown. Not that the Pirates weren't a first-rate organization. I just wasn't with them long enough on the major league level to really absorb as much as I needed to. I had headed off to Caracas, Venezuela, to play winter ball and wasn't there but a week or two when my mother called to report that the papers were full of stories about a rumored deal that would bring me to the Yankees. That was the first I'd ever heard of it. I had done pretty well in the minor leagues, and the Pirates had made it clear they thought highly of me. I believed I was going to be in Pittsburgh for the rest of my career.

The rest of my career in Pittsburgh ended up being a few more weeks.

CHAPTER 3

The Good with the Bad

Whether I was going home on the F train to Brooklyn as a teen or driving over the George Washington Bridge back to Jersey as an adult, winning and losing clung to me like the dirt on my slide-stained uniform—alternately an emblem of pride and a symbol of baseball's original sin. Heaven and hell. I've been to both in my days in New York baseball, but in either case, given a choice of where to play, there was no place I would rather have been than my hometown.

Fortunately, I was able to put some distance between myself and thoughts of New York City and the trade rumors that were swirling around me. I went to Venezuela to play in the Winter League, still believing that I needed more work on my game, especially if I was to master all the techniques necessary to play second base effectively in the major leagues. I enjoyed playing in Venezuela, but didn't like being away from family. If I wanted to succeed, that meant making sacrifices. This was the era before telecommunications expanded—back in the late '70s, only CEOs or the CIA made regular phone calls to Latin American countries. So when word came down that Gabe Paul, the Yankees' general manager, was calling from New York to talk to me, I immediately suspected that some kind of coup was going on.

"Welcome to the Yankees," Gabe said. "You're coming home."

I was almost as numb when I heard Gabe's words as I was when Steve Demeter had told me five months before that I was going to the big leagues. I hadn't really put any stock in the trade rumors. Now I found out they were not rumors at all. Faster than you can say Bobby Richardson I was a New York Yankee second baseman. I was going back to New York City. I couldn't wait to tell Gretchen. The Mets were my team as a kid, but New York is New York. I was going to play my next big league game in front of my family and friends, in the newly renovated Yankee Stadium. I liked the sound of this a lot.

"Thank you, Mr. Paul," I said.

The official account of the trade states that on December 11, 1975, the Yankees traded George "Doc" Medich, a twenty-seven-year-old pitcher who had won forty-nine games in the previous three years, in return for Ken Brett, Dock Ellis, and me. Given Dock's playoff explosion, it was no surprise that he was dealt. Despite my excitement about being able to play in New York, I was a little bit hurt. The Pirates were the team that drafted me and nurtured me in my first years as a pro. They were one of the finest organizations in Major League Baseball and were on a run of success that any team would envy—from 1970 to 1980 they would win their division six of those years. From 1965 to 1975 the Yankees failed to win their division. You take the good with the bad was what I'd been raised to believe. Now I was going to have to put those words to the test.

You can look at a trade one of two ways. One team doesn't want me. Or another team does.

The Pirates had been like my first girlfriend, and now she was rejecting me. All the way back in high school they had been one of the original teams interested in me. They weren't my only suitors back then, but our courtship had gone on for a long time.

By the time I was a senior at Tilden High School in Flatbush, Brooklyn, in the spring of 1972, scouts from seventeen big-league organizations had come out to see me play. I didn't keep track, but Herb Abramowicz, the athletic director and head baseball coach, did. He knew who was there, and why, and it had nothing to do with the amenities. The Tilden field didn't even have a dugout. We just sat on a bench along a chain-link fence, with the guy closest to the plate always wearing a glove, so he wouldn't die by foul ball. Five or six feet behind the fence on the third-base side was the school building itself. (No, there wasn't a lot of foul territory to cover in the big city.)

The Twins were regulars at my games. Their scouts would set up behind the third-base fence. The Mets came out too. Their scout was named Len Scott, and he was the one I was the happiest to see. The Mets, after all, were my team. Everyone else was scouting me as a shortstop, but Len Scott told me the Mets liked me as a catcher, even though I was a welterweight. I didn't catch too often, but I gunned down a couple of base runners and made some good blocks one game when Len was there, and I guess he never forgot that. Whenever Len came to Flatbush, Coach A and I would have the same conversation.

"Coach, can I catch today? I really want to catch," I'd say.

"No, you can't. You're my shortstop. You are not a catcher."

Herb wasn't just a good coach. He was as protective as a father, forever looking out for me. He always batted me leadoff instead of my usual number-three spot when scouts were at the game, so they'd maybe get to see an extra at-bat. No matter how often I pestered him to let me get behind the plate—I liked the equipment and loved being involved in every pitch—he would never let me sway him.

"I'm not going to let you get hurt catching for one team when sixteen other teams see you as a middle infielder," he said.

Herb would get annoyed at the scouts all the time because every one of them wanted to run me before the game, time me from home to first. "You're going to wear the kid out before he even plays," Herb complained to a scout once. "Why can't one of you time him and be done with it?"

"That's not how it works, Herb," the scout replied. "We all have to clock him for ourselves." I can still see Herb walking away, shaking his head, grumbling beneath his bushy mustache about how silly it was for me to run over and over again, as if all the stopwatches were different. If they had just asked, Herb would've told them: "Hell, yes, he can run."

I saw more of one scout than anybody else. His name was Dutch Deutsch. He worked for the Pittsburgh Pirates. He was a square-jawed, square-bodied man with dark hair, an aluminum beach chair he'd set up behind the plate, and the salt-of-the-earth demeanor that most baseball scouts possess. If you ask me, scouts are some of the best people in baseball, and some of the most knowledgeable. They run around from ball field to ball field, and where I'm from, they are often doing it at 42-degree games in April, all in the hope of finding the proverbial diamond in the rough. They're underpaid and overlooked, doing what they do because they love watching games and finding players, a task that's much harder than most people realize. Scouts aren't scouting how good a kid is now; they are scouting how good he can be, where he is going to project a few years down the road. There is a big difference. How do you know when a player is going to stop improving? How do you get a read on who will be able to hit a big-league curveball and who won't? It's tricky stuff. In 1984 the Mets had the number-one overall pick and drafted Shawn Abner. They passed on Mark McGwire. Eight years later, the Cincinnati Reds took an outfielder named Chad Mottola and didn't take a shortstop named Derek Jeter.

So you never know.

The first time I met Dutch Deutsch was before one of those frigid early-spring games. He came up to me beforehand, introduced himself, and told me he was looking forward to seeing me play.

"Thanks for coming out," I said. We talked for a minute or two, and then he handed me his Pirates business card. I'd never held a business card before. Not too many people who I knew in Brownsville were walking around with them. (Gang members didn't typically use them much either.) When Dutch Deutsch gave me his card, it was almost like a portal to another world, a big-time world.

A big-league world.

In my impressionable, seventeen-year-old mind, it meant that maybe I could be a Pittsburgh Pirate one day, that maybe my long-held dreams could come true.

This is for me? To keep? I thought as I ran my finger over the yellow background with the swashbuckling Pirate on it. It took me back to all the times I'd stood in front of the mirror and done my Pirate stances: the great Roberto Clemente, with his big leg kick and his slashing swing; Matty Alou, with his hands choked almost halfway up the bat; and Willie Stargell, with his signature twirl of the bat, which looked like a matchstick against his big body.

Dutch wasn't a big talker, but I always knew when he was there, and always made extra sure to do everything right when he was. He didn't need to sell me on the Pittsburgh Pirates one bit. It probably seems from another millennium to long-suffering Pirate fans, but the Bucs of that era were in the hunt every year. They weren't only the defending World Series champions, they were a regular rainbow coalition, and I liked that about them too. They had star players who were white (Richie Hebner, Steve Blass, and Bob Moose), black (Stargell, Al Oliver, and Dave Cash), and Latin (Roberto Clemente, Manny Sanguillén, and Vic Davalillo). They had Dock Ellis in the rotation and Dave Giusti in the pen. The Pirates won ninety-six games and the NL East that year, 1972, and had a ton of young talent in the pipeline.

On June 6, I officially joined the pipeline.

That was the day of baseball's annual June free-agent draft. The Pirates' top pick was a shortstop named Dwayne Peltier, a big, blond-haired California kid who looked as if he'd stepped off the cover of a Beach Boys album. I heard he got a $60,000 signing bonus. Six rounds later, the Pirates called my name, with the 167th pick of the draft, right after the A's selected a pitcher from Alabama named Clarence Harrell and the Orioles selected an outfielder from Georgia named Nathaniel Clayton. I never met Clarence or Nathaniel, but I'm sure they had the same dream I did.

There wasn't much press about the draft in those days. This was long before webcasts, and even before ESPN became the worldwide leader in sports news. Nobody was blogging about who the Expos or Angels should take with their first picks. Scott Boras wasn't compiling dossiers to prove why the youngsters he was advising were worth a gazillion dollars. Mr. Abramowicz found out about the Pirates' selecting me from a newspaper reporter. About 1:00 PM, just after lunch, he called me into his office. It was a cramped, windowless space bulging with file cabinets and training equipment and desks covered with game schedules and papers. The air smelled like liniment.

"Congratulations, Willie," Herb said. "Dutch Deutsch and the Pittsburgh Pirates drafted you on the seventh round today." He reached across his desk to shake my hand. I don't think I even moved. I let the words sink in for a minute. The Pittsburgh Pirates. Seventh round. After all those years playing for funeral homes and grocery stores and the Junior Mets, I just sat there and smelled the liniment and thought about what it might feel like to put on a big-league uniform, a Pirates uniform.

"Thanks, Coach. Thanks a lot. This is great," I said. If my reaction sounds low-key, well, it was. It was a major moment in my life, definitely, but as I sat there in Herb's office I can't tell you that it felt like some watershed event. I was happy for sure, but I knew this was just the beginning—that there was a lot of work to be done and a lot of people to convince. Having your name called was no guarantee. Hell, ten of the guys chosen on the first round that year—including Dwayne Peltier and a catcher the Mets coveted much more than me, Richard Bengston—never made it out of the minor leagues. I don't remember getting giddy or cutting out of school or getting carried around on anybody's shoulders. Honestly, I thought I had a good chance to be drafted and would've been more surprised if I hadn't been. Maybe I was trying to affect some professional detachment, wanting to act cool.

Mostly I just wanted to start playing some ball.

The next step was to sign a contract. I didn't have an agent or a clue about how these things were supposed to be handled, so I followed the Pirates' lead. Dutch made it clear from the beginning that I wouldn't be anywhere near the Dwayne Peltier bonus neighborhood. More likely I would be in the loose-change neighborhood. I didn't care. I wanted to sign. The Pirates knew that.

And the Pirates took advantage of that.

Shortly after the draft, Dutch Deutsch showed up for one of my games at the Parade Grounds. He acted as if he'd been there before, and I am sure he had, scouting the Torres or Joe Pepitone or John Candelaria, another Brooklynite the Pirates took that year (on the second round). There were close to 1,000 fans in the stands and a couple of guys in suits along with Dutch Deutsch. I was playing an American Legion game with Cummings Brothers Post. Dutch came over and shook my hand and explained that he was hoping to sign me quickly so I could get right down to Bradenton, Florida, to get started in rookie ball. Of course, I'd already been drafted, but I was still eager to put on a good show that day, maybe earn myself a few more bucks. I trotted out to short in the first inning. I was very aware of being watched. I paid close attention to my form, got down nice and low on the grounders in warm-ups, and fired my throws to first.

I didn't have to wait long for my first chance. With one out in the top of the first, a routine grounder came pretty much right to me. I got in front of it. Got set.

And then I let the ball go right through my legs. I turned and looked behind me and saw the worst sight an infielder can see: the ball you booted bouncing into the outfield. Oh geez, of all the times to commit a horrible error. I didn't think it would make the Pirates retract their draft choice, but it definitely wasn't the impression I was looking to make.

"He looked like the Golden Gate Bridge on that one," one of the suits said. I learned about this comment from my old friend Joe Laboy, who was in the stands alongside them. Joe immediately took charge of the Neighborhood Defense Network.

"Hey, you know how many rocks are on that field?" Joe said. In my first at-bat, I blistered a line drive to right-center and got a triple out of it. Joe naturally wanted to make sure it was fully noted.

"Look at that kid run!" Joe exclaimed. It probably wasn't the most subtle attempt of a representative of mine to do my bidding, but it was the first.

It was the strangest day I ever had at a ball field. At the end of each inning, I'd leave the dugout and walk over to a nearby car where Dutch and the suits were waiting, spikes click-clacking on the asphalt. We'd talk for a minute or two, then I'd clack back to the game. I remember doing this about half a dozen times. Maybe it was only two or three times, I don't know, but in my memory I see myself doing more clacking than hacking that day.

Mr. Williams, the father of my friend Gordon and my baseball coach, was there to advise me. My father—who almost never could get time off from work to see my games—was there too. The car was pretty crowded. We—well, Mr. Williams—went back and forth over the course of a few innings. With each passing inning I could sense that Dutch Deutsch was getting increasingly antsy about getting this done. (Scouts are always ready to get naive kids to put their John Hancocks down. It's not evil, just business. And the kids? Like me, they always want to sign. Level playing field? Nope.) The Pirates were offering me $5,000 to sign. Dutch was ratcheting up the pressure.

An ultimatum? It was short of that, but not by much.

"I've got this contract right here—a contract for you to be a professional baseball player for the Pittsburgh Pirates. Do you want to play ball or not?" Dutch paused and let me digest the weight of the moment. He looked serious and almost threatening. "I have a flight back to Pittsburgh in a couple of hours. I'd really like to have this signed contract in my hand when I do."

I felt my insides tighten. My whole future, my life dream, was tied up in those papers in Dutch Deutsch's hand. Do you know how many times I drove by Shea Stadium when I was a kid, staring at it from the back window until it disappeared from view? Do you know how often I told myself, *I'm going to play in that park some day?* I wished that I had more time to think. But I didn't. I was not going to play a game of chicken with a professional baseball team. I was not. With the grudging approval of Mr. Williams, I grabbed his pen and the contract and signed my name—not Mickey—and became a member of the Pirates organization.

We shook hands, and I headed back to the field. Mr. Williams saw Joe Laboy and gave him a hug. "Your buddy is a professional ballplayer," Mr. Williams said. I'd played ball with Joe for a good piece of my life. He looked as happy as if he'd been drafted himself.

And how did I feel? I felt great. Five thousand bucks? My father didn't make a whole lot more than that in an entire year. I wasn't fretting over the money Dwayne Peltier got. In the Randolph orbit, this was some serious dough. As soon as the check came in, I bought my parents a console TV, and I bought myself a blue suit at a discount clothing store on the Lower East Side of Manhattan. Somewhere there is a photo of me in that suit, all 100 percent polyester of it, probably thinking I should be on the cover of *Esquire,* or at least *Ebony.*

A couple of days later, the suit and I headed for Bradenton and the compound they call Pirate City. I hadn't even graduated from high school yet, but my grades were fine and my tests were done, so the Tilden administrators let me go a couple of weeks early—though it took a lot of badgering on Coach A's part to get it done.

"What's the purpose of high school? Isn't it to help kids get ahead and get a job?" Coach A argued to the resistant administrators. "Well, he's got a job, so why not let him get started at it?" The Pirates were more understanding when it came time for me to leave Pirate City for a few days to go back to Brooklyn for graduation. I was the first in my family to graduate high school. It would've crushed my mother if I'd missed it.

It's hard to believe anyplace could be hotter than summer in Bradenton, on the humidity-drenched west coast of Florida. We put in full days in the broiling Florida sun, and the sweat never stopped pouring off me. I didn't have any weight to lose, but I lost it anyway. On day 1 there was another adjustment to make: I was no longer a shortstop. The Pirates already had a promising shortstop in their system, Craig Reynolds, who they drafted first in 1971. Now they had a bunch more money tied up in Peltier. The left side of the infield was getting crowded.

They told me they thought my arm was better suited to playing second. I was an all-city shortstop and I took a lot of pride in that, but Mr. Abramowicz had already forewarned me that they might want me to switch positions, and short of them making me a peanut vendor, his attitude was: wherever they want you to play, go play it the best way you know how. Ernie Banks changed positions. So did Mickey Mantle. Was I supposed to tell the Pirates, "Sorry, guys, I'm going back to the ghetto"?

Like a dutiful soldier who doesn't ask questions and does what he's ordered to do, I took on the task of becoming a second baseman. I did have some thoughts about Jackie Robinson playing the same position, and in my head I ran down the list of other guys who had made it into the Hall of Fame at that position. I wasn't thinking that I might join them someday, but I wanted to know what the standards for excellence were. I knew that second basemen typically weren't expected to hit for much power or really be any kind of major offensive threat. Turning the double play, being rock-solid overall defensively, and maybe stealing a few bases were all more important.

I did a little bit of research, and the one name that stood out for me, because he was a Pirate and because one home run he hit was such a part of baseball history that I couldn't help but have heard of him before, was Bill Mazeroski. He's still the only player to hit a walk-off home run to win Game 7 of the World Series. Most of the names on the list solidified my ideas about what an ideal second baseman should be. To me, the one exception was Rogers Hornsby. In his twenty-three seasons, he had 2,930 hits and 301 home runs, and he hit .358. Impressive numbers for anyone playing any position. Like I said, I didn't have my sights set on topping those numbers, but it was good to know what the gold standard was. Later on, Ryne Sandberg of the Chicago Cubs would be considered a strong offensive second baseman. Just to put into perspective how good Hornsby was, in seven fewer seasons Sandberg had 2,386 hits and 282 home runs and hit .285, a full 73 percentage points lower. Amazing.

A Pirates coach, Gene Baker, was instrumental in helping me make the transition. He was there in rookie ball, and I was too green to know it but the man was a Negro League legend. To me, he was this older black gentleman, a very dignified man who was worthy of my respect simply because he was a coach and my elder. Later in my career, when I became a bit of an amateur historian about the Negro Leagues and was more conscious of the role that black players following Jackie Robinson played in the game, I was even more impressed with Gene Baker. He had a nice major league career with the Cubs and the Pirates. He also became the first African American manager in organized baseball when the Pirates named him to head their Batavia team in the New York–Penn League. In 1962 he became the second black coach (after Buck O'Neil) in the major leagues.

He spent hours working with me, hitting me hundreds of ground balls, talking about positioning, helping me with my footwork around the bag, and demonstrating the kind of dedicated approach to teaching that later on made me want to be a coach. He passed on in 1999, and I regret not ever getting in touch with him to really thank him for all that he did for me.

I also owed a thank-you to God and my parents. I don't know if it was my natural athleticism or what, but I immediately felt comfortable with playing the position. I felt like I'd been there all my life and had never played shortstop. The Pirates really knew what they were doing because in no time my natural assets, quick hands, and quick feet helped me develop the rhythm needed to play second base. That doesn't mean I didn't work hard at it, because I did, but seeing some positive results early on made it easier to do that.

ON THE DAY I was officially introduced as a Yankee, in the winter of 1975, Dock Ellis and I had a snowball fight outside the Stadium. We winged a few at each other—Dock wasn't wearing his curlers, and he wasn't on LSD as far as I know—and then I went up to the Yankee offices to see Gabe Paul. Gabe had a contract for me to sign. I still had neither an agent nor any idea of my value to the Yankees. I was terrified to negotiate and ready to agree to almost any number the Yankees threw out there.

Maybe I wasn't as naive as I was when Dutch Deutsch first signed me, but I was still pretty green.

The contract Gabe put in front of me was for $19,000, the major league minimum. When he put the paperwork on the desk, he looked at me sternly, as a schoolmaster would.

"Don't look at the hole in the doughnut. Look at the whole doughnut," he said.

I thought about asking him what he was talking about, but decided not to. I did as he asked and regretted it almost immediately, especially after I told Dock about what happened. Dock was his typically restrained self.

"You stupid son of a bitch!" Dock said. "You are a goddamn fool! You think the Yankees made this trade to get my tired ass? To get Ken Brett? No, you idiot, they wanted you. You were the key to everything. And now Gabe Paul talks to you about doughnuts and you sign for what they put in front of you."

Because of my naïveté, I was woefully underpaid that year and as a result remained underpaid for most of my career. Few people have any tolerance for ballplayers complaining about money, and I don't blame them. Who wants to hear a fiscal tale of woe from someone in the top 1 percent of the income chart in this country? The fact remains, however, that for the industry I was in, and for a guy who made six All-Star teams, I got shorted pretty regularly. Most of that was nobody's fault but my own, for not recognizing my value and negotiating accordingly. I know people in other businesses, and they tell me that the same thing is true in any business. When you're starting out, companies take advantage of a lot of new hires, especially those in their first few years in the business. If you don't negotiate hard and get what you really deserve at the start, you're always going to be operating out of a deficit the rest of your career.

But when I was a victim of the owners' collusion to keep salaries down in the late 1980s, it was definitely *not* my fault. I was a free agent, a pretty attractive free agent, and for a long time there wasn't a single offer to be found. How does that happen exactly? My highest salary for a season was $1.1 million. Again, you won't hear me pleading poverty, because that would be offensive to people who really are struggling to support their families, but when you see one guy after another come to the Bronx and score a huge payday and then leave again, without ever winning anything, you start to wonder when it will become your turn.

When it goes on long enough, it starts to eat at you.

When I reported to Fort Lauderdale in the spring of 1976, though, money was the last thing on my mind. I was there to win a job and went about it in my usual way: I shut up and played ball. I didn't want to be rude or disrespectful to anybody, but I also wasn't going to be carefree and frivolous. And no matter what Dock Ellis told me about being the key to the whole deal, I sure wasn't taking anything for granted.

The first guy to puncture my armor was the late Catfish Hunter. He was another player I grew up watching, and I could hardly believe I was sharing a uniform with him now, after he became George Steinbrenner's first big free-agent catch. Just to put things in perspective, in 1975 Catfish would earn $640,000. He was one of four players in six figures that year, and Ken Holtzman, another free-agent signee, was next in line at $165,000, followed by Graig Nettles and Thurman Munson at $120,000 each. Catfish was a big fish obviously.

No one on that '76 team held that salary against Catfish. Everybody loved the guy. He was one of the best teammates you could ever have, and a needler without peer. He had the rare gift of being able to deliver his barbs without anybody getting mad at him, partly because of his homespun, North Carolina farmer drawl, but mostly because there was never any mean-spiritedness behind what he said. He saved some of his best lines for Reggie, his old teammate from Oakland. After they came out with the Reggie! Bar, Catfish said, "It's the only candy bar that when you unwrap it, it tells you how good it is."

I'll tell you what sort of guy Catfish was. In that first spring we were playing an intrasquad game. Catfish was on the mound. First time up, I got a good pitch to hit and drilled a line-drive single. Second time up, I got another good pitch to hit and lined a double to right-center. I stood on second base, feeling as good and confident as I ever had as a ballplayer. I came out of that game thinking, *Wow, if I can hit like that off Catfish Hunter, I think I'm going to do all right.*

Only later did I realize that Catfish served those cookies to me on purpose. "Cookie" is ballplayer slang for a hittable, batting-practice fastball. Catfish wanted to help out a kid teammate, help him get properly baptized as a Yankee. He was a highly prized and highly paid pitcher. His spot in the rotation was secure. What did he have to lose by boosting a rookie's confidence? Nothing. What did he have to gain? An even more confident second baseman who could contribute to wins. A smart move on his part. I never got a chance to thank Catfish for that, but I know that's exactly what he was doing.

It was during those early days in spring training that I came to know our manager, Billy Martin, a whole lot better. I know that a lot of other players don't hold Billy Martin in very high regard, but I do. I guess it was because he and I played the same position and had the same "take no prisoners, this is war" approach to the game that from the very beginning he seemed to respect and like about me. I'd heard of Billy growing up when he was the manager of the Twins teams that featured Rod Carew and Harmon Killebrew. I'd seen footage of him as a Yankee player making a nice play on a ball that Jackie Robinson hit over the mound. Billy ranged over, made a shoestring catch, and with that the very quick Mr. Robinson was out.

When I went to the Yankees, I was pleased to be managed by a man who was a part of the second base brotherhood. I thought I could learn a lot from him, and I did. In some ways, Billy was like that inexplicable father who has four sons but seems to favor one of them and gives the other three a lot of crap. I can't explain why that was really, but Billy always treated me well, asked about my family, and reserved his bad-tempered behavior for others. As trivial as this may sound, we both had wives named Gretchen and maybe that made it easier for Billy to remember mine and to ask about her.

The first time I saw Billy Martin was that first spring training with the Yankees. He was hitting ground balls to some of the infielders; to Billy, even routine practice was to be approached with intensity. I could see him bearing down with that fungo bat in his hands, and I tried to match his intensity. As the session progressed, Billy started to hit the ball harder and harder at me and to my right and to my left. I was determined to not let him get one past me. We were both sizing each other up, and I believe we came to the same conclusion. I was as tough as the calluses that developed on that man's hands from all those ground balls he tried to rocket past me.

I also knew that Billy liked small ball—bunting, moving guys over, stealing bases—and that was my game as well. That first spring training, I walked in there not thinking that the job was mine, but also not really thinking about how my competition for the position was going to be. I was just focused on getting the job done, doing the little things that I needed to do to play the game the right way. I think that my not thinking about what my possible role was going to be and focusing on just playing the game the way I'd been taught made that first Yankee spring training less intimidating than it might have been.

That was especially helpful to me at the start of that first year on the Yankees, when I went hitless in nine at-bats before getting my first American League hit, and my first big-league home run, off Jim Palmer. It came in our fourth game, in Baltimore, in support of Danny Murtaugh's favorite pitcher, Dock Ellis, and helped me relax as we returned to the Stadium two days later.

It was April 15, 1976, the grand reopening of the renovated Yankee Stadium. The sunshine was brilliant. When I walked down the tunnel into the dugout and looked out on the field, it looked as if it had been dipped in gold. I gazed up at the massive upper deck and thought, *It looks like it goes all the way to heaven.*

I had a couple of dozen family members and friends on hand to mark the occasion, and there were dignitaries there as well: Mrs. Babe Ruth, Joe DiMaggio, Mickey Mantle, and Whitey Ford. Bob Shawkey, who started the first game in Yankee Stadium when it opened in 1923, threw out the first pitch in the remodeled Stadium too. We all came away happy. The Yankees won, 11–4, and I went 2-for-4 with two runs scored and a stolen base. I wound up hitting .400 in April, and with Billy Martin batting me eighth and looking out for me, I adjusted comfortably to the baseball rhythms in the Bronx.

The thing that strikes me now about that first game in the then-new Yankee Stadium was how the Yankees' ceremonies were always such great combinations of drama and history. Having just recently attended the retirement ceremony for Mariano Rivera, I can say that the organization continues to excel in that regard. More on Mo and that wonderful night in the Bronx later on, but as a young player, I don't think I appreciated as much as I do today the fact that Mrs. Babe Ruth was there the first time I put on the home pinstripes.

So many people have asked me about "the Yankee Way"—the organization's sense of tradition and its effect on the mind-set of players. Going back to my comparison of the Willie Stargell finishing school in Pittsburgh with the Yankees as "college," here's where that analogy falls apart. Yes, I did receive more of an education with the Yankees, but it wasn't as though, after getting that phone call from Gabe Paul, or when I showed up for spring training, I was handed a syllabus for the course or a handbook of student conduct that I was to follow.

We talk about "intangibles" in sports all the time and use that word because it describes things that we can't easily pin down statistically or physically, that we can't define in precise and measurable ways. When I joined the Yankees, no one sat me down and explained, say, the ten things I had to do to follow the Yankee Way. Some of it I picked up by observation, and the rest I just kind of sensed. I know that's not a very good explanation of the Yankee Way, but in some intangible way things did feel different in the Yankee clubhouse and on the field in that stadium.

Today we might talk about it in terms of branding, but back then I just felt that putting on that uniform, which had been unchanged for more than half a century except for wool and flannel being replaced by polyester blends, made me a part of the history and tradition of the organization. Compare what I was wearing in my short stint with the Pirates to the Yankee uniforms. Those buttonless jerseys and the elastic-waistband pants may have been fly in the disco era, but looking back on that and the uniforms of other teams like the Padres and the Astros and some others, I have to wonder, "What the hell were they thinking?" Baseball's appeal to the fans has always been about its history, and those attempts to make players look contemporary now seem kind of laughable. At the time I didn't mind, but when I joined the Yankees—and even later when I managed the Mets and was involved in changing the mind-set and culture of the organization—I understood even more what I had sensed in my first full year in the big leagues.

Being a New York City native, I'd heard and read about Mr. Steinbrenner taking over in 1973 as owner of the Yankees. He had talked about changing the Yankee culture and restoring the team to its historic legacy. I knew that he was a very ambitious guy, and he was a presence during spring training. During one spring training years later, his office was housed inside a trailer parked outside the ball field. I'd see him walking into and out of that thing, like a construction foreman minus the hard hat and the rolled-up blueprints, and was struck by how he carried himself. I can't say he strutted, but he was kind of like those ships he'd made his money with—he cut through the air with a businesslike demeanor that said, "Out of my way." By then I'd been with the team for a few years, but I still treated him the same way I had during my rookie season—like a school's principal. When I saw him coming my way, I'd alter course and sail off in another direction. When we did finally meet, I was as polite as I could be, just as my parents had taught me, and he was definitely Mr. Steinbrenner, and not George and not the Boss, to me.

George Steinbrenner might have seemed like a meddling micromanager, and we didn't always like his rules about facial hair and hair length and all the rest of that, but in retrospect, I can see why he was doing the things he was. Later on, when I left the Yankee organization, I felt a difference. How much that Yankee tradition contributed to winning, I can't really say, but I know that history and its effects linger. Knowing that you were stepping to the plate where all those greats had dug in as well might not translate into hitting twenty points higher, but it did have an effect on how you felt about yourself.

One part of the Yankee tradition didn't have the effect on me that you might think. Monument Park was originally a tribute to Miller Huggins, the manager who died suddenly in 1929. Like a lot of other ballparks, the original Yankee Stadium had a flagpole that was in the field of play. With the center-field fence standing 500 feet away from home plate, it wasn't like that flagpole was wreaking havoc on outfielders and knocking down fly balls. Eventually, various other Yankees got plaques like Huggins did, memorial plaques went up on the fence, and the fence was moved in to 461 feet. By the time I played there in 1975 the monuments were outside the field of play and the center-field fence was now 417 feet from home. I cite all these facts because I have no factual basis for the reason why I never went out there. Visiting players would go there, my teammates would, fans could tour the monuments, but I never went through there. Maybe it's my country boy roots and my ancestors' superstitions getting hold of me, or maybe it was all just my way of showing respect in a different manner, but I would have felt like I was tromping around in a cemetery to go back in there. It's not that it felt disrespectful to go in there, but the idea of doing that also felt a little creepy to me. That's all on me and doesn't reflect on anyone who has anything to do with the Yankees, but I was a bit squeamish about that place. I'd peek out there and look at the plaques from a distance, but that was it. Sorry if that disappoints anyone.

Maybe it had something to do with the fact that the left-center-field alley, especially when the fences were so far back, was called Death Valley. I clearly remember having a discussion on the bench that first game at home in '76 and us saying, you don't want to hit a ball out there. No way it's going to go out. Of course, Danny Ford of the Twins hit one out there, to the exact spot I was thinking was Death for Fly Balls. Shows how much I know about things supernatural.

In a lot of ways, the Yankees of 1976 were a team in transition. Six new pitchers were added to the staff, Mickey Klutts and I joined the infielders, and four new outfielders joined the team. Not a complete overhaul, but a significant infusion of new talent. From 1960 to 1964, the Yankees had gone to the World Series each year. From 1965 to 1975, their best finish was second in the newly formed American League East in 1970 and 1974. That was a long drought by Yankee standards. The '75 club had won eighty-three games but finished twelve games out of first place behind the Orioles and the Red Sox. Billy Martin had come on board as manager in August 1975, George Steinbrenner had owned the team since '73, and Gabe Paul had become the GM in '74.

In spite of so many changes—and this was a pattern that would repeat itself—one of the constants was that no matter how much chaos later ensued, when the first pitch was thrown, we were ready to play. I was among the guys who were really into it. Even though throughout the league and throughout the country we were celebrating the bicentennial, you couldn't have told by me. That is, not until the All-Star Game in Philadelphia. All the major sports held their All-Star Games in that historic city in '76. President Gerald Ford threw out the first pitch, and I had the honor of being named to the squad as a rookie, joining my teammates Thurman Munson, Chris Chambliss, Mickey Rivers, and Sparky Lyle on the roster. A knee injury kept me from playing—Bobby Grich of the Orioles started and was replaced by Phil Garner—but being among guys like George Brett, Rod Carew, Carl Yastrzemski, and Carlton Fisk, to name just a few, was an honor and a privilege. Mark "The Bird" Fidrych was on the mound, and just seeing that guy, somebody who created such a media sensation with his gyrations as well as his stuff on the mound, was something I'll never forget.

By the time we beat the White Sox at the Stadium 5–0 in our last game before the All-Star break, we were nine and a half games up, nineteen games over .500 at 50-31, and I was having a great time. I felt like I was doing what I was expected to do—using my speed to get on base and be a disruptive force once on. I was hitting .273 but had 39 walks and was 24 out of 30 in stolen base attempts. I had struck out 24 times, which I wasn't too happy about. As a contact guy, I prided myself on not striking out, and I was determined to do better at that the second half. I ended the year with 39, so I did cut down on them some.

I learned more baseball from Billy than anyone I ever played for. To this day, when people ask me who my favorite manager was, I say Billy Martin. I enjoyed playing for him. That doesn't mean he was the best manager, and some of the things he did over the course of a game sometimes defied reason or were clearly a product of Billy's healthy ego. Going to the Yankees, I knew Billy had a reputation for not liking young ballplayers, but he went out of his way to help me, and one of the first lessons he taught me was never to take any guff from anyone.

I wasn't very far into my rookie year when Billy one day told me to follow him out of the clubhouse and down the hallway beneath the right-field stands. When we got near the indoor batting cage, he turned and brought me to a little corner. Hanging from a board on the ceiling was a speed bag. I had no idea what Billy was up to.

"This will really help quicken and strengthen your hands," he said. And then he gave me a demonstration, *pop-pop-pop-pop-pop*, his hands flying, the bag dancing. It was an amazing exhibition. You'd always hear stories of skinny little Billy beating up the marshmallow salesman and big guys like Dave Boswell, his pitcher with the Twins, but if you ever saw him on the speed bag you wouldn't have been surprised at all. Man, his hands were strong, and they were fast. I wasn't there when Billy decked Boswell, but I heard every detail about it.

There were many more valuable lessons that Billy Martin taught me on the field. If a guy was coming into second base high and hard, Billy showed me the perfect retort: you drop down with your throw to first. It's amazing how getting buzzed by a fastball is all most runners need to learn not to mess with you. It was a good piece of baseball wisdom, and I didn't have to wait long to apply it.

We were playing the Baltimore Orioles in the middle of May 1976. The Orioles' newly acquired slugger, Reggie Jackson, was on first base. Reggie had a well-known swagger, and the muscles to back it up. I knew he'd played defensive back at Arizona State, and that's about how he looked. As he took his lead, Reggie hollered to get my attention. I turned and looked at him. He smiled, a look that had a lot more menace to it than friendliness.

"Hey, rookie, you better look out, because I slide real hard," he called out. Reggie kept staring over at me, the smile now a glare. "Look out, rook. I'm coming at you."

I tried not to pay him any mind. Or rather, I tried to act like I wasn't paying any mind. Reggie Jackson, of course, could've knocked me into left field if he wanted to, but I don't scare easily. If you showed fear where I'm from, people would take advantage of you. I was also Billy's well-schooled pupil, and I had his voice trailing through my head: don't back down from anybody, ever. Don't let anybody intimidate you, ever.

Well, after the last of a series of increasingly hostile Reggie-glares, wouldn't you know the batter hit a grounder to third baseman Graig Nettles. I raced to cover the bag, preparing to turn the double play—with Reggie on my mind. And here he came, thick thighs churning, arms pumping, coming at me hard, as promised. I straddled the bag and waited for the ball from Nettles. My heart was pounding. So was Reggie, toward me. When he was almost on top of me, I caught the ball, pivoted in front of the bag, and fired the ball to first, three-quarter underhanded. My throw would've made the late Dan Quisenberry proud. It pretty much headed right for Reggie's forehead. So he did the only sensible thing.

Hit the dirt.

By the time he got up, our double play was complete and Reggie was screaming.

"You crazy little son of a bitch! Who the hell do you think you're throwing at?" That was the gist of it, though there probably were some other select expletives Reggie worked in too.

I tried to suppress a smile, not entirely successfully. Over Reggie's shoulder, I saw Billy in the dugout. He wasn't suppressing anything, beaming and nodding like a proud papa, watching his kid grow up before his eyes. Reggie slowly dusted himself off, muttering and glaring all the while. I trotted toward the dugout, not gloating, but privately enjoying the way it played out. It may not have been the moment I officially knew I had arrived in the big leagues.

But it was close.

I also knew that I still had a lot to learn, and I was fortunate to have several mentors along the way. Playing for the Pirates had shown me one way to have a winning atmosphere, but as my time with the Yankees lengthened I'd learn that the Pirates' way wasn't the only way.

What fascinates me the most about winning is its improvisational nature. Before you start scratching your head wondering how I could throw in a five-dollar word and concept like that, bear with me. I mentioned in the introduction that I am a lover of jazz music. I have a collection of more than 10,000 recordings in various genres, and among my personal heroes is the jazz saxophonist John Coltrane. For a while, I considered calling this book *A Love Supreme,* in honor of his 1965 album of that name. But if I'd done that, I wouldn't have been doing justice to Miles Davis, Charlie Parker, and a few others. Those guys are all geniuses, obviously, but if it hadn't been for the influence of another one of my personal heroes and baseball mentors, Roy White, I might not have ever gotten to hear and appreciate "The Trane."

Roy White spent his entire baseball career as a Yankee outfielder, from 1965 to 1979. When I came along in 1976, Roy took me under his wing a bit. To me, Roy was the epitome of 1970s cool. He worked a full Afro, studied the martial arts (karate to be specific), and loved jazz. He was a veteran, of course, and though there were certain new guy–veteran things that went on in most clubhouses (more on some of that later), Roy and I hit it off. I was still a youngster and easily influenced, and I took up karate and later tae kwon do because of his influence.

Mostly, though, Roy impressed me because of his demeanor, a product of that Eastern martial arts composure. I'd see Roy sitting there, listening to his jazz recordings, looking at peace with the world, unaware of the chaos going on around him. Roy was cool in another sense—he was just one of the most tranquil, easygoing guys in the world. That's not to say he wasn't competitive, but he went about it in his own laid-back way.

Even when Roy was angry and exploded, he still did it with his unique coolness. In '77, Roy was struggling quite a bit at the plate. He was hitting line drive after line drive, and they weren't dropping. That's sometimes harder to deal with than not making good contact. To that point, Roy had never gone off the way some guys would have done, slamming helmets, swearing, busting bats, and what have you.

Instead, Roy would come back to the dugout looking like he'd just retrieved the newspaper at the end of the driveway. He'd sit on the bench, calmly observing the game, and then trot back out there once the inning was over.

Well, on this particular night—I believe it was against Baltimore and the soft-tossing lefty Scott McGregor—Roy had had enough. He hung a rope on a slow-breaking ball that went right to their shortstop, Mark Belanger.

Very calmly, Roy walked to the end of the dugout, shelved his helmet, racked his bat, and then delivered a series of chops and kicks to the water cooler. In a few seconds, the device was leaking all over. Roy turned back around, his face blank, and took his seat on the bench as if nothing out of the ordinary had happened. The rest of us were too shocked to say anything immediately, but later on in the clubhouse Roy got some third degree and ribbing.

Come to think of it, maybe that was Roy's bit of improvising. He hadn't planned on taking out that watercooler and casting us all in a Bruce Lee action movie; he just went with the moment. That's not exactly what I'm talking about with improvising and winning. What I am saying is that you can strategize a team's structure and go into a particular contest with a game plan, but it's always going to be the adjustments and variations, pitch by pitch, out by out, and game by game, that make winning the game and winning championships feel like a jazz ensemble playing with a melody.

It's also good to have a mix of players around—young guys like me and veterans like Roy and the others—to play off one another. Technically, I was still a rookie, but I wasn't much into the "rookies are dogmeat" program. If somebody said, "Hey, rook, go get me a cup of coffee," or, "Hey, rook, carry my bag," that didn't sit well with me. I didn't want people telling me what to do, and I wasn't going to take crap from anyone. It's a good thing I never went to college and tried to join a fraternity, because the minute they started with the hazing, I would've been in people's faces in a big way. What can I say? When I feel slighted or feel that somebody's trying to get over on me, I don't like it one bit. I was a serious-minded twenty-one-year-old who was busy making his lifelong dream come true. Lightening up didn't come easily to me. It didn't come easily at all, though the captain, Thurman Munson, did his best to break me down.

One afternoon early on he came into the trainer's room and saw me in the whirlpool getting some therapy for a cranky knee.

"Hey, get out of there, rook," he growled. "You got no business being in the trainer's room at your age." I might have smiled. Might have.

Thurman had the personality of sandpaper (large grit). He showed his warm, fuzzy side about as often as Halley's Comet comes around. What I completely failed to pick up on was that when he gave you grief, that was his version of affection. The message finally got through during a batting-practice session about a month into the season.

I was in the cage, getting my hacks, when Thurman chased me out.

"That's it, rook. Five is all you get."

I reluctantly stepped out and watched Thurman and a couple of other veterans take eight swings. I was not happy about being short-changed. I jumped back in, and after my fifth swing, again I heard the voice of Thurman Munson.

"Get out of there, rook. You're done." Now I was really ticked off. They were messing with me. They were screwing me out of at-bats. If they thought I was going to roll over in the face of this blatant double standard, they didn't know me at all.

"What do you mean I'm done?" I said. "I only got five. All you guys got eight. What's up with that?" I paused. "I am not getting out of the cage."

"Get out of the cage," Thurman said, stepping toward me.

Almost instantly, I bowed my back and took a step forward, as if I was ready to go with him. The idea of me, a skinny rookie, mixing it up with Thurman Munson, a strong, beefy veteran, was ridiculous, but what can I tell you? I was a headstrong kid.

He came right over to me, right in the cage. Batting practice got very quiet.

I wasn't sure what he was going to do. I braced myself. A terrifying thought crossed my mind: *Am I about to get punched out by Thurman Munson?* Almost in my face now, Thurman looked straight into my eyes. His fists didn't move, which was a major relief. "Relax, would you?" he said. "If I didn't like you, I wouldn't get on you, okay?"

"Okay," I said.

From then on, Thurman and I were great buddies. I was able to get beyond the bark and the bite and see him for the softhearted man he truly was. I was the new kid, the baby, and he made me feel special. He gave me a hideous yellow T-shirt with green block letters that spelled R-O-O-K on the front. I cut off the sleeves and a bit of the neck, and wore it under my uniform most of that season. It's still in my dresser at home, a fraying reminder of one of the best ballplayers I've ever shared a field with.

As rookie years go, I couldn't have asked for a whole lot more. I hit .267 and stole 37 bases and was named a reserve second baseman in the All-Star Game. I couldn't play because of a chronic knee problem. It wasn't worth risking injury, so I was one those "we'll only use you if we really need you" guys. That really was the only downer the whole year. For the whole season, the knee kept me out of more than thirty games.

We dominated the AL East, winning by ten and a half games, and maybe what was most impressive about that was that we were a much better team on the road than at home, going 52-27 away from the Stadium. That was because we had tough-minded pros like Thurman, Graig Nettles, Lou Piniella, Roy White, and Chris Chambliss, though the guy who really made us go was John Milton "Mickey" Rivers, our center fielder and leadoff hitter. It seemed like every time you looked up, Mickey was doing something to get the team jump-started.

ONE OF THE CONSTANTS during my first few years with the Yankees was our annual playoff confrontation with the Kansas City Royals. Some people are shocked when I say this, but at the time, and still looking back on it today, in some ways those series against them were as big to me as the World Series itself. We went at each other regularly, and we went at each other hard. We built up a mutual respect, but that didn't mean there wasn't a lot of animosity between the two teams. To this day, if I see George Brett or Hal McRae or any of the other Royals of that era at some function or another, the reception is always cool.

Who can blame them for being pissed off at us? From 1976 through 1980, we faced them four times in the American League Division Series. We beat them three out of those four times. Maybe the guys who booked their golf tee times, the fishing trips, and the hunting expeditions liked us, but the players themselves sure as hell didn't.

Today "win or go home" has become a cliché, but those were the prospects we faced on Saturday, October 9, 1976. We'd split the first four games of the series, each team winning one game at home and one on the road. Back then, the games were split 2-3. We started out on the road, so that meant that game 5 was at the Stadium. After an eleven-year wait for postseason baseball, you can bet Yankee fans were in full throat as the first pitch was thrown shortly after high noon. Because this was a five-game series and it wasn't the World Series, most fans probably don't remember what a classic, taut game that was. Even today, given all that I've witnessed and participated in, that game was the most nerve-racking I ever experienced.

The Royals jumped ahead immediately in the first, scoring two runs. Ed Figueroa was on the mound for us and got the first two outs. Then George Brett doubled, and big John Mayberry homered. Talk about a quick strike attack. In the bottom of the inning, we scored two and eventually were leading 6–3 heading into the eighth. That's when George Brett homered to tie it. The Yankee fans went a little bit nuts, throwing debris on the field and eventually holding up the start of the ninth inning. The PA announcer was pleading with them to stop. Billy was so angry that I thought he was going to run upstairs and read the fans the riot act, and quite honestly, I'm surprised the umpires didn't pull the Royals off the field and make us forfeit the game.

Mark Littell, a twenty-three-year-old reliever who hadn't given up a run in the series, was on the mound. He stayed out there through the delay, every now and then throwing a warm-up pitch. Littell had been one of the best relievers in the league all season, pitching to a 2.08 ERA and giving up a single home run in 104 innings. I don't know if he had ever dealt with circumstances like this before.

Our hottest hitter in the series, Chris Chambliss, led off the bottom of the ninth. Littell's first offering was a fastball up in the zone, out over the plate. Chris stayed back and then jumped on it. It sounded good, really good, when he made contact, driving a high fly ball to right-center. Sitting in the dugout, I wasn't sure if it was going to carry over the fence or not. We all sprung off the bench toward the steps to follow the ball's flight. McRae, playing right field for the Royals that night, raced back to the track, to the wall. He leaped.

When he came down, I thought the ball might be in his glove. It was hard to tell. McRae stood ramrod straight against the fence, center fielder Amos Otis alongside him. McRae's glove was empty. The Yankees were American League champions, after a twelve-year hiatus. Chris threw both arms overhead as he neared first base. Almost instantly, fans began pouring onto the field by the thousands. It was a scary and out-of-control scene, just total bedlam. As Chris tried to make his way around second, the bedlam got much worse, Chris getting knocked down, throwing his forearms, trying to fend off fans and get around the bases. All I could think of was that he had to touch all four bases for the home run to count. If he didn't do that, the homer would be nullified and we'd go into extra innings.

Of course, by the time Chris got halfway around the bases, the plate had already been dug up and hauled off. There was nothing left to touch but the dirt.

I ventured onto the field to try—futilely—to run some interference for Chris. I couldn't get near him, so I turned to head back toward the dugout steps. Above the din I heard a familiar voice.

"Larry! Larry! Over here!" I looked into the crowd, and there in the middle of a mob of fans by the railing of the box seats, next to the dugout, trying to get down to the field but being restrained by a security guard, was my father. I'll never forget the look on my dad's face. It was an equal mix of ecstasy and terror, for he'd never been engulfed in such chaos before, or been strong-armed by a rent-a-cop.

I raced over to the railing and told the guard, "That's my father. Let him go! Let him go!" The cop was reluctant at first, as if he wasn't sure if he believed me.

"Trust me. He's my father," I said. Finally, the cop released his grip. I helped my father get over the railing, and he came down on the field. We walked down the dugout steps together, then up the runway to the clubhouse, where the celebration was already raging. My father wasn't a baseball man, and I know that he thought that all the time I spent playing ball as a kid was time I could've spent much more productively. But now he was here with me, surrounded by the spray of champagne and the whoops of joy and George Steinbrenner hugging everything but the clubhouse pillars, and it was great to have him there.

We'd made the transition from winners to losers, finally getting the Yankees to the playoff promised land of the World Series. There we would face Cincinnati's Big Red Machine.

It was a thrill to be in the World Series for the second straight season, but it was even more special because I would be playing against Joe Morgan, a guy who I tried to emulate when I was in high school. Back then, everybody had a thing against the Reds. They were so good, and they were all about the competition. Players didn't fraternize much back then anyway, but I remember being on the field with Joe at All-Star Games and in the World Series and being struck by one thing. *I'm taller than this guy?* I couldn't figure out where all his power came from. He had this kind of slappy swing, something I tried out myself when younger, but the ball just jumped off his bat. He had that timing mechanism, where he flapped his arm like a chicken wing before the pitcher delivered, and he was a little fireplug. I'd check the box scores to keep up with Joe's numbers, but I knew that we were very different kinds of players.

Outside the game, Joe and I never got real close and became what I call cordial friends. But the intensity of my imagined rivalry diminished once he stopped playing. Joe served as a kind of mentor/counselor once I decided that I wanted to manage. He had the same aspirations as I did, but in broadcasting, where the opportunities were less fraught with the politics of the game and perceptions than managerial positions were. He was invaluable to me, and I can't thank him enough.

I have to thank him and the '76 Reds for another reason. We suffered a bicentennial beat-down at the hands of those guys. Sure, we took some satisfaction in having returned the Yankees to the Series, but that whipping left a bad taste in all our mouths. Only one thing was going to rid us of that—some World Series champagne.

CHAPTER 4

Keeping My Eye on the Ball Game

'll always remember the picture of Reggie Jackson in the Oakland A's dugout after losing the 1971 playoffs to the Baltimore Orioles. He was slumped in pain. He wanted to win, *bad*.

I was in the middle of my senior year of high school that October, and I would rush home to watch the games on NBC. Curt Gowdy and Tony Kubek did the announcing for the final game of the Series, when the Orioles swept the A's with their 5–3 victory. That game was played in Oakland, so I had a chance to see the whole game. I can't say that I was a huge Reggie Jackson fan, but you couldn't be a lover of the game and not know who he was. I watched him flailing away at the offerings of the crafty left-hander Dave McNally. Reggie was 0-for-4 in that game. He'd homered twice in the previous games, but came up empty with the Series on the line.

Reggie was in his fourth full season with the A's in 1971, and while he was productive, he hadn't matched his incredible breakout year of 1969, when he hit 47 home runs and drove in 118 runs as a twenty-three-year-old. Still, the image of him sitting in the dugout absolutely crushed by that defeat stayed with me. He seemed so humbled by the game, and as you of course know, the world "humble" isn't one that often gets used in connection with Reggie. That's what this game can sometimes do to you.

The word "humble" also isn't one that you often think of when looking back on the Oakland A's teams of that era. I think that it's a measure of the man and the team that Reggie and the A's bounced back from getting swept and went on to win World Series titles the next three seasons. I can see now that the A's of that period and the Yankees who became known as the Bronx Zoo had some things in common—and not just the former A's whom the Boss brought over to play. Both teams had colorful owners. Charlie Finley was one of the game's great innovators, and the A's were literally colorful with their green-and-gold uniforms. Like Bill Veeck before him, Charlie Finley was an innovative promoter of the game. One of his ideas involved getting his players to grow mustaches to keep up with the fashion trends of the '70s. Rollie Fingers's handlebar mustache and the Vandyke facial hair on Catfish Hunter and others all contributed to a kind of anti-establishment flair. They were also known for their clubhouse tension, and other on- and off-field escapades earned them all kinds of headlines.

So maybe that was why in the off-season, following our embarrassing loss to the Reds, the Boss signed Reggie to a contract for five years and nearly $3 million. George had to wine and dine Reggie, who had higher offers from the Expos and the Padres. He sold Reggie on the idea that only New York City was large enough to accommodate his personality. To his credit, Reggie didn't just follow the dollars—he wanted to be with a winner.

Of course, Reggie's reputation preceded him. Even though players didn't fraternize a whole lot back then—in fact, I rarely said anything other than a brief "Hey" to an opposing player—word got around that Reggie thought a whole lot of himself and his abilities. Back then, I'm not sure anyone used the word "swagger" to describe Reggie's approach to the game. Mostly the press described him as "confident," but some less kind words were used by his former teammates.

I was following all the ups and downs of the negotiations through the *New York Post,* and I was thrilled when, the night before the press conference announcing Reggie's signing, I was asked to attend. I remember thinking at the time that my being included in the press conference was a sign that I'd really arrived as a Yankee. I was there with

Roy White and Thurman Munson and Mr. Steinbrenner. I remember slipping into my double-knit church-wedding-funeral suit and feeling pretty darn good about myself and the prospects for the 1977 season.

Looking back on it, I see that my appearance at the press conference as a representative of the team was equal parts Roy's influence and convenience—I lived nearby in New Jersey and I could get there easily. Given how Mr. Steinbrenner later treated me (not particularly generously), I don't think he was trying to send any kind of signal that I was that big a part of the Yankees. I was just a convenient solution to a problem. He needed a show of solidarity, and I was a good soldier who happened to be housed nearby.

I helped put the Yankee hat on Reggie's head on November 29, 1976, and I was thinking this was an early Christmas present for the rest of the Yankees, for all of New York, and for me. Reggie's power was legendary. Graig Nettles had led us with 32 home runs in '76, and a trio of guys, Oscar Gamble, Thurman Munson, and Chris Chambliss, followed him up with 17 each. We had a total of 120 for the season, placing us behind the Red Sox, who hit 134 that year. Home runs weren't the most important statistic, obviously, but having that big bat of Reggie's in a lineup that already featured the league's Most Valuable Player, Thurman Munson, as well as Graig Nettles and Chris Chambliss, certainly wasn't going to hurt us. Oscar Gamble wasn't with the team in '77, but, no disrespect intended, I think everyone agreed that Reggie would be able to produce better numbers even if he had an off year.

I think that adding Reggie to the mix was a good thing. Sometimes competition among teammates, particularly really competitive ones, can bring out the best in guys. I think that was the case with Reggie and Thurman and Graig. Reggie seemed to believe that this was now his team. He projected the sense that he welcomed the idea of having guys climb on his back so that he could lead us to the promised land. I know that didn't sit well with Thurman, who thought that this was *his* team. He was right. He'd been with the Yankees longer, he was the reigning league MVP, and as a catcher he commanded a ton of respect from the pitchers as well as the position players. Graig was a very, very bright and articulate guy. He used his wit as a weapon, a whip, and a welcome mat—and sometimes as an un-welcome mat. He was a proud and accomplished player, someone who rarely trumpeted his own considerable accomplishments, and he and Reggie were bound to clash.

I know that a lot of people believe that you have to learn to win. Our getting swept by the Reds in such a humiliating fashion was a painful lesson. Say what you will about Reggie, but he was a part of those winning clubs in Oakland, and in my mind that meant something. We were a team on a mission, and since Reggie wasn't going to take over my position on or off the field, he posed no threat to me and I posed none to him. We got along well, and that put me in the minority. That was okay. Nobody else tried to sway my thinking about him. I was focused on getting the job done, and I pretty much blocked out whatever distractions went on.

One of the big changes I've seen in the game is how spring training is handled. When we reported in '76, there was no big meeting to set the tone, no "State of the Yankees" address that set out our goals. The staff just rolled out the bats and balls and we got after it. Truth is, they didn't need to have any kind of meeting to let us know what was expected. We knew. We were so fired up about the opportunity to get that Reds sweep out of our memory that no one had to remind us of what the end zone looked like.

The composition of the team was ideal for a championship run. We had a few young guys like Mickey Rivers and me. It just so happened that we were the speed element on the team as well. We also had a solid group of veterans who could see the finish line of their careers coming and wanted to win another championship—or a first one—before time and opportunity slipped away.

In addition to Reggie, we added pitchers like Dock Ellis, Ed Figueroa, and Catfish Hunter. We knew that the bar had been raised, and we had no problem with those high expectations. Even though not every one of the guys had suffered the kind of blowout that the guys from the '76 team experienced being swept by the Reds, the sense of revenge was something you couldn't help but detect. We pulled together and rallied around each other in a tough town, playing for a tough owner.

I eventually came to realize that one of the Boss's most important acquisitions that off-season was another player who had championship experience. Sometimes understanding your role on a squad is almost as important a contribution as what you do on the field. Paul Blair, a teammate of Reggie's during his one season with the Orioles, in 1976, understood his role, and more important, he accepted it. Paul was one of the best center fielders in the game, playing twelve full seasons with the Orioles during their great run from the mid-'60s to the mid-'70s. He was a decent hitter, but in his last two years in Baltimore he had finished just above and just below the dreaded Mendoza Line. Fortunately for him, he was better known for his defense and was a multiple Gold Glove winner. He was going to serve as a late-inning defensive replacement, a guy versatile enough to play all three outfield positions in 1977 and, in addition to those three, short, second, and third in '78. I learned a lot from Paul. He had designs on being a coach after his playing days were over, and he was eager to share the wealth of knowledge he had picked up from playing for the great Earl Weaver and alongside guys like Frank Robinson, Brooks Robinson, Davey Johnson, Mark Belanger, and a host of other great players.

More important, he was a great clubhouse presence. Some guys are great in the clubhouse because they work hard and keep their mouths shut and lead by example. Some guys are more vocal. We had a number of vocal leaders—Thurman and Graig among them—who could use verbal jabs to keep guys on their toes or back on their heels, as necessary. Paul had a way of giving guys crap that I'd not seen before. He was genuinely funny, and he had the habit of calling guys "Darling" in such a disarming way that you couldn't help but laugh.

One of Paul's "darlings" was Reggie.

That came into play on one of the most infamous days in Reggie's tenure—June 18, 1977. We were playing the Red Sox at Fenway, and the Saturday afternoon contest was part of NBC's *Game of the Week*. At that point, both teams had won thirty-six games, but the Red Sox led us by a game and a half. Going into the bottom of the sixth, we were trailing 7–4, and Mike Torrez, who had started, was still on the mound. He got the first out, then Fred Lynn singled to right. Jim Rice stepped in and hit another ball to right. I was busy focusing on the runners, so I can't say for sure that Reggie loafed after the ball, but Rice came into second base. I stood nearby, and then started making my way toward my position once the ball was back in Torrez's hands. Billy came out of the dugout to make a pitching change, and then, because we were the visiting team at Fenway and our dugout was on the third-base line, Paul Blair came trotting out onto the field. I was near my second-base position, and as Paul came by I heard him say to Reggie, "You're out of the game, *dahlink*."

That was bizarre. Pulling a guy out of the game in the middle of an inning like that, especially a game against a rival and on national television, was sure to do one thing—embarrass Reggie. Paul said those words like he was enjoying the hell out of being asked to replace Reggie. I knew that a lot of the guys resented Reggie, and maybe Billy was trying to make a point about hustling, but in my mind that crossed the line. Maybe that was Billy's way of gaining the loyalty of the rest of the guys, letting them know that he was on their side of the Reggie debate, but there's enough blame to go around for what happened next. Reggie and Billy confronted each other, and Billy eventually had to be restrained by Elston Howard.

Being on the field, I couldn't hear anything that was being said, but the whole episode seemed unnecessary. I sometimes wonder how things might have played out if it hadn't been a nationally televised game. You have to understand that, back then, there was only one way to see a game outside of your home market on television. As a result, the incident got a whole lot of attention. Of course, this being New York, it was going to get a lot of play anyway, but outside New York that might have been the nation's first glimpse of the animals on exhibit in the Bronx Zoo. If Billy was trying to fire us all up, his attempt had the opposite effect: we lost the next three and fell four and a half games out of first.

I also believe that Reggie had a positive influence on guys like Thurman and Graig especially. Like I said, competition among teammates can be a really good thing. Graig had a monster year in '77, hitting 37 home runs and driving in 107, while Thurman also continued his MVP-type year, hitting .308 while homering 18 times and driving in 100 runs. Reggie proved his worth as well, hitting 32 out of the park with 110 RBIs, while hitting a more than respectable .286. As a team, we scored 831 runs, 101 more than we did in '76. I don't know if my teammates would be willing to give Reggie any credit for that kind of increase, but I sure do. We won only three more games that year than we did in '76 (100 versus 97), but we needed every one of them. We finished two and a half games ahead of a very good Orioles team to capture an AL East title. The division was so competitive that the Red Sox also won 97 games but finished tied for second with Baltimore. If we were a zoo, then the AL East was a real jungle in 1977.

At the time, I never really bought into the whole "Bronx Zoo" theme—the idea that our team was more of a circus than Ringling Bros., coming soon to an American League city near you. The more I think back on it, though, well, it was pretty crazy, with the managerial changes and the clashing egos and the almost constant sideshows. The thing was, though, I was so used to that kind of chaos—first with Dock Ellis during my brief stint with the Pirates, and then in those first few years with the Yankees—that it all seemed, if not completely normal, then at least what I'd come to expect. Maybe fortune smiled down on me by having me exposed to those things early on and blessing me with the ability to keep my head down and ignore the chaos going on.

In a way, being accustomed to all kinds of nonsense going on around me and not getting too distracted by it goes all the way back to my days in Brownsville. I witnessed stabbings, beatings, all kinds of other criminal acts, and some of the worst of humanity. It's not that I wasn't affected by it or didn't care and grew callous, but I did develop a sense of self-preservation and a focus from an early age that was much needed to make it in Brownsville. I had to learn to keep my head on a swivel and at the same time develop a kind of filter that helped me block out some things, and those abilities would later help me out with the Yankees. I knew that what was going on behind the scenes and on the field were not matters of life and death. Being able to just go about your business when the place seems to be going down in flames is an undervalued skill, in my mind.

From an early age, I'd been taught that by the best. My mother took us every Sunday to Pilgrim Baptist Church and nourished our spiritual souls every other day. She didn't just read the Bible. She lived it. Minnie Randolph was and is our spiritual beacon, the nonstop nurturer, the person more than anyone else who has taught us to believe in ourselves and to think positively, even in the face of despair. I don't know if it is her Christian faith that frees her of any lingering resentment about the years of hardship, or if she's just really good at hiding it, but as a mother she has a wonderful way of empowering you and uplifting you. You just have to work hard, live the right way, and trust in the Lord.

It's a pretty simple formula, if you listen to Minnie Randolph.

You also must always carry yourself in a way that reflects God's grace and brings honor to your family. That's what my mother insisted on. Even as a grown-up, if I mess up in that department, I am going to hear about it. I sure found out in August 1978, my third year with the Yankees. We were playing the Orioles on ABC's *Game of the Week*. I was up at bat against Jim Palmer in the top of the fourth. When Palmer threw a breaking ball, I started to swing, but held up. Steve Palermo was umpiring first. Steve and I came up together through the minor leagues, and this was his second year in the majors. He wound up umpiring for fourteen years before he suffered a crippling spinal cord injury as a result of being shot in the back outside a Dallas restaurant in 1991 as he tried to help a robbery victim in the parking lot. It happened on July 7, the day after my birthday. I was in Cleveland, playing for the Brewers at the time, and was just sick about it when I heard the news.

Even for someone who was accustomed to street violence, I was struck by the randomness of the tragedy, a good man doing a good thing and almost dying because of it. (Steve ultimately wound up making a tremendous recovery and learned to walk again, and now he works as an umpire supervisor for Major League Baseball.)

Anyway, in all my dealings with Steve over the years, I always liked and respected him, never had any trouble with him at all. I had no reason to think that was going to change. Then Rick Dempsey, the Orioles' catcher, appealed plate umpire Larry McCoy's call to Palermo. Palermo had his hands on his knees at first base, staring straight ahead. I started to set myself in the box, preparing for the next pitch, when I looked toward first and saw Steve Palermo straighten up, raise his arm, and ring me up with an emphatic jerk of his right hand. I froze for a moment, in complete shock. There was no way I'd gone. It wasn't even close. As I began the walk back to the dugout, I shot Palermo my best "you blew that and you know it" glare.

On the bench the guys started giving Palermo a brutal time of it. I walked by Reggie Jackson.

"Did you go?" Reggie asked.

"No way," I said. "I held up. I know I held up." I sat down next to Reggie on the bench. He started talking to me about my swing. Reggie always wanted to talk about hitting. Graig Nettles and a few other guys stayed all over Palermo. They were riding him pretty hard. Palermo wasn't happy about it. Finally, Palermo had heard enough and walked over to our dugout. He pointed around, looking for somebody to run. He pointed at me, and then he shouted:

"Randolph, you're gone!"

I couldn't believe my ears. I had never been thrown out of a game before. This was a complete joke. Honest to God, I wasn't doing anything but sitting in the dugout, talking to Reggie. The injustice was too much to take. Without a shred of forethought, I bolted from the dugout and charged at Palermo, completely out of mind. I didn't care about national TV or Howard Cosell or anything else. I just lost it completely. I arrived at first and got right in Palermo's face, veins bulging from my neck, curse words pouring out of my mouth.

"How can you run me? I didn't say a frigging word!"

"I heard you. I heard all of it. You're gone!" Palermo said. Now I was even angrier. If I was going to get tossed unjustly, I was going to get my money's worth.

"You're horseshit and the ejection is horseshit," I said. "It's the biggest piece of horseshit umpiring I've ever seen." Only the strong arms of the first-base coach prevented me from getting into more trouble.

Back in Brooklyn, my mother took in all of this on TV and was not pleased, not at all. If she had been at the park she probably would've marched onto the field and dragged me away by the ear. She had to settle for chewing me out on the telephone the next day. "Don't you ever embarrass the family like that again," she said. "If you do, I will put you over my knee." I was twenty-four years old—and she wasn't kidding. Later I got a letter of apology from American League president Lee MacPhail about the incident; it made me feel better, but to my mother it was irrelevant.

CLEVELAND WAS ALWAYS AN interesting place to play, and '77 was no different. Mr. Steinbrenner was from that city, of course, and the whole Indians versus Yankees rivalry, the Big Apple versus the Mistake on the Lake, was always something unique. For the Labor Day weekend that year, the Indians' brass came up with a promotion idea. They passed out I HATE THE YANKEES "hankees." That's no typo by the way—that's what they called them, and that's how they spelled it.

I liked going to Cleveland, but I hated playing in Municipal Stadium. If Cleveland was the Mistake on the Lake, then Municipal Stadium was the son of that "mistake," and the apple didn't fall far from the tree at all. The home of the Indians was a cavernous, damp, dank place that could just suck your soul right out of you.

That wasn't true, though, for that Labor Day 1977 series against the Indians. We came in riding a seven-game winning streak. Nearly 28,000 fans packed the place—well, not exactly "packed," since the monstrosity had a capacity of about 70,000. Battling the low sun and shadows of a September afternoon, and with the fans waving those I HATE THE YANKEES "hankees," we lost that doubleheader, 4–3 and 5–4. The "Curse of the Yankee Hankee" was born.

At the start of the next season, in April 1978, we traveled to Texas to face the Rangers and another Yankee Hankee promotion. Ironically, we faced Dock Ellis, who had gotten himself into trouble in '77 by getting into an inevitable free spirit versus authority clash with the Boss. At one point in the spring Dock had said, "The more we lose, the more Steinbrenner will fly in. And the more he flies, the better the chance there will be a plane crash." About a month later, Dock was on a flight to Texas without the rest of his Yankee teammates. The Curse of the Yankee Hankee worked. Dock ended up beating us 5–2.

The stories of Mr. Steinbrenner's quick temper and impulsive actions have been repeated and repeated. What doesn't get reported on as frequently is his great generosity. I said earlier that I liked going to Cleveland but didn't like playing in that horrible stadium. (That crowd of 28,000 on Labor Day was followed by a game the next day with only about 5,000 showing up. It felt like we were playing in a meadow in Yellowstone National Park.)

Mr. Steinbrenner held a financial interest in a restaurant called The Theatrical. Well, a lot of drama took place there. Mr. Steinbrenner graciously allowed us to run up a tab at the restaurant, so nearly all of us took advantage of the free meal and drinks whenever we were in town. Some of the drama was food-related—contests over who was going to be able to eat his weight in steak, lobster, and other menu offerings. Some of it was alcohol-fueled. One night I was having dinner with Roy White at a corner table when Billy came in with Yogi Berra and Elston Howard, his de facto bodyguards. The minute Billy arrived at the bar, this huge guy—he must've been six-foot-six and 300 pounds—lurched over to him. The guy—think offensive lineman in a rumpled tie and jacket—was plastered. He started getting on Billy, saying the Yankees suck, they're going to lose tomorrow, blah, blah, blah. Yogi and Ellie tried to nudge the guy away. More blah, blah, expletive, blah, blah. Billy just sat there, never said a word, and nursed his drink. From my experience in observing Billy Martin, that was a very bad sign for Mr. Lineman. The guy kept on him and was getting more animated, and the next thing I knew Billy was wheeling around, bringing up his right hand, and just flattening the guy.

Yogi and Ellie made sure the man didn't get up right away—not that there was a great chance of that, but just to be safe. Billy decided it was an excellent time to finish his beverage in his room.

Incidents like the Yankee Hankee and Billy's first-round knockout helped to punctuate what could be a long season threatening to turn into a complete blur not only when you look back on it but while you're living it. Over the course of a 162-game season, each game counts equally in the standings. If you fail to win a playoff spot by half a game, the difference could have come as a result of some uninspired play in early May when you were playing in a cold-weather city and couldn't feel your hands and all you wanted to do was get back in the dugout and out of "the Hawk"—the chilling wind that seems to cut through clothes and flesh. Or it could have been that final game of the year when everything was on the line and you weren't totally into every pitch.

Of course, as much as you want to give 100 percent every day and on every play, it's simply not humanly possible, and probably not advisable, to push yourself that hard all the time. So there's this conflict going on in your mind all the time—go as hard as you can, keep some in reserve for when the postseason comes around, have some fun and enjoy the game, but remember that any play can have serious consequences.

What was interesting to me about that '77 team was that during the dog days of August we showed what we were made of. On August 6, we lost to the Mariners, 9–2, to fall to 4-4 on a nine-game Western swing. We also fell five games behind, our largest deficit, and were in third place behind the Red Sox and the Orioles. The old saying about playing .500 on the road has some merit, but getting thumped by the Mariners, an expansion team in its first year of operation, and possibly being swept by them to finish the trip 4-5 was not something that would sit well with us or with Billy and the Boss.

Mike Torrez was huge for us that season, and he scattered six hits in our 7–1 win. That put Mike just one game above .500 at 11-10, but we really needed that win and he delivered. It was a strange game in that Tom House, who later went on to some fame as a somewhat controversial pitching coach, retired me to start the game and then exited with an injury. We then jumped on his replacement, John Montague, in the third inning. Up again in the leadoff spot, I started things off with a double, and before the inning was over we'd scored six runs, with Graig delivering a key double and Paul Blair homering. Up and down the lineup that inning, we produced.

It's hard to speculate on what might have happened, but if we had lost that game, I can imagine that the long Sunday night cross-country flight back to New York would have been interesting—and I don't mean because we'd have all been wrapped up in reading a good book.

As it turned out, we didn't play again until the following Wednesday, and those two days off probably helped us as much as that victory. We got hot as an August night in New York City can be, winning twenty-three out of our next twenty-six games to go from being five down to four and a half games up. That was as impressive a run of good baseball as I'd ever been a part of. Some days we just hammered the ball, like the 15–3 destruction of the Angels when Mickey went 4-for-5, drove in three runs, and raised his average to .322, and then there were the pitchers' duels, like Ron Guidry besting Doyle Alexander of the Rangers 2–1.

Another key contributor to that success was Sparky Lyle. He closed out the month of August winning three games in a row out of the bullpen. On the 29th, we trailed the Royals 3–2. Sparky came in to replace Catfish in the top of the eighth. In the bottom of that frame, we scored three times with two outs when Chris Chambliss hit a clutch home run. The next day we blew a 5–3 lead against the Mariners when they scored three times in the eighth to tie us. We won 6–5 in the eleventh, with Sparky going three and two-thirds innings without allowing a run. Finally, on the 31st, we again lost the lead to the Mariners in the eighth, but then won on a Graig Nettles walk-off homer. Sparky got the win with another two innings of shutout ball. In that three-game stretch, he pitched seven and two-thirds innings and gave up six hits and no runs to increase his record to 12-4. In that last game, he gave up a couple of fly balls after Torrez surrendered a double, so he did blow a save, but no one held it against him for vulturing a win. Sparky felt like crap about it, and I saw him letting Mike know that he deserved better. But those comeback wins, despite losing leads late, said a lot about the makeup of that club. We weren't going to lose.

And we kept up that mentality and learned how to win in another classic Royals versus Yankees playoff series. We opened at home against a Royals team that had won 102 games. Former Reds veteran pitcher Don Gullett took the mound for us, but it was clear that he wasn't the same dominant pitcher he had been with the Reds. He had a great regular season, going 14-4, but he was plagued by arm troubles, which would end his career the next season. By the third inning, we were down 6–0, and Don was out of the game.

I have to say this, though. Don Gullett was a warrior. These were the days before advanced imaging techniques like MRIs and guys being treated with every possible medical advancement. Don was hurting, but he was one of those "I'll rub some liniment on it and go out there and give it all I've got" kind of guys. No, he didn't get the results we'd hoped for, but the man earned our respect.

We scored a couple of times to avoid the shutout, but losing at home—again with that two games at home and three on the road format—didn't bode well for us. We weren't panicking, but like most of the 54,930 who made their way home in the evening twilight from the Stadium, we knew that the following day was a must-win. I liked our chances, especially with the matchup of Guidry versus Andy Hassler. Andy was a good major league pitcher, but Ron could be lights-out at any time.

I was seeing the ball pretty well and went 2-for-4 the next day, driving in a run in our 6–2 win. The story of the day, however, was Ron Guidry: he went all nine, allowing just three hits. His battery mate, Thurman, also came up big, going 3-for-4. To that point, Reggie had been struggling a bit, with just one hit in eight at-bats.

We went to Kansas City knowing that we had to beat them two out of three. I made no visits to Gates Bar-B-Q for barbecue sauce. Too much was on the line for anything but complete focus. That was even more true when we lost game 3, 6–2, and now faced elimination. I felt bad for Billy. We'd gotten to the Series the year before, we'd had some upsets along the way during the regular season, but we'd battled back, and now we faced an enormous task. Generally, after the season is over, the manager will address the players as a group. As fiery and ornery as Billy could be, I don't think I'd ever seen him as emotional as he was after that '76 sweep the Reds put on us. Say what you will, but Billy cared very deeply about the organization and about winning. He was red-eyed with near-tears, and his voice was painful to hear, there was so much hurt and disappointment in it.

I can't speak for the rest of the guys on that '77 team, but part of my motivation to get back to the Series and to win it all was to help vindicate Billy and ease some of the pain that he felt. Like I've said, for whatever reason, maybe because I played the same position and played it like he did, Billy treated me decently. Some managers you win for, and some you win despite them, or maybe even to spite them, but as much as I wanted to succeed for myself, I wanted to please Billy. It was clear to me that Billy was devoted to the game, that he'd paid enormous personal sacrifices to it, and it just seemed to me that the universe should somehow be fair and get out of Billy's way and allow him to succeed. Billy treated me fairly, and I wanted the baseball gods to do the same for him.

Walking into the clubhouse on October 8, 1977, I was as on edge as I'd ever been before a ball game. I could tell that the rest of the guys were feeling it a bit also. It wasn't that they were tight, but they were purposeful. I remembered some of the guys telling me about Sparky Lyle and his superstition about his glove. Back in '72, he was having a terrific year, and he was using a three-year-old glove, a beat-up and tattered thing, but it was his gamer and he was having such a good year that he kept using it despite how decrepit it was getting. Then someone stole it out of the bullpen, and Yankee management had worked like Sherlock Holmes to crack the case and get the glove back for him.

Lots of guys have good-luck hats, bats, rituals, etc., and I would be willing to bet that there was no greater accumulation of them than there was in that fourth game of the Royals series. It wasn't so much that we felt like we needed luck, but that we wanted this game to be like any other. If you normally wore eyeblack, you put it on. If you ran ten sprints right after batting practice was over or just before you took the field, then you did that. It wasn't so much that you didn't want to jinx yourself, but that you wanted to get into your usual routine, do the things you'd done that had allowed you to win 100 times that season. Sparky was legendarily superstitious, and in some people's minds it was the Curse of Sparky Lyle as much as the Curse of the Bambino that kept the Red Sox from getting into the winner's circle, but it was Sparky's breaking out of the usual routine that made this game so special.

We were facing the tough left-hander Larry Gura, but we put some good at-bats together in each of the first three innings and took a 4–0 lead. Unfortunately, the Royals scored two in the bottom of the third and two again in the fourth to chase our starter, Ed Figueroa. We'd picked up another run and were ahead 5–2 going into the bottom of the fourth. Billy brought in Dick Tidrow, who allowed a double and a walk while getting one out. With two out, the game now 5–4, and the dangerous George Brett coming to the plate, Billy made a stunning move. He brought in our closer, Sparky Lyle. To that point in the series, Sparky had appeared in two of the first three games, pitching two and two-thirds innings and giving up a run on four hits. Relatively speaking, he was rested, but I don't think that Billy expected him to finish the game. With two runners on and Brett coming up, Billy must have figured that this was a pivotal point in the game. Later, when asked about the move, Billy said that he wanted his best pitcher out there.

I can't imagine how that move would have been scrutinized and analyzed today, and how Billy might have been crucified, if it hadn't worked out the way that it did. Sparky was masterful, going five and a third innings and allowing only two hits and no walks. I was surprised by the move, but never really questioned Billy's unorthodox approach to using his closer. We scored one more run to make it 6–4, and Sparky's performance was a season saver. Today closers come in and throw in the mid- to high 90s for the most part, but Sparky beat you with a combination of guile and guts that was unsurpassed.

We headed into game 5 with a renewed sense of hope. Sparky's performance had lifted us, and I'd like to say we rode that high to an easy victory, but it was anything but easy. Ron Guidry had started game 2 and won in a complete game. He took the hill to start game 5 on two days' rest, and he clearly didn't have his best stuff. The Royals jumped on him in the bottom of the first for two runs. When he gave up another run in the bottom of the third, Billy came out and got him. That just goes to show that Billy couldn't pull a rabbit out of his hat every time. He gambled on Guidry, but he drew an inside straight when he brought in Mike Torrez. Mike shut down the powerful Royals offense for five and a third innings on just three hits, pulling a Sparky Lyle, and our offense eventually woke up.

The legendary Whitey Herzog had to do some bullpen manipulations of his own, since he didn't seem to trust Mark Littell, who'd been victimized in the '76 playoff game by Chambliss's home run. We'd scratched out a run in the top of the third, but went into the eighth with their starter, Paul Splittorff, still on the mound. He'd been masterful in mixing his pitches all afternoon, throwing that really good overhand curveball and high fastballs that were so tempting. I led off the eighth with a single, and that brought Whitey out of the dugout. He brought in Doug Bird to face Thurman, and the move paid off as our catcher went down on strikes. That brought up Lou Piniella, and he drove a ball into right field that allowed me to get to third. With the right-hander on the mound, Billy went to the bench and brought in Reggie to pinch-hit for Cliff Johnson. That's right. This was the most important game of the season, and Billy was playing the percentages, not starting the left-handed-hitting Reggie Jackson against the lefty Splittorff.

That was part of Billy's genius, though. As a manager, you're under a lot of pressure to make the right calls all the time. So how do you sleep nights knowing that you're taking your $3 million man, one of the best power hitters in the game, and sitting him down? Billy didn't seem to have any problem with it, and Reggie rose to the occasion when he singled off of Bird on a 1-2 pitch. That brought me home, and Lou aggressively took third on a ball hit to center field. That was all we got, though. Nettles lined out hard, and Chris Chambliss rolled over one and grounded out to second. We were down by a run. Mike needed to hold them there, but he seemed to run out of gas after getting the first two outs in the bottom of the eighth. He walked the next two, and in came Sparky. He got out of it, and we had one last chance.

The Royals brought in one of their starters to begin the ninth, Dennis Leonard. Dennis had been tough on us in game 3, going the distance and allowing four hits and two runs. He was a tough right-hander who'd won twenty games that year, and he also had one save. So it was completely out of the ordinary for him to be brought in in that situation. The Royals, like a few teams back then, had a closer by committee. (I should say that the term "closer" wasn't even in use back then.) Leonard's job was to stop us, but he didn't get much of a chance to do that. A Paul Blair single and a Roy White walk put two runners on and brought up the top of the order and Mickey Rivers. Herzog went with the percentages and brought in another starter, this time the lefty Larry Gura, to get Mickey. Rivers didn't cooperate. On a 2-2 pitch, he singled to right, plating Blair and getting Roy over to second. That was it for the starters turned relievers.

I came up to face Mark Littell. With the count 3-1, I knew Littell didn't want to load the bases for the clutch-hitting Thurman. I sat dead red and got the fastball I was looking for. I made solid contact, but hit it on the line to center. Fortunately, it was deep enough that Roy was able to score to give us the lead. We added another run on an error and went into the bottom of the ninth up 5–3.

Sparky did his thing and induced Freddie Patek to hit into a game-ending 5-5-3 double play. I've never been as happy to turn two as I was that day. Satisfaction mixed with relief and a healthy splash of joy was the locker room drink of choice. Someone later told me that Tony Kubek summed up our remarkable comeback by saying that, in comparison to the Royals, the Yankees knew how to win. That was true of those series, but we still hadn't gotten what we really wanted. The Dodgers were the team standing in our way now.

Believe me, I understand that Reggie Jackson pounding out three home runs in Game 6 of the '77 World Series is indelibly printed in the minds of baseball fans. That is as it should be. I had chills running up and down my spine in that one. We won the Series with that Game 6 victory and Reggie's clutch performance. I'm a team player, and I have to give it up to Reggie and my teammates. Allow me a bit of time, though, to talk about my own little Reggie moment.

To me, Game 1 of the Series was a classic. Given how bright Reggie's star shone in Game 6, it's easy to be blinded to the fact that that opening game had everything you'd want to see in a World Series game. It went twelve innings, with me leading off the twelfth with a double deep into the corner in left field. I thought it might get out, but that would have been too much to believe. After all, I'd also led off the sixth inning with a deep drive to left, this one clearing the wall and tying the game at 2–2. I would have bigger thrills in the game as a Yankee, but as far as personal feats go, it's tough to top that Game 1. Scoring the winning run on a Paul Blair single, I'm not sure my feet even touched the ground. Believe me, I made sure they touched home plate, and being mobbed and jumping into the arms of the *dahlink* Paul Blair was a mighty nice slice of baseball heaven.

Guys like me don't often get to figure in the spotlight, and I understand that it had to shift to other players and other games, but I sure enjoyed those moments. Hometown boy did good, but he certainly didn't do it alone, just the same as Reggie didn't. In that Game 1, Don Gullett gutted out eight and a third innings. Sparky blew the save, but hung in there for three and a third innings of one-hit baseball to pick up the victory. Paul Blair came in as a defensive replacement for Reggie and wound up driving in the winning run. Most important, we recovered from losing the lead in the top of the ninth to come back and win it. The Stadium was rocking as I headed for home, and I can't be sure if it was my own excitement or the fans' thunderous cheers that had my heart rattling around inside my chest.

I never got a chance to experience the kind of prodigious offensive display that Reggie put on in Game 6, and I don't know if I could have survived the outpouring of emotion when it was clear, except to the most diehard skeptics, that our 8–3 lead, which we took in the bottom of the eighth after Reggie's monster drive to center field off Charlie Hough settled into the night, was going to hold up. Notice the "our" and the "we" in that previous sentence.

When that pop-fly bunt settled into Mike Torrez's glove to end the years of frustration that Yankee players and fans had experienced, I remember looking around at the guys all charging toward the mound. We were united in purpose, just like we'd been that entire year. I also think it's meaningful that baseball is the one sport where championship-winning players all pile onto one another in one mass of limbs and hearts. What other major sport has the kind of 162-game grind that baseball does? How many other athletes spend three-quarters of the year together in the singular pursuit of a goal like a World Series title?

I experienced a deep joy and satisfaction that remain, even after all these years and all those championships, very hard to describe. I do know that I was incredibly happy for Billy, especially given how hard he had taken the previous year's loss. We'd experienced a crazy year, but the thing about Billy was that he wasn't afraid to put his faith in the people he trusted. That trust was always hard-earned, but the rewards felt richer as a result. Another thing about Billy was that he was all about the team concept. He could be petty and hold grudges and not hold his tongue or his liquor, but he cared about team and about winning. He also understood the role he played in that championship season, and he gave credit where credit was due. I'm not sure he always got the credit he deserved from the powers that be, but I do know that we appreciated him for what he was—an imperfect man and an imperfect manager, but a guy with as much heart as anybody I'd ever met.

I've been asked on several occasions how different it is to win a World Championship as a player versus as a coach helping to lead a team. I hope someday to add a third part to that question—what it's like to win one as a manager?

I think that the answer is obvious. Nothing compares to winning a World Series title as a player—especially when you contribute directly and regularly to your team's efforts. Coaching a team to the win is satisfying, don't get me wrong, but since your involvement is more indirect, so is the thrill you get. It's almost like the pleasure you get from seeing your children succeed at something. You're proud, you know that you played some part in it, and you're glad that they are getting to experience something really wonderful.

I could cop out and say that one isn't better than the other, that they're just different. That wouldn't be truthful. Flat out, hands down, winning a ring as a player is a more satisfying experience. Which is the greater accomplishment? Well, that's another question entirely.

Leading and playing are both very, very difficult tasks. You take them on at different points in your life, so you come to these jobs with different experiences and perspectives. But one difficulty shared by everyone who wins a baseball championship, whether as a player or as a coach, is the length of the season. When guys talk about the grind, those conversations are taking place in the clubhouse, in the manager's office, and in the coaches' office. The 162-game season is far longer than the season of any other professional sport. The days themselves are long. No, ballplayers aren't doing the same kind of hard physical labor that some folks do, but when you add in the travel, being away from family but still being a part of a family and all that goes into that, and the pressures that come from being part of a team in New York City, you get worn down physically, mentally, and spiritually.

Fortunately—and I mean that with the largest capital F you can think of—we do get to be involved in a game we all love. No offense to anyone in these lines of work, but if I were a doctor, lawyer, CEO, or anyone who puts in long hours at a high-stress job, I don't think I could hang in there. Dealing with the same levels of stress but getting to have those three to four hours a day out on the field—that I could do.

After all, the game is fun, and so are a number of other things that go along with it.

CHAPTER 5

Paying the Price

A fter winning that pennant in 1976 and then winning it all in 1977 and 1978, we were living the lives of rock stars. Everywhere we went we were mobbed by fans. Even on the road, fans would be lined up outside the ballpark, outside our hotel, and in the lobby, all wanting a piece of us. Some just wanted an autograph and a handshake, but others were looking for a little bit more physical contact than that. Fortunately for me, I was a young married man with a growing family, and I took those responsibilities and my vows seriously. I don't know how some of the other young guys on the team dealt with what was not so much temptation as demands on their time and energy.

But I did enjoy the adulation of the fans. Though I got used to the idea of people wanting autographs, that doesn't mean I ever got angry about them asking for one. During my first few years in the league especially, I still felt strange when people approached me. This was before the era of professional autograph-seekers and memorabilia businesspeople. These were real fans who loved the game, and I kept thinking, *Really? You want me to sign something?* I was especially pleased when kids came up to me, because I remembered what it was like for me as a Con Ed kid going to those games. Man, how much I looked up to those players. I felt like I owed it to the game that had been very good to me to be good to those who supported the game.

That doesn't mean that I was like some overeager brown-nosing schoolboy. I had my fun as well. I didn't lead the life of a hermit. I went out with the guys and had a few drinks, went to dinner and, in cities like Chicago, went to clubs to hear music, but I couldn't do that every night on the road. I would have been worn down to a nub and not been able to do my job. If I gave in to temptation, it was in places like Kansas City, which was famous for its barbecue. Gates Bar-B-Q was a legendary spot for good down-home eating, and I'd make sure to stop by when I was in town. And I'd also buy a bunch of bottles of sauce to take back with me.

One of the treats that comes with winning a World Series Championship for a New York team is the victory parade. It's easy to forget that in the mid- to late '70s New York City was struggling just like the Yankees had been. The city was on the verge of bankruptcy. When we beat the Dodgers in '77 to win the Series, some people thought that we'd done the city a great service by boosting its morale. That summer had been a particularly rough one. A major blackout darkened the streets, riots broke out in Brooklyn, and the "Son of Sam" serial killer was on the loose.

Mayor Ed Koch was not a big sports fan; he caught hell in the press for only staying for two innings on one Yankee opening day, for example. But even though the city was having trouble paying its bills, he authorized a ticker-tape parade. I don't know how much it cost the city for the extra security and the cleanup and what-not, but I know that I enjoyed the hell out of the trip through the Canyon of Heroes. An estimated 2 million people lined the streets of Lower Manhattan to cheer for us. I know that for professional athletes it's easy to become jaded, to grow tired of people wanting something from you—an autograph, tickets, a bite out of what they think is your oversized and undeserved ego—but, man, to just hear all the noise and see all the paper raining down on you as you're driven along is a surefire cure for being blasé about baseball.

I've said that I'm a student of baseball history, but I have to confess that I had only a vague sense back in '77–'78, and even later into the '90s and the new century, what important moments and figures had been celebrated in New York with a parade. So I did some research, and my jaw dropped when I realized who and what had been honored in this great city with a parade—a tradition that goes all the way back to the 1880s, when people took to the streets unofficially to mark the opening of the Statue of Liberty. Parades had been held since then for Charles Lindbergh, Amelia Earhart, Jesse Owens, General Eisenhower, Connie Mack, Winston Churchill, astronauts, presidents, world leaders, and popes.

And little Mickey Randolph from Brownsville in Brooklyn and the rest of the Yankees also passed along that same route. Can you imagine?

Earlier I stated that baseball is unique in having the victory pile on the field as a sign of unity. Well, I'm not naive enough to fail to understand that our pileup on the field had another symbolic significance. It was a clash of egos, and I'd imagine that some guys wanted to deliver a few kidney punches and head butts while in the middle of celebrating. My good friend Roy White, who'd played and conducted himself so admirably for so long during the lean years, left the clubhouse celebration feeling like he hadn't really contributed to our efforts, since he'd appeared in only two games and gotten only two plate appearances. If a quality guy like Roy was so upset about how things had transpired, then you can imagine what was in the hearts and minds of some of the rest of the guys.

You didn't have to imagine what Lou Piniella—ironically, the guy who replaced Roy in the lineup—was thinking. He told a reporter that he was happy the season was over and he didn't think the club could take any more of the off-field stuff, not another year, not another week. He acknowledged something that I didn't really want to believe. "You don't have to be one big happy family to concentrate on playing ball. But if everything isn't going to be tranquil, next year we'll be a good fourth-place club."

I also read later that Thurman said he wanted to be traded to the Indians. That came in the middle of the celebration, and maybe he was just giving a reporter a hard time, but his feud with Reggie produced more headlines and headaches than anything else I can remember.

Still, we won it all, and that can do a lot to soothe any mental and emotional aches and pains you might have. At least it did for me. Maybe we were deluding ourselves, but I really believed we had what it took to be a winner for a very long time. I wasn't alone in that altered state of consciousness. Famously, the Boss said after the '77 season, "I'm not going to touch this team. How can you touch a club like this? We're just going to try to get them all back together and do it again."

Even Billy and Reggie were part of the cover-up. Reggie stood there with his arm around the shoulders of his other nemesis and said, "I'll tell you, nobody better catch Billy Martin and me in a bar together and try to give us some crap. We'll be hell together, won't we?"

We did go through a lot of hell the next year, in '78, but we were also a hell of a team when it really mattered.

Mr. Steinbrenner was mostly true to his word and kept the team largely intact. We lost Mike Torrez to the Red Sox via free agency. The Boss's one big acquisition was Goose Gossage to serve as our closer. That didn't sit well with a lot of the guys. Sparky had been outstanding in '77, saving games and saving our asses so many times that he won the Cy Young Award and finished sixth in the MVP voting. That's astounding for a relief pitcher. How Billy was going to utilize Sparky and Goose was one of the key questions, but it was a good question to have to answer—having two guys of that quality to come out of the pen gave us a huge advantage over most other clubs. It also helped that Goose was such a great guy. He was coming into a tough situation in the clubhouse, and he handled it well.

Sparky was one of the team's leaders and a legendary prankster, leading the league in issuing hot feet and all that. He was tough as nails on the field and was always surrounded by guys in the hotel bar afterward. Goose was about as intimidating a presence on the mound as you could imagine. His demented woodsman hair and mustache, his arm-flailing delivery, and his "I'm going to throw this damn ball as hard as I can, so see if you can catch up with it" style was different in a lot of ways from Sparky. The two of them combined for thirty-five saves that season, Goose getting twenty-six of them, and they both appeared in almost the same number of games, so somehow that transition worked itself out.

What wasn't working was a lot of our bodies. Catfish's shoulder troubles had him out of the lineup for two months. Don Gullett was reduced to starting only eight games for us. At various times Bucky Dent, Mickey Rivers, Roy White, and I also missed significant time with injuries. I played a lot of the '76 season with a lateral meniscus tear in my knee. We didn't have MRI exams back then, but when I felt my knee pop early that season, I knew something was wrong. Ice, wraps, and aspirin became a part of my everyday routine. Because my knee was bad, I compensated for the weakness and changed my stride a bit and that had my hamstring barking at me as well. They were nagging injuries, and only after the World Series was over did I get them examined and have the full extent of the knee injury diagnosed and taken care of.

It wasn't as if we were playing awful baseball, but we just never got into any kind of hot streak. By June 26, we were eleven games above .500 and nine and a half games behind the Red Sox. To their credit, the Red Sox were thirty games above .500 at 51-21. Only one other team in baseball, the Giants, had reached the forty-five-win mark by that point.

I chose to sum up where we were on June 26 for a reason: that's when things got a little bit testy. On that date, Reggie received what he thought of as a demotion. He wasn't going to play right field full-time anymore and would take a few turns as the designated hitter. More harmful to his pride, though, was being dropped from the cleanup spot to sixth. Reggie wasn't having a terrible year, so it's easy to understand that he might have felt like he was being made a scapegoat.

And it wasn't like the lineup change suddenly transformed our season. From June 27 to July 16, we went 6-10 and fell thirteen games behind the Red Sox. The next night, a Monday game against Kansas City—of course—things came to a head. We'd already lost the first two games of the three-game series to our archrivals. The game got off to a promising start: we chased Paul Splittorff in the fourth inning and took a 5–1 lead with a mostly healthy Catfish on the mound. He made it into the fifth before Sparky came on. Then Goose started the seventh inning, with the score 5–3. That meant that he was expected to get the usual three-inning save. Again, can you imagine that going on today?

Unfortunately, Goose couldn't hold the lead. More unfortunately, I contributed to that blown save. In the top of the ninth, after one out, George Brett singled. Hal McRae hit a ground ball to me. It would have been a tough chance at a double play, but I booted it. A couple of hits later and the only thing that was turned that inning was our 5–3 lead into a 5–5 tie. Things got really weird in the bottom of the tenth. After Thurman led off with a single, Reggie, batting fourth and DH-ing, came up. Billy had the bunt sign on for the first pitch, but when that didn't work, he took it off. But instead of following the new sign, Reggie kept trying to bunt the runner to second base. I sat there on the bench watching as Reggie squared around—or attempted to in his own unique way—in a failed attempt to lay one down. I kept looking at the third-base coach, Dick Howser, to see if Reggie was doing what Billy wanted. No bunt sign was given.

To Billy's credit, given his past history with Reggie, he didn't call time-out and talk to Reggie or club him over the head, and he didn't pull him and use a pinch hitter. Instead, after the game, Billy announced that Reggie was suspended indefinitely. Later the suspension was made more definite—five games. That wasn't Billy's idea, of course, that was the Boss's intervention.

We flew off to Minnesota, and Reggie flew off to California to serve his time. The Boss was in full support of his manager telling the press that, though he understood there were mitigating circumstances on both sides, "there has to be a boss and leader, and Billy Martin is the boss and leader of this ball club." We all know how long that lasted.

Reggie didn't return to the lineup until well after his five days were up, not until July 28 at home against the Twins. In his absence, we went 8-2 and cut six games out of the Red Sox's fourteen-game lead on us. Billy was quoted as saying that Reggie's suspension was the best thing that happened to the club—and that was *before* we went on that ten-game hot streak—but I don't think that taking out one of your team's most productive hitters and causing all kinds of friction is the best way to go about things. In my mind, it was just like Reggie had been injured. We had to pull together a little bit more as a result. I know that I was in the minority in that regard. We all wanted to pull harder, but I know that a lot of guys wanted to show Reggie that we didn't really need him to succeed. That wasn't a healthy attitude.

That last statement is obvious. The Yankees were healthy on the field, but things were awful off the field. On July 23, we beat the White Sox 3–1 in a Sunday afternoon game. We were all sitting around O'Hare Airport waiting for our charter to Kansas City. We'd won all five games of Reggie's suspension period. Billy enjoyed BS-ing with the members of the press, and it was reported that on Saturday night he had been full of jokes and stories. By Sunday some switch had been flipped. Billy was in a foul mood. He then fired off the words heard 'round the Bronx: "The two men deserve one another. One's a born liar, the other's convicted."

Billy was also peeved because he suspected that George Steinbrenner was working behind the scenes to trade him to the White Sox for their manager, Bob Lemon. All this was crazy nonsense to me, but less than twenty-four hours later Billy had tearfully resigned, Dick Howser had taken over for a game, and then Bob Lemon was in fact our manager for that season's sixty-eight remaining games. To Bob's credit, he came in and said that he felt his role was to just get out of way and let us play the game. He was a very smart and well-respected baseball man, and it was obvious to everybody that all the clubhouse distractions had been hurting. Bob was such a quiet guy and such a contrast to Billy that he was exactly what we needed at that moment. Peace and tranquillity helped us a whole bunch the rest of the way.

Even now, I still feel sad about all those events. I know that it can't be as simple as, "Let's just go out there and play the game," with everybody setting their egos and their agendas aside. I tried to do that to avoid getting all caught up in it, but it's impossible to block everything out. I have great admiration and affection for Billy, and I hated to see him self-destruct like that. I also admired and had affection for Reggie. I don't know why he wanted to push Billy's buttons the way he did. I guess the only thing I can say is that as much as we're ballplayers, we're also human beings, and that's where that imperfection I mentioned earlier applies to every one of us.

In spite of the tension with Billy, that season did have several moments that approached perfection. The "Boston Massacre," when we went into Fenway in early September down four games and swept them in a four-game series by the collective score of 42–9, approached that impossible standard. By the time Cleveland came into town the final weekend of the regular season, we were up by a game over the Red Sox. That's when the joy and the agony, the perfect and the imperfect, decided to play a kind of doubleheader on me.

In the first game of the series, we were facing David Clyde, the former hard-throwing phenom who was rushed to the big leagues at the age of eighteen and had his career ruined by arm injuries. Still, he was effective against us, and we went into the bottom of the eighth inning trailing 1–0. We'd all been scoreboard watching, and unless something cataclysmic happened, the Red Sox would hold on to their 11–0 lead over Toronto and win that game.

We got a leadoff single from Cliff Johnson, Mickey Rivers bunted him over, and I came up. I hit a ball down the third-base line and busted my ass toward first, hoping to beat the throw. About three-quarters of the way down the line, I felt like a gazelle and a cheetah had clamped onto the back of my right leg. I knew my hamstring was done for, but I kept going. I was safe, but done for. Brian Doyle came in to pinch-run for me.

Fred Stanley, who came in to run for Cliff, couldn't advance, so we had runners at first and second and only one out. Three singles later, we were up 3–1, and then Goose shut the door. I know that fans like to play the what-if game, and I know that logically, just because one thing happens it doesn't really have an influence on what does or doesn't happen later, but please indulge me.

If I hadn't beat out that ground ball, we would have had a runner on second and two out. Who knows what might have happened, how the pitcher's strategy might have changed, how the hitters would have responded, etc. I'm not trying to say that because of me we won that game, leading to Bucky Dent's later heroics in the playoff game, or that my being out of the lineup was the only reason Brian Doyle got to step up big-time and compete like he did. What I'm trying to do is illustrate how all these factors of the grind and giving it your all can come into play.

I was an intense guy, but as the old saying goes, the spirit was willing but the flesh was sometimes weak. I had a few leg problems throughout my career, knee stuff mostly, but that hamstring was always my Achilles' heel (if you'll let me slide on the anatomical mix-up) because there was an imbalance in my muscles. I was always trying to strengthen the front of the leg (the quadriceps) to help stabilize my knee.

Regardless of why my hamstring popped, and despite the pain, I kept thinking, *Please let us win, please let us win.* I wanted to get back to the playoffs and the World Series in the worst way. The idea of grinding through that entire season and the upheaval and the comeback and then not getting to play at the end was heartbreaking. The so-called Boston Massacre was such a thrill that I really wanted to be a part of putting a fitting end on the Red Sox season. I was so happy that we won it all, but to not be a part of it on the field, to not be contributing—that was a bitter, bitter pill to swallow.

I didn't have an on-field view of the events of the one-game playoff, but I was there. Talk about an electric atmosphere. This was more like an electrocution. You could just feel the Boston fans' hatred. They wanted that game, as did the players, in the worst way. I really wanted to be in there because I always did well in Boston. The thing about the rivalry was that you had instant motivation. Fans booing you is always an added incentive to do well. Since the most and the loudest boos I ever heard came from Fenway fans, the better I did in games against the Red Sox.

What I remember most clearly was Bucky Dent's at-bat when he hit the home run. As sore as I was, I could feel for the guy when he fouled a pitch off his foot and ankle. I could see him wincing, and he came back toward the dugout to walk it off, just hobbling around. His ankle had been bothering him on and off for most of the year. I know that our manager, Bob Lemon, said in later interviews that he would have liked to have pinch-hit for Bucky before he got up there, but even more so after fouling off that pitch. Like I've said, you never know how things might turn out and winning is so unpredictable. Well, imagine if Bucky hadn't fouled that pitch off his foot and instead just tapped it down toward third base but not in fair territory? He wouldn't have come back toward the dugout. That's when Mickey Rivers got involved. Mickey knew that Bucky was understandably focused on just walking off the pain and didn't realize that his bat was broken—not busted in half like you see so many times now, but just a hairline fracture. Mick yelled at him, "Hey, homey. Your bat's busted." And he made sure that Bucky got a fresh one.

You know the rest.

Watching the rest of the playoffs and the World Series games from the bench was tough. Like I started off this chapter talking about, this was more like the pleasure you get from watching your kids succeed. Sure, I'd played and contributed most of the year, but not being out there when everything was on the line was a lot more painful than that hamstring injury. I was thrilled that we won, and I celebrated the victory, but it just wasn't the same. And even though to some extent it felt like watching my kids do something great, it was different, since these guys, as childish as some of them could act, and as much as I loved them for that, were my peers, my teammates.

Mickey was one of the guys I always looked out for. He was acquired on the exact same day I was—December 11, 1975—coming over from the Angels with Ed Figueroa in a trade for Bobby Bonds. It was as good a day of trading as any Yankee general manager has ever had. Gabe Paul basically won the pennant for the Yankees that day. Going 55-30 over the next three seasons, Figueroa was a steady sinkerballer who inhaled innings and kept us in the game just about every time out. And Mickey, well, he was, in his own way, as valuable to us as Thurman. I think everybody on that team would tell you that.

Mickey became one of my favorite teammates in about as short a time as it took for him to run to first. Which was shorter than any player I've ever seen. Mickey was a sweet-natured man, and trusting to a fault. We were neighbors in Hackensack, New Jersey, one year, and he'd visit with everybody in the neighborhood, sign autographs, get them tickets, whatever. One day I saw him flip the keys to his Cadillac Brougham to a guy he'd just met a few days earlier.

"Mickey, what are you doing?" I said.

"He's just going for a little spin. He'll be back," Mickey said.

Everybody loved Mickey. He could make me laugh even when he wasn't trying to be funny. "What was the name of the dog in *Rin Tin Tin?*" he asked once. Another time he said, "Me and Billy and George are two of kind." My pal Mickey often seemed to be in the middle of a bunch of the fires that broke out—usually because of money. Mickey's biggest vice was the racetrack. He'd go all the time, and he couldn't have won all that often, because he always seemed to be broke. The Boss frequently had to deal with Mickey's money problems, usually by giving him an advance on his paycheck. Billy would also get involved, often giving him a couple of hundred dollars out of his own pocket, partly out of kindness, partly out of practicality, because he knew that when Mickey was happy and motivated, he was the kind of guy who could take over a game.

When Mickey got to the park after a rough day at the track, he'd go looking for Bill "Killer" Kane, our traveling secretary.

"Tell Billy I need an envelope," Mickey would tell Killer.

"Okay, Mick," Killer would say.

If Mickey got his envelope, he'd run through a wall for you. If he didn't, he'd play in a much lower gear, or not play at all. It was always a juggling act keeping him satisfied. If it had been anyone else, guys on the team probably would've gotten ticked off about it, but Mickey was the sort of teammate who would do anything to help you out. Even if you started out mad at him, you couldn't stay mad at him.

Unless, of course, you were his wife. Her name was Cookie, and Cookie had no trouble at all staying angry at Mick. I found that out one afternoon in the players' parking lot outside the Stadium.

It was about 3:30 PM. I had just pulled into the lot when I spotted Cookie pulling in right behind me. She was driving a two-seat Mercedes.

"Have you seen Mickey?" she asked.

"No, I haven't. I just got here myself," I said. "What's the matter?"

Mickey and Cookie would have some real knockdown fights when they got angry. I was hoping that wasn't where this was heading.

"He didn't come home last night," Cookie said.

"I don't know, Cookie," I said. "I don't have any idea where he is."

At that moment I looked up and saw Mickey's brown Brougham turning the corner and making the left turn into the players' lot. I looked at Cookie. I saw her eyes get big and fiery.

Oh shit, I thought.

As soon as Mickey pulled into his spot, Cookie, back behind the wheel now, pulled in right behind him to block him in. Chris Chambliss, who had also just arrived, was walking toward the Stadium entrance.

"Chris, stay here, something is going to go down. Mickey might need our help, because Cookie is on the warpath."

"No way, brother," Chris said. "I don't want any part of that."

In the next instant, Cookie put her car in reverse, gunned the engine, and rammed the Mercedes hard into Mickey's Cadillac, smashing the bumper and jolting Mickey's car violently. Then she put it in reverse again, gunned it, and rammed him again.

"Cookie! Stop! What are you doing? Stop!" I yelled.

"Get out of my way! I'm going to kill him," Cookie screamed, and then bashed into the car one more time.

Mickey, meanwhile, was frozen in his car, hands clutching the wheel. And here came Cookie again, smashing Mickey's car once more, Mickey again getting bounced around as if he were a bobblehead doll. This time, though, she got hooked up on his fender and couldn't get free.

Two cops arrived and opened the door and dragged her out of the car. I went over to check on Mickey. His hands were still wrapped around the steering wheel. He looked to be in shock. He was trembling.

I reached out for his arm.

"Mickey, c'mon, it's okay now. Let's get into the clubhouse."

He wouldn't budge.

"C'mon, Mickey. Let's go. It's okay." He told me the same thing he told Bull Watson in the Oakland trainer's room.

"Turn me loose!" he said. I tried to calm him down.

"C'mon, Mick, let's just get into the clubhouse and things will be all right."

As the cops questioned Cookie, I finally convinced Mickey to unwrap his hands from the wheel and let me take him into the Stadium. I don't know whether Mickey got an envelope that day, but I know he was real happy to be out of his car and away from Cookie.

What made Mickey Rivers such a great ballplayer was also what created these dangerous situations. He was playful, full of fire, and wanted to win no matter who the opponent was. Some players learn how to channel their passions, and others don't. On the field, Mickey's passions usually worked for himself and his team.

But that same passion doesn't work off the field. Most players struggle with the different roles they play on and off the field. I was lucky to have Gretchen, who had understood me since I was a kid and who protected me like a warrior but also expected me to act like a man off the field. Other players aren't so lucky.

Later on, as a coach and as a manager, I felt the same protectiveness and had similar expectations for my on-field "kids." Seeing them grow and achieve was its own kind of pleasure. Maybe not being able to play in that '78 Series was preparing me for what was to come. Of course, I still had a lot of playing ahead of me.

And then there was Mickey's famous jab at Reginald Martinez

Jackson: "No wonder you're all mixed up. You got a white man's first name, a Spanish man's second name, and a black man's third name." Reggie and Mickey would get into it all the time. Once, in front of a pack of reporters, a slumping Reggie told Rivers he should learn how to read and write. To which Mickey replied, "You'd better stop readin' and writin' and start hittin'."

Sometimes, though, the exchanges weren't so harmless. On the team bus outside Chicago one night, Reggie and Mickey got into a dissing match, back and forth and back again, and when the conversation turned to what guys were going to do after their playing days, Reggie said to Mickey, "You're going to be driving this bus." Suddenly the bus got real quiet. You could sense that a line had been crossed, that this was somehow a real cheap shot. You could get on a guy for how he dressed, how he wore his hair, and just about anything else, but going after a guy about his intellect was definitely a below-the-belt blow.

I felt protective of Mickey. A lot of us did, not because he wasn't the most educated guy on the club, but because he was guileless, almost naive to the reality of how hard a place the world could be. Mickey was quiet after Reggie made that remark, but I know it stung him.

No more than a day or two later we were in Oakland, getting ready to play the A's. Reggie was lying on a training table, getting a rubdown or some sort of treatment. Next thing I knew there was a loud crashing sound from the trainer's room. When I ran in there to see what was happening, I saw the table overturned and Mickey and Reggie rolling around the floor, throwing punches from everywhere. Mickey was on top of Reggie, just flailing away. He had rage in his eyes, and when Mickey got like that, it took a small army to subdue him; he was much stronger than he looked in his uniform. A couple of guys got down on the floor and pulled Mickey off, holding him in a viselike grip, even as Reggie was yelling at Mickey and Mickey was screaming, "Turn me loose! Turn me loose!"

Fortunately, no one turned him loose.

At the end of the day Reggie is not a fighter—he's a lover. He wants attention, and he doesn't want the other side to intimidate his team.

But he doesn't want to play baseball like a hockey player. I remember one time when Reggie was playing for Baltimore, the year before he joined the Yankees. Dock Ellis was coming in tight on the Orioles, and Reggie started screaming from the dugout: "Hey, you bleep, don't hit him, hit me!" And so Ellis hit Reggie. And nothing happened. Make love, not war.

IT'S HARD TO SAY when the Bronx Zoo really came to an end, but to me it was never about the trading of Billy Martin or the end of the decade or even Reggie Jackson's departure from New York after the '81 season. No, for me, what ended the Zoo was a plane crash.

I was home that afternoon, August 2, 1979. Gretchen was watching TV when a bulletin came on.

"Willie! Come quick!" she said. I heard the alarm in her voice. I raced into the family room. The words and images I saw and heard on the screen still seem incomprehensible. The captain of the Yankees, my beloved teammate, was gone. I felt almost physically ill as I stood in front of the television and looked at the pictures of my friend and a plane wreck and a tragedy that would change a family's life forever. Thurman Munson dead? No. It couldn't be. I had just seen him the day before, said good-bye to him after our game in Chicago. It never occurs to you when you see someone every day, someone you love like a brother, that one day you might say good-bye and that will be it.

Thurman died on a Thursday, and we flew to Canton for the funeral on Monday. We had a game with the Orioles that night and decided that we wanted to play. The funeral was one of the most painful days of my life. To see Thurman's wife, Diana, and their three young children, mourning their loss, was too much to bear. Mostly what I remember is seeing everybody crying, all of us, including people I'd never seen cry before—people like Reggie Jackson. Everybody knows about the bitter falling-out between Reggie and Thurman soon after Reggie joined the club in 1977, the trigger being a *Sport* magazine interview in which Reggie proclaimed himself "the straw that stirs the drink" on the Yankees. What far fewer people know is that Reggie and Thurman eventually got beyond the frostiness and established, if not a full friendship, at least a mutual respect. Ray Negron, an old friend and longtime Yankee official who has been everything from a batboy to a clubhouse kid to a personal assistant to George Steinbrenner, tells a story about being at an airport bar with the two of them, watching in total surprise as Reggie and Thurman shared a hamburger—one of them taking a bite, then handing it to the other guy.

So yes, Reggie took Thurman's death hard too.

Flying back to New York and playing that Monday night game was as hard as anything I've had to do as a ballplayer. I put on my "Rook" T-shirt and solemnly got into my uniform. When I led off the bottom of the first, all I kept thinking was, *I have to honor Thurman. I have to play the game he would've played.*

I ripped a single in my first at-bat and got another hit later. The Orioles were fifteen games ahead of us in the standings, but that didn't matter. To me, it felt like a World Series game. It had that much intensity, though you couldn't necessarily tell by the scoreboard. In the bottom of the seventh, we were down 4–0, getting completely locked up by Dennis Martinez. With two outs, Bucky Dent walked just ahead of me. I got a pitch to drive, turned on it, and hit a double to left.

Next up was Bobby Murcer, maybe Thurman's best friend on the team. He had just rejoined the Yankees after being traded from the Cubs midway through the season. As Bobby took his stance in the left-handed batter's box, I wondered what he must have been feeling, how hard it must have been for him to think about baseball, let alone hit one.

The next sound I heard was a crack of the bat. Bobby had gotten ahold of a pitch. He had knocked the ball over the wall in right. It was suddenly a 4–3 game.

As we came up in the bottom of the ninth, we were still down a run. There was but one thought going through my mind: *We have to find a way to win this game.* Tippy Martinez, the former Yankee, had come on to pitch for the O's. He hadn't given up a run in over a month.

Bucky worked out another walk, and then I squared around to move him along. It was not my best bunt. Far from it. It rolled toward the mound, toward Tippy. He bent down and picked it up. I dug down the line as hard as I could; a double play would've been crushing. As I neared the bag I saw Tippy's throw to first sail past Eddie Murray, the first baseman. I turned and sprinted to second, just behind Bucky, who was now on third.

There were 36,000 people in the park that night, but it sounded like an SRO crowd, that's how electric it was. Up came Bobby Murcer again. The crowd was standing. It was almost as if they were demanding a storybook ending. Having just come back from the National League, Bobby hadn't seen Tippy much and had never gotten a single hit off him. He settled into his closed stance, in a deep crouch. Tippy wound and delivered. Bucky led off third, and I got a big lead off second.

C'mon, Bobby. You did it once. You can do it again, I thought.

The pitch came in, and then Bobby uncoiled, his bat firing through the zone, making solid contact, driving a ball the other way, on a line to left. Bucky came around to score, and I was right behind him, and when I crossed the plate the game was over. We had won, 5–4, on the most emotionally wrenching day most of us would ever have on a ball field. An instant after I scored, we all ran to embrace Bobby. Only one other time in his career had he ever driven in five runs in a game, and it sure wasn't when he had gone to the plate full of grief. We were hugging each other, holding each other up, and I remember as we moved en masse from the field to the dugout that it was almost as if we were literally lifting each other up, finding strength in togetherness.

I don't think I have ever felt more completely spent after a game. Being together was the only way we were ever going to get through this. The only way. I was never prouder of the Yankees than I was that night, the way we came back against the first-place Orioles, the way we honored Thurman. It was one of the most gratifying games of my career.

At the time of Thurman's passing, our record stood at 58-48. We finished the remainder of the season 31-23 for an overall record of 89-71, eighteen games above .500 but in fourth place and thirteen and a half games behind an enormously talented Orioles team that won 102 regular-season games. They eventually lost in the World Series to my former mates on the Pirates. This may be hard to believe, but that year the Eastern Division had five of its six teams finish above the .500 mark; the lone exception was the Toronto Blue Jays, who'd only begun playing in 1977.

I think it says something about the man and the ballplayer that Thurman was the first player to be named captain of the Yankees since Lou Gehrig had held that position, forty years earlier. I wrote about how Thurman treated me as a rookie; ironically, according to his teammates Gene Michael and Bobby Murcer, the "be seen and not heard" view of rookies did not sit well with Thurman. He was as confident as anybody I'd ever been around, and he backed every bit of it up with his performance on the field.

Who knows how many more victory celebrations there might've been if Thurman hadn't gotten in his jet in Chicago and flown home to Canton that summer night in 1979? If he hadn't gone off to the Canton airport to practice takeoffs and landings the next day? Thurman had just traded up his propeller plane for the jet, and I read later that aviation experts said that it was way too much airplane for an inexperienced pilot. I don't know about that, but I do know if somebody told Thurman he wouldn't be able to fly that plane, he would've been in a real hurry to prove them wrong.

Thurman was a man who loved to compete, at everything.

CHAPTER 6

The More Things Change

L osing Thurman in the middle of the '79 season was the most traumatic experience I'd ever had in my days in baseball. You lose guys to injury all the time, and you try to make up for their absence knowing that at some point you're going to get them back in the lineup. That wasn't the case with his death. There's no real way to account for your grief, and there's no book that you can turn to for advice on how to handle the loss of a team leader. Management made a decision to keep Thurman's locker as it was. He'd always been holed up near the trainer's room, and I remember walking past it each time feeling this strange buzzing sensation in my gut, an uncomfortable reminder of what was missing in our lives. I think it was a great tribute, mind you, but I felt unsettled, and I think that carried over to the rest of the team and our performance.

Numbers don't entirely take the measure of a man, and that's also true of the '78 and '79 teams. On offense, we hit one percentage point lower in '79 than we did in '78. We scored 1 fewer run and had 46 fewer hits and 25 fewer home runs. How much of a difference Thurman's absence made in those last two categories is debatable. Our pitching staff suffered, and some of that may also have been attributable to Thurman not being behind the plate. The '79 staff's ERA was 0.65 runs higher, they allowed 0.63 more runs per game, and they gave up 125 more hits overall. Some of that, however, was due to injuries, changes in personnel, and other factors.

I know that we missed Thurman as a person and as a leader. I don't like using his absence as an excuse for our losing, for finishing fourth in our division and winning eleven fewer games than we did in 1978. Thurman would have kicked our butts for using anything as an excuse for not winning. Something was missing, however. Sparky Lyle had been traded in the off-season, and that may have accounted for some of the decline in pitching as well. They call them "intangibles" for a reason: without those two guys, I'm not sure any team could have recovered fully. Nobody called them a "three-peat" back then, but it sure would have been nice to have had a stand-up triple on our résumés.

Not even Billy Martin's return could get us on track. Billy's tenure was brief, though, and we entered the new decade with Dick Howser at the helm. Mr. Steinbrenner also went out and got Rick Cerone to solidify us behind the plate. We had a great regular season in '80, winning 103 games to beat out the Orioles for the division title. Graig Nettles was limited by injury to just 89 games, but Reggie had a monster season for us, belting 41 homers and driving in 111 runs while also hitting .300. He finished second to George Brett in the MVP balloting, and Goose, who had 33 saves, finished third. Rick Cerone also was in the running, with a .321 average, 14 home runs, and 85 RBI for the season. I wasn't so bad myself: I had another All-Star season while hitting .294 with 119 walks and 30 stolen bases. Top to bottom, on the mound, and out of the pen, we had some great talent. You can't win 103 regular-season games without it.

The postseason was a different story. The Royals swept us in three games. I had one of my finest postseason series performances, hitting .385, but that was little consolation. We lost. We got swept. We got embarrassed. That had happened to us in '76, and those of us who remained with the club used that embarrassment as a motivator in '81.

Memories from the previous postseason fueled us during the first half of the '81 season, when we went 34-22 before the infamous strike interrupted play for fifty games. Good thing we did, because we stunk up the place a bit when play resumed. Dave Winfield had signed with us—more on him later—and he seemed to be one of the few guys on the team who was able to stay on track throughout the interrupted season. Dave was twenty-nine years old and coming into his prime as a hitter, and we needed him.

Because of the strike and the split season, we met the Brewers in the first round of the playoffs. They were a very talented squad led by Robin Yount, Paul Molitor, Cecil Cooper, and Sal Bando. And coming out of their bullpen was Rollie Fingers, another former member of those great A's teams, who was both the Cy Young winner and the MVP in the American League. The two games away and three at home format helped us out. We won twice on the road and then came home needing only one victory to advance. It took us until game 5 to get that last win. Fortunately, game 5 wasn't a complete nail-biter—we won 7–3—after we lost game 4 at home 2–1. We had barely been edged out in that game, leaving runners on the corners in the bottom of the ninth when Fingers worked his magic against Rick Cerone. I don't think Yankee fans would have had much patience for any kind of shenanigans on our part.

We faced off against a revived Oakland A's franchise in the American League Championship Series. Tommy John, who'd come over to us in the off-season prior to the '79 season and had subsequently gone 44-18 in his first two seasons, set the tone for us by winning game 1, 3–1, which should remind some readers that the man gave more than just his name to what is today a fairly common orthopedic surgery procedure. We ended up sweeping Oakland three straight to win the 1981 pennant. In the last game, in Oakland, I broke a 0–0 tie in the sixth inning with a home run off of Oakland starter Matt Keough, and then Nettles cleared the bases with a three-run double in the ninth to clinch it.

Mr. Steinbrenner wanted to celebrate. He got the team together at a big banquet hall near the Oakland Coliseum. Nettles, who was named the Series' MVP for hitting .500 with 9 RBI, was there with his wife, Ginger. Just about all the players and their wives were there. Music pulsed through the night, and we enjoyed a nice spread of food. It was our chance to be together before flying home to begin the World Series against the Dodgers.

Ginger put her pocketbook down on a chair. Reggie moved it and took the seat. Nettles had little use for Reggie to begin with, and he took big exception to Reggie doing this. Heated words were exchanged, Nettles let fly with a right hand, and then all hell broke loose, the two of them throwing haymakers at each other. The fight broke up quickly, but the festive mood was wrecked. What I remember most about the aftermath was Mr. Steinbrenner doing everything he could to keep the party going.

"C'mon, guys, love each other and have a good time," he said. "Get out on the dance floor with your wives. This is a celebration for our team." But nobody wanted to celebrate anymore. We all went back to our rooms.

The drama didn't overshadow what we'd accomplished, but it also didn't help bring the team together right before the Series. We were up against the Dodgers in a rematch of our '78 World Series. I think that was fitting, given how the strike had affected the fans, disillusioning so many of them. We could all go back to simpler times in a way. I wish that there was a simple explanation for how we could take a 2–0 Series lead and wind up losing in six games. Sure, it's easy to point a finger at Dave Winfield getting one hit in twenty-two at-bats, but history is filled with stories of superstars—and Dave was certainly that—having a bad Series.

On paper, the two teams matched up well, but in all honesty, I've got to say that we had a better club, better starting pitching, and a better, more veteran closer. We lost Games 3, 4, and 5 by one run in each. In Game 3, Fernando Valenzuela pitched a gutty complete game in beating us 5–4, even though we out-hit them 11 to 9. Game 4 was another tough loss. I homered and tripled in my first two at-bats, then walked once and was held hitless after that in an 8–7 loss. Too many lost opportunities to mention.

I can still feel the sinking sensation in my stomach and chest when the Dodgers' Steve Yeager followed up Pedro Guerrero's home run off of Ron Guidry with one of his own to wipe out our 1–0 lead in the top of the seventh inning. Ron had been lights-out to that point, giving up a hit in the first and second innings and then retiring fifteen of the next sixteen hitters he faced. He got ahead of both Guerrero and Yeager, but then they hit no-doubters into roughly the same section of left-center field. Those hits happened so suddenly that the feeling of cresting a hill while speeding in a car settled into me, a kind of negative thrill. The 9–2 wipeout at the Stadium to end the Series was no thrill at all. The World Series had been a repeat of the regular season—great start, lousy finish.

I DON'T THINK ANY of us could have imagined that was going to be the last pennant we would win in the 1980s. Unimaginable. Impossible. Ludicrous. Mystifying.

How could a collection of guys who had been described as knowing how to win suddenly turn into a team whose best finish over the next nine years would be second in 1985 and 1986? That '85 season was particularly hurtful to me. With Yogi Berra at the helm, we got off to a 6-10 start; George Steinbrenner immediately fired him and brought in Billy Martin. You know how I felt about Billy, so for me to say that I was hurt by that firing tells you how much respect I have for Yogi. There was no way that Yogi didn't deserve to finish out that season. None. We were sixteen games into the season.

I heard that a lot of meetings were always going on behind the scenes with the management and on-field staff. I was never part of them. I got to the ballpark that day and there were more media types around than usual. That got my attention. Something was up. I peeked in Yogi's office and he wasn't there. I felt my heart drop. Afterward, I read some of the same accounts that fans did. George wanted Yogi to resign. Yogi refused. George fired him. Yogi never spoke to us, and I never saw him come to clear out his office.

The Billy-Yogi back-and-forth from '83 to '85 was as ridiculous as it was unproductive. Out of all the firings and hirings, seeing Yogi get axed stirred up the most reaction among the players. We couldn't believe that he didn't even get a chance to make it to the All-Star break. We were pissed, partly because we felt like we'd let Yogi down. We'd heard all the rumors and we were, to be honest, pressing too much at the start of the season. Sure, we went 91-54 under Billy the remainder of that year, but I think we could have done that just as easily under Yogi's leadership.

Looking back, I see some things that make me wonder if there really was such a thing as the Yankee Way during that stretch. I'm not saying that a lack of team unity was the only cause of the subsequent slump during the mid-'80s. I do think it was a factor, but what does it also say when you have an owner who is preaching love one another and team and then cuts a manager loose after only sixteen games, and a manager who meant so much to the franchise?

I still have a lot of respect and affection for Yogi. I got to know him because Elston Howard was one of my great mentors in the game. Yogi and Elston were great friends, nearly inseparable, so when I went to Elston for advice, Yogi was there. I think that my being so respectful of Elston and his baseball knowledge impressed Yogi. A young guy like me wanting to hear what his elders had to say meant a lot to Yogi, someone who has such respect for the game and the Yankee tradition. I felt the same way about Yogi, and I have to say that in a lot of ways, he was the one who welcomed me into the Yankee family. He was my connection to the glory years of the franchise, and he always felt that the Yankees were something special. Through him, I got to meet a lot of the other players who came to the Stadium for old-timers' games. It always saddened me that Yogi wasn't around the ballpark for all those years. I missed hearing him say to me, "Hey, Shorty, how ya doin'?" He's always been such a down-to-earth guy and never put on airs.

One bright spot during these difficult years in the mid-'80s was the race for the batting title between Don Mattingly and Dave Winfield, which went down to the last day of the season. A lot of people wanted to make the contest a racial thing. Some thought that the New York fans being behind Donnie much more than Dave had to do with racism. I never saw it that way. Donnie was a young, homegrown Yankee in his first full year in the big leagues, a consummate overachiever, a guy who wasn't big and couldn't run and who made himself into a star through sheer effort. Except maybe for Bo Jackson, Dave was the greatest athlete I ever saw in baseball. He could've been a professional athlete in three sports. Not that Dave didn't work at the game— because he did—but his gifts were such that he made it all look easy. The Yankees signed him to the biggest contract in pro sports at the time. He was a first-round draft pick. Donnie was a nineteenth-round draft pick. New Yorkers have always loved the underdog, and Donnie was the embodiment of an underdog. The more you saw him the more you liked him and the more you wanted him to do well. From the start, Don Mattingly was an impossible guy to root against.

The first time I saw Donnie was in spring training of 1980. I could tell you I saw greatness in him right away, but I'd be lying. Sometimes you see guys come up and you think immediately, *This guy has a real shot,* or, *This guy has no shot.* Donnie wasn't like that. Nothing about him knocked you over in the beginning, and I had real questions about how a guy who was five-ten or so would do as a big-league first baseman. He started out as an outfielder, and he was an opposite-field slap hitter, kind of like Brett Butler. Later on, after he learned to use his hips better, he transformed himself into a guy with good power. For two or three years he was on a streak where he was as good a hitter as I'd ever seen. When he was healthy, like he was from 1984 to 1989, he could rake: during that period, he averaged 27 home runs, 114 RBI, and .327.

It was no wonder that he was "Donnie Baseball." He came along when I was the team's captain, a role I took more seriously as time went on, and Donnie and I spent a lot of time together and remain very close.

What I did notice from the outset, though, was an aura about him . . . a sense that he belonged. Don Mattingly wasn't cocky. He just acted as if he knew he would be around for a while. And "a while" didn't take long to arrive. Very subtly, very steadily, he made you a believer. He played a lot of outfield his first couple of years, but by the time he got ensconced at first he would pick everything. He was the best I ever played with around first base, scooping balls in the dirt, the 3-6-3 double play, everything. I could shade another step up the middle, knowing he was there to my left. Was it an accident that the Yankees led the league in double plays (177) in his first full year at first? I don't think so. You felt like you were playing next to Superman, and at the plate he may have been even better. For the five or so years when he was at his peak, Donnie just raked the ball, day after day, week after week. When he hit .352 in 1986, it seemed as if he went the whole year without missing anything. You know how many times he struck out that season, in 742 plate appearances? Thirty-five. Even then, he would be in the cage more than anyone on the team, hitting off his tee, doing it for hours. I used to walk by and kid him, "In search of the perfect swing, Donnie?" He'd smile and go right back to work. Work is what got him where he was, after all.

So it wasn't as if the Yankee teams of that era weren't trying or didn't have good teammates. Guys did enjoy being around one another. That's one of the things I most enjoyed besides the competition—getting to know different guys and being exposed to things that a New York City guy might not normally have known about. Jazz was one of those things, though exposure to it would seem inevitable for anyone working in one of the cultural capitals of the world.

Jazz can help explain what was wrong with those '80s teams. A great jazz ensemble has to be selfless. Everybody gets a chance at their solos, but the main thing is getting every element to mesh together. That didn't happen with those clubs. We didn't jell in the best way possible. Guys were cool with one another—not as in chilly but as in cool—but we didn't have that same kind of chemistry, the sense of brotherhood, that we had in '76–'79. In the '80s it seemed like Mr. Steinbrenner opened his pocketbook more and it was like Pandora's box opened up as well.

I have to admit I felt slighted sometimes. There were times when I felt underappreciated and underpaid. When an organization is preaching team and family in one breath and then brings in free agents and pays them very highly and touts their abilities in another breath, then there's going to be some disconnect. Even if you throw out the money issue, it seemed like in that era ownership was spending big money on power and offense and neglecting pitching. And it seemed the more money that the Boss spent, the more he felt like he had to speak up and voice his dissatisfaction and provide his input on how things should be done on the field. That whole sideshow eroded morale and took away our focus.

One of the guys from those '80s-era teams who would have fit in pretty well with the late '70s teams was Dave "Rags" Righetti. The big left-hander was an interesting character, to put it mildly. His quick wit and sense of humor, which ranged from dry to slightly off center, made him one of my favorite teammates. He seemed to be able to keep some of the nonsense that was going on in perspective. On August 6, 1983, he started a game against the Detroit Tigers. We won 12–3 and Rags got his first win since July 15. Of course, what was noteworthy in the media was that the night before Dave Winfield had tossed a ball during the game and killed a seagull. Now, I like animals of all kinds, and having a seagull get pegged and killed was tough, but to have Dave Winfield detained by Toronto police for what was an accident—Dave had a rifle for an arm but no malice in his heart—was a little bit silly.

But that's how things seemed to go back then. The next day the newspapers focused on the seagull incident. Billy was in good form, telling reporters that he thought that maybe we'd be a little off our game since we got home so late due to waiting on the runway for the plane to take off because of the "jailbird." Thing was, Dave Winfield wasn't the only one on the hot seat at that time. Billy was under review for a possible suspension because of some remarks he'd made about the umpire Dale Ford.

Rags took all of this in stride, and when he was asked about it he said that it was all part of being a Yankee. He added that for his entire time with the Yankees that kind of press attention and weirdness was going on, so it seemed normal. It didn't seem normal to players from other teams, and they relished the opportunity to come into the Bronx and stir up things by beating us. These guys read the tabloids, and I've had many tell me years later that they loved winning against us and then seeing what the *Post* and the *Daily News* were going to say. It was fun for them to come in, get a shitstorm of controversy going, and then fly on out of there while we were left scrambling in their wake. We all developed a kind of shrug-it-off attitude and approach to the media circus, but, combined with losing, those years were exhausting mentally.

It was good to get away from the game for a while during the off-season.

One activity I never thought I'd get involved in took me to the mountains of Colorado courtesy of Goose Gossage. Goose was a hunter, and he had a big spread out in the central mountains of Colorado, his home state. At the end of every season, Goose would start talking about deer hunting. He's a good old boy, and I really love him, and he'd ask me to join him and a few of the guys. Our wives were also good friends, and it made sense to Goose that even though I was an inner-city kid, I would enjoy the wide open spaces and roughing it.

"Let me put you on some deer. We'll sit up there, we'll drink some beer and hang out with the boys."

"Yeah, Goose. Sounds great. Definitely."

And of course, when the off-season came around, I'd find other things to do. Goose kept putting the pressure on, in a friendly way, and I started thinking more and more about it. Finally, in the off-season after the '84 schedule was over, I said to myself, *You've got to do this.* A couple of my buddies in our New Jersey neighborhood were hunters, so I contacted them for advice. Eventually one of the guys took me to a gun shop and got me set up with a good hunting rifle and a nice scope, and he even took me to a range a few times to teach me the fine art of squeezing off rounds. I enjoyed learning a new skill.

Goose repeated his offer for probably the sixth or seventh time the following fall, and when I told him I would finally join him and the guys, he said, "BS. You're not coming. You've been saying that for years."

I finally convinced him that I was going to make it out there. He told me that I'd better be sure because we weren't going to be heading back to his ranch each night. We were going to be riding out on horseback, pitching tents, cooking over a fire, the whole deal. I knew better than to tell him not to worry about me and my skills as a horseman— I'd ridden them a couple of times in Prospect Park as a kid.

I had this image in my mind—a mix of an old ad for Marlboro cigarettes and the movie *City Slickers*. Nothing could have prepared me for the reality of the experience. Colorado and its mountains were spectacular. We were in a large valley, but there were some rolling hills and steep-sided and rocky gullies and trails leading into pine forests. I'd gone out and gotten the best winter weather gear I could—a down jacket, polypropylene long underwear, a heavy wool hat, lined elk-skin gloves, heavy waterproof leather boots.

Goose's cousin was going to serve as our guide, and Ken Griffey Sr., Don Baylor, Roy Howell, and Bruce Kison (a former Pirate teammate) and a couple of other guys Goose knew joined us. It was impossible to not get into the spirit of things. On what people in Colorado call a bluebird day—the sky was the same deep shade of blue as that creature's feathers—I was going out in the manly pursuit of meat and antlers. We set out in a beautiful grassy valley, the breeze light, and in the distance the bare limbs of the aspen and the stands of pine trees provided a beautiful backdrop.

We set up camp that first night, and Goose's cousin cooked us dinner. I'd stood there earlier trying to do my best to help put up the tent. After dinner, sitting around a campfire watching sparks fly into the night sky, the whiskey warming my insides, sharing in the baseball talk, all was right in the world.

The next morning when I got up all was white in the world. A snowstorm had come in overnight. What seemed to me to be about a foot of snow blanketed everything, and a cold gray mist limited visibility to a couple of feet.

"Ain't this great?" Goose bellowed. "Willie, it's your turn to do the cooking. Let's get those bacon and eggs going."

All I wanted to do was crawl back inside that sleeping bag and hope that somehow I could be teleported back to my home on the range in the New Jersey suburbs.

Later that day we were on the horses negotiating a very steep trail cut into the side of a slope. It was icy, and the horses were slipping. I wasn't enjoying this at all, and at one point when we took a break, I said, "Hey, man, Steinbrenner is going to fire us all if any one of us comes back with a broken leg or if this horse falls on me!"

The guys all laughed, and I did too, acting like I was joking.

I battled the cold for the next couple of days, and then on the fifth day I understood what buck fever was all about. We had gotten up early and settled into a meadow. The low late November sun helped warm us a bit, but when a group of about five deer came out of the trees, my temperature really rose. I don't know why those deer acted the way they did, just kind of casually strolling and munching on the grass. Most of the time they'd been very skittish, but these dudes (they were all bucks) seemed completely oblivious to us.

I started shaking, and I could feel my legs kind of go numb. We were all lying on the ground, with our rifles resting on bags.

I kept thinking, *I've got to do this. I've got to get this buck.*

I squeezed the trigger once and then again. One of the bucks seemed to spring into the air and then collapse. I looked out of the corner of my eye, and I saw Goose laying his rifle on the ground.

Son of a bitch, I thought. *Goose shot that thing for me.*

I didn't have time to debate things with him. The deer had taken off, and we followed the blood trail and then put the buck out of its misery.

Goose kept saying, "Man, you got him!"

He seemed so excited for me that I didn't want to ruin things, so I said, "Yeah. Can't believe it. Lucky shot."

He denied it later when I told him what I thought had just happened. To this day he denies that he was the one who took that buck down. Regardless, it was a great feeling to be out there with the guys, and you can't ask more of a teammate than to have him do what Goose did for me—helping me experience something like that, whether I was the one who fired the shot or not. Besides, when Goose Gossage tells you something and he gives you that same look he used to intimidate hitters, you just smile politely and say, "Thank you very much, Mr. Goose."

Maybe more than any other year, I couldn't wait for the off-season in 1985. I needed a break from the craziness. I decided to get away for a day, right after the World Series, and booked a fishing trip in early November, figuring it would be good to get out on the water and reel in a few fish. My former teammate, the pitcher Rudy May, introduced me to a captain who had a fishing boat and a shop in Huntington, Long Island, and the captain and I, along with his son, went all the way out to Montauk Point, the eastern tip of Long Island, to fish for bluefish or blackfish or sometimes striped bass. I'm not much of a swimmer or a water person, but I loved being out on his boat and putting the line in the water.

The day was gray and kind of gloomy. The air was chilly, the wind biting. You tend not to forget too many details on days when you almost die.

We were out on the Long Island Sound, the body of water between Long Island and Connecticut. It's not especially big or wide open compared with your neighborhood ocean, but it's not completely protected either. We headed out to sea with five people on board, including the crew. After getting pretty far out into the Sound, we dropped anchor and started fishing, and we were reeling them in, catching dinner and then some. It was one of our better trips, fishing-wise. I was having a really good time.

As the afternoon went on the wind started kicking up. The water was getting pretty choppy. I didn't really even think about it. The boat's captain knew what he was doing. I was just happy the fish were biting. The waves began getting bigger and bigger. We decided it would be a good idea to head back in, or at least closer to the shore. There was no reason to take any risks.

When the captain went to start the engine though, it wouldn't turn over. He did some trouble-shooting and discovered that the line of the anchor had somehow gotten caught up in the propeller. He tried to untangle it, but couldn't. Now the weather was getting heavier. The boat was starting to rock back and forth. He didn't want anyone to panic, so he was staying extra calm, but this was definitely not normal—even I knew that. He tried the engine a few more times. He primed it, tried a few other things. It just wouldn't start.

He looked at us and said, "Get your life jackets on."

It's never good when the captain tells you to get your life jacket on.

Waves were spilling over the side now, and seawater was coming in, and the pump he had going couldn't get rid of it fast enough. We radioed for help. The waves kept slamming against the boat, and the back of it started to get submerged. He told us to get to the front of the boat and spread out to keep the weight evenly distributed. I was bundled up like a mummy, hanging on to the top of the cabin as the boat rocked back and forth, back and forth. The farther the stern sank into the water, and the more I felt the stinging wind in my face, the more I was thinking I had caught my last fish and played my last ball game. I thought about Gretchen and the kids, and about the death threats against Eddie Lee Whitson, and about how I was suddenly facing a death threat of my own, in the angry waters of Long Island Sound. I thought about how the Yankees would have to get out the black armbands again, five and a half years after we lost Thurman Munson. I even thought about the lead story on the eleven o'clock news and the newspaper headline: "Yankee Second Baseman Willie Randolph Missing at Sea."

I was also thinking how bizarre it was that I survived the Tilden Houses and the streets of Brooklyn, but I might not survive a fishing trip off of Long Island.

I had no clue how long the boat would stay afloat, how much water it could take on. I just knew that even with a life jacket I was probably not going to last long in such churning, frigid waters. I kept saying prayers, asking God to protect us, and kept looking for another vessel, any vessel. My heart was pounding, taut with terror. My stomach wasn't feeling too good either. My new fishing pole had already floated out to sea, and I was thinking that now I was about to do the same, dead at thirty-one years of age.

Finally, on the horizon, I made out the silhouette of a good-size ship heading toward us. It was a Coast Guard cutter. It seemed to take forever to get to us. I prayed that we'd stay afloat a few more minutes. I kept looking at the ship and thinking, *Why can't you go faster?* At last the cutter pulled alongside us, and the crew and my captain quickly got to work. In short order, they brought us on board and hoisted the front of the boat out of the water with a thick chain, and the cutter slowly began the trip back in, with our boat in tow. As we headed back into port, I pretty much had one thought:

Man, am I glad there is a US Coast Guard.

When we got back on land, we thanked our rescuers and said goodbye. I was in such a daze, I still can't remember the drive home to New Jersey. The Long Island Expressway? The Throgs Neck Bridge? The George Washington Bridge? No data. I walked in the house, and Gretchen took one look at me and said, "What's the matter with you?" I spent most of the next week in a state of numbness, still shaky when I relived the whole thing, and incredibly grateful that my prayers had been answered. It was a long time before I went out on another fishing boat.

OUR STRUGGLES AS A team during the 1980s did little to please Mr. Steinbrenner. Yet despite his notorious volatility and the team's inability to make it to the playoffs, I managed to stay on his good side. The toughest part about our struggles as a team was that they came during a period when I felt like I was the most comfortable in my skin as a baseball player. I marvel sometimes when I think about how young and inexperienced in the ways of both the baseball world and the world at large I was when I became a major league ballplayer. As my time with the Yankees went on, I matured in lots of ways, as a player, as a husband, and as a father. Over time, I felt more comfortable taking on a leadership role with the Yankees. That also had to do with my tenure with the team and not just being in the league. By

1986, when I was named captain, I'd been with the Yankees for more than a decade. Ron Guidry, or as we all called him, Gator, also served as co-captain.

Being the captain of the Yankees, even if it wasn't a perennially playoff-bound Yankee team, was still an amazing honor. This may not sound humble, but I thought I had earned that title. The club made no big deal out of it, and there was no fanfare involved, but joining the ranks of guys like Ruth, Gehrig, Munson, Nettles, and later Mattingly and Jeter, is huge in my mind. It helped ease some of the sting of other slights. I was always proud to be a Yankee, but co-captain of the team made my association with the club even more special. I'd joined an even more special and select group of players.

I found out I was going to be made team captain in a utility closet. Billy had been dropping some hints about a change in my status, and before the Old-Timers' Day game, I was walking in the tunnel that led from the dugout to the clubhouse when I heard Billy calling my name. He was in a utility closet, and not wanting prying eyes or ears to be in on our secret, he hustled me into that cramped space. There, in the middle of all kinds of pipes and conduits in the dim light of a bare bulb, Billy shared his thoughts with me. Unlike in pitching and hitting, location didn't matter. I was feeling pretty good about myself and how the Yankees felt about me.

Of course, there were always times when that "feel good" wasn't so good.

Early in the 1980 season, Gretchen and I learned that our baby daughter, Chantre, then one and a half, needed an operation. They were calling it minor surgery, but I didn't care what they called it. If they were putting my daughter under with anesthesia, it wasn't minor. We were in Detroit, and I told the team I had to leave for a day.

Mr. Steinbrenner called and told me that he was not happy. He tried to talk me out of leaving. It was not his finest hour, in my opinion. Of course, I know how much he wants to win. I respect how much he wants to win. But how do you tell a man that he should stay on the job when he has a baby undergoing surgery?

"Willie, I'll tell you what. I'll have Gretchen and your daughter taken to the hospital in a limousine, and the driver can stay with them the whole time," the Boss said. "Maybe that will make you more comfortable."

"Thanks, George, I appreciate the offer," I said. "But I need to be there for my family. I don't think Gretchen wants your limo driver sitting next to her holding her hand when her daughter is having surgery. She wants me next to her."

Gene Michael was our general manager at the time, and he was in an impossible spot. I think Gene understood and even agreed with my decision, but Mr. Steinbrenner was all over him, and he had to try to get me to change my mind. Gene called me up to his suite in our hotel. He looked at me with great earnestness.

"Willie, George is very upset about this. He understands your feelings, but he doesn't want you to leave the team, even for a day. If you do leave, he is going to be incredibly angry about it."

The bottom line of this story is passion. George Steinbrenner always wanted in the worst way to win baseball games. He bought the best players, hired and fired managers, built a regional TV network to create a gusher of revenues—and he played the role of Patton, accepting no excuses for failure. When the Yankees lost a World Series, he declared himself "embarrassed," called the season a "failure," and said we "owed" New Yorkers championships. The *New York Daily News* cartoonist Bill Gallo depicted him in a spiked Prussian military helmet.

I always respected George Steinbrenner's will to win. I also want to win, every day. But I also want to care for my family.

"Tell George to do what he has to do, the same way I'm going to do what I have to do," I said, and then I walked out.

A few years before, I'd been faced with a similar situation, except that time I didn't just leave, I literally escaped. It was the winter of 1975–76, and Gretchen and I had gone to Valencia, Venezuela, so I could play winter ball. The playoffs were about to begin. I got a call from Gretchen saying that our baby, our oldest daughter, Taniesha, was sick and not getting better. Gretchen didn't think she was getting good advice from the doctors. She was worried.

A league official told me there was no way the team would let me leave, no way that I could leave.

"You watch me," I said.

Gretchen and I found a cab driver, threw him some extra money, and asked him to pick us up in the middle of the night at my hotel. I pulled a hat down low, hopped in the backseat, and got to the airport as fast as I could. The club knew nothing about it. Part of me felt bad about bailing on the team, just going AWOL like that. I'd never done it before, and I've never done it since. But how could I stay in Venezuela when our little girl was sick? Life is full of hard decisions, close calls. This wasn't one of them for me. If your family needs you, you go. And you don't let anything stop you.

The flip side of that family obligation and loyalty issue caught up to me in 1988. I was going into my thirteenth season with the club, and I'd never been a free agent before. I was really looking forward to the opportunity to test my market value for the first time. You remember Dock Ellis yelling at me for signing that first contract with the Yankees for the minimum? Well, to a certain extent I'd remained underpaid ever since. I understood that the big free agent signings meant that the huge dollars weren't going to be there for me. When guys like Reggie or Dave Winfield or whoever the latest sexy free agent to come in was, even the other superstars who'd been treated well, guys like Thurman or Graig, felt a bit slighted. The way salaries were escalating, you could sign a huge deal one year and two years later feel like you were underpaid, and believe me, guys knew who was getting what.

So I went into '88 thinking that this was going to be my year to make up for some of my past failures to really demand what I deserved and management's failure to reward me for performance, loyalty, and longevity. Given everything that had gone on behind the scenes, I guess you could say that I deserved combat or hazardous duty pay.

Lady Luck didn't smile on me. In early May 1988, I strained ligaments in my right wrist. The injury wasn't bad enough to require surgery, but it did affect everything I did on the field, particularly swinging the bat. That season it seemed like I spent more time on the trainer's table than I did at home or on the field. I suppose I should have just gone on the disabled list and let it heal. At one point, I went to Lou Piniella and said to him, "Look, Lou. I'm hurting the ball club, man. I'm just not up to par at all." I hated the idea that I was letting the team down and letting a former teammate down.

Lou and I had some history when it came to dealing with injuries. Back in '86, Lou's first year of his first stint as manager, I was having my usual hamstring troubles. I came back off the DL to play a game against Boston, and I reinjured it. I was devastated. I went into the clubhouse, sat on the stool in front of my locker more frustrated than I'd ever been in the game. I started crying and whipped my equipment bag across the clubhouse. Lou came in and saw me sitting there sobbing. He knew how bad I wanted to play and to win. We spoke for just a few minutes, Lou trying to console me and help me keep things in perspective.

I don't know if in '88 he had that scene playing in his mind when I spoke to him about my wrist, but he said, "Willie, we need you out there. Even if you're only at seventy-five or eighty-five percent, we still need you."

I did what Lou wanted me to do.

My bum wrist was a factor in the .230 average I put up that year. That was a huge drop-off from '87, when I'd hit .305. Not exactly the kind of year that you want to have when your contract is up. Still, I was optimistic that the Yankees wanted me back and that they'd understand that an injury is an injury and I'd tried to play through it the best I could. Supporting that notion was the fact that Dallas Green, who was hired on October 7 to replace Lou Piniella following our fifth-place finish, seemed like he was hoping I'd be back. I'd gone into the Stadium to clear out my locker, and he was there doing some promotional stuff for the Yankees shortly after his hiring.

Dallas had a reputation as a tough-talking, no-nonsense guy, and he told me that he was counting on me to contribute and be a good clubhouse leader. Of course, I understood that he wasn't the one doing the hiring and the negotiating and all that, but I figured he must have had some conversations with management, in particular Bob Quinn, who was the general manager who had replaced Lou Piniella as general manager, who resigned that position in May before Billy was fired in June for his involvement in a drunken brawl in Texas and Lou agreed to take over as field manager. That last sentence is a mess, I know, but it reflects how much of a mess that season was. It also reflects how much of a mess Billy was when he showed up that next morning after getting tossed against a stucco wall of a strip club. A bouncer "escorted" Billy out of the place, and when he walked into the clubhouse the next day, he looked awful. He had a patched-up ear, but you could still see it looked pretty mangled. I felt bad for him. He was deteriorating physically from the drinking and the stress. I wanted to say something to him, but you just didn't do that kind of thing. We were all adults and responsible for ourselves, and I don't think going up to Billy and saying, "Hey, Skip, look, I'm concerned about your conduct and your health," would change anything. If the situation was reversed and I was the manager and he was the player, of course I would have intervened somehow. Given how things turned out for Billy, I'm sorry that things were like that.

Looking back on it now, I'm kind of ashamed to have thought that anybody within the organization had any idea about what was going on that year or the next.

As it turned out, Dallas Green may have had plans for me, but the Yankees didn't. On November 24, 1988, in a weird trade that wasn't a trade, Steve Sax of the Dodgers signed as the new Yankee second baseman, and on December 11, I signed as the new Dodgers second baseman. I didn't want to leave the Yankees, but I was glad to have the opportunity to play for a great organization.

I don't want what I'm about to say to diminish respect for the Dodgers or Yankees, but a sad chapter in baseball was being written at the time. The owners were never happy about free agency, and their successful attempts at collusion to limit player movement and keep down salaries illegally have been well documented. I was part of a group of players included in a settlement in October 1989 in what came to be known as "the Collusion II case." The arbitrator ruled that we'd been unfairly victimized, and we were awarded "new look" status. That meant that we could test the waters of free agency without voiding the contract we were currently working under. A complicated mess. The owners were forced to pay $38 million, and the players' association distributed that among the guys named in the case. Believe me, that wasn't how I was hoping to be rewarded, but it was just one of the harsher realities of playing at that time.

Again, I don't hold any ill will toward the Dodgers and the way they went about signing me. I liked the different vibe of living in LA, and I had a great '89 season, returning to All-Star form and status. We finished fourth, and it wasn't any fun to be out of the race, but I got to see an entirely different style of managing under Tommy Lasorda.

Tommy was a colorful guy, to be sure, but he always had our backs. I saw that personally when Rob Dibble of the Reds, a six-foot-four, 235-pound wild man, threw a 100-mile-per-hour fastball over my head. At that stage of my career and life, I didn't need that. Hell, at any time of my career and life I didn't need that. It was absolutely a message pitch, because we were beating up on him and he was frustrated. The benches got all riled up. I stayed pretty calm (I was in no great rush to charge the mound to visit a pitcher of that size), but Tommy Lasorda was on the top step screaming at Dibble with every curse word in his vocabulary (and Tommy has a lot of them), letting him know in no uncertain terms we would get him back for this. Tommy's mood got even worse when he read that Dibble basically called me out, saying, "If he wants to do something about it, he knows where I am and can come and get me."

There were some guys you knew would hit you without a second thought. To them it was just a normal part of competition. ("Normal" would not be the word chosen by the targets.) Jack Morris would hit you, especially later in his career, when he wanted to make sure you knew that he owned the inside part of the plate. Nolan Ryan would too; you think his 158 career HBPs were an accident? What would set Nolan off more than anything was guys trying to bunt on him. He hated it. He didn't seem to consider bunting smart baseball; he thought you should hit your way on base. I remember seeing him stalk off the mound one time after a rookie (I can't remember who) fouled off a bunt against him. He moved toward the plate, with that slow, purposeful Texan gait, and I heard him say in that slow, purposeful Texan drawl, "I wouldn't do that again, son." He might as well have been Marlon Brando threatening somebody in *The Godfather.* The "son" had the good sense not to attempt another bunt in that at-bat. In fact, I'd wager that he never attempted another bunt in his life against Mr. Ryan. It just wasn't worth it.

Nolan never said that to me, because he didn't have to. When I bunted on him (which, believe me, I did very, very rarely), I made sure I got it down in fair territory. I didn't want him walking toward me from the mound, whispering sweet nothings. I had a wife. Children. I had a life I wanted to lead, one that did not include a crushed temple. Mostly, with Nolan, I just waited him out, because he was often wild high. A walk was definitely as good as a hit against Nolan, and way, way better than a bunt.

The pitcher with the funniest approach to hitting guys, though, was probably Bret Saberhagen. If you kept fouling balls off him, getting him into a ten- or eleven-pitch at-bat, he would just hit you. When we were teammates with the Mets in 1992, I asked him about it. I was left with the impression that he didn't want to waste any more pitches on guys he was struggling to get out.

You can't argue with his logic.

Pitchers, of course, have been throwing at hitters for as long as baseball has been played. And retaliation for those HBPs has been around just as long. It's part of baseball's unwritten code: you get my guy, I'm going to get yours. Almost nobody wants to talk about it, and almost everybody lies about it. But that's the code, and it gets enforced all the time, no matter how much pitchers and catchers and managers might deny it. How many times have you heard a pitcher who you know absolutely drilled a guy on purpose say, "The pitch got away from me"? How many times have you heard a manager say, "We were just trying to pitch him in, and he got a little too far in"? It's all such a crock.

No manager I've played for was more aggressive in meting out justice than Tony La Russa. After I joined the A's in 1990, I recall a game when Yankee starter Tim Leary gave up a homer to Jose Canseco, then plunked Mark McGwire. Tony would always go nuts when they came anywhere near McGwire, and he was the same way more recently with Albert Pujols. I think Tony knew that Mark could be intimidated and would get a little squeamish about it, so Tony would protect him by going on the offensive wherever possible. I remember him screaming at pitchers in the other dugout, letting them have it for messing with his guys.

Before the series was over with the Yankees, Dave Stewart of the A's took the mound and proceeded to hit Don Mattingly, Bob Geren, and Mike Blowers. Dave walked two guys in eight innings. Funny how he kept losing control and hitting guys. Funny that Tony didn't mind at all.

Playing for the A's in 1990 gave me an opportunity to get back into the World Series. Funny how life sometimes provides you with bookend moments. My first World Series with the Yankees ended up with us being swept by the Reds. My last World Series as a player also resulted in the Reds sweeping us. I had a decent Series, going 4-for-15, but what I remember most is the sight of guys like Mark McGwire, Jose Canseco, a young Gene Nelson in the bullpen, Dave Stewart, Carney Lansford, and the inimitable Rickey Henderson going at it.

I was still eager to play and signed with the Brewers for the 1991 season. I knew that I was going to be playing a platoon role, sharing time with the left-handed-hitting Jimmy Gantner. You have to take advantage of opportunities, and when the Brewers' third baseman, the young stud Gary Sheffield, went on the disabled list with a wrist injury, Gantner took over his spot and I played second base full-time. I got into 124 games, hit a career-high .327, and drove in 54 runs, the most since I'd knocked in 67 for the '87 Yankees. Not bad for a thirty-six-year-old.

I went my whole career without getting hit in the head, but toward the end of my last year, with the Mets in 1992, I got as big a scare as I ever had at the plate. The Mets were playing the Pirates, and Bob Walk was pitching. Walk was a big guy, six-four and probably 235 pounds. He didn't throw that hard—a distinction your body doesn't draw when a ball slams into it—but just the same, he didn't want you leaning over the plate. Fine, lots of people don't. But Walk crossed the line. I always thought he had some headhunter in him. On this night he came on in relief in the seventh inning, and manager Jeff Torborg sent me up to pinch-hit for David Cone. On his third pitch, Walk wound and delivered, and right away I knew this was trouble. The ball was coming right at my head. Maybe it was an innocent mistake. I don't know. In the moment, I didn't much care about the whys or where-fores. Instantly, I got this blast of panic. There was no time to do anything. None. You've got a sick feeling, and a bad feeling, one that I can sum up like this:

Oh man, this ball is coming at me and it's going to be here in a millisecond and I'm going to get hit in the face.

I could see the seams clearly. I could almost read NL president Bill White's signature on the damn thing. In that instant, I could almost feel my reflexes slowing even as the ball was hurtling toward my eyeballs. It was as if time stopped. I put my hand up in self-defense, and thank God I got it up in time. The ball slammed into my hand, and it hurt like hell. Later I found out it was broken, but at least I didn't get the ball in the face or head.

I stayed in the game and scored when Daryl Boston hit a homer off Walk—which suited me just fine. The incident reminded me, though, that I was not a kid anymore and that the next time maybe that hand wouldn't get there in time.

After a seven-week break and a ton of rehab and strengthening exercises (and let me tell you, rehab is seriously tedious), I returned for the final game of the season. I wasn't going to end my season on the disabled list. And if this turned out to be the end for me as a player, I sure wasn't going to end my career on the DL either.

No way that was happening.

I went hitless in my first three at-bats and then stepped in against a big Pirate rookie named Steve Cooke in the ninth. I worked the count to 3-1, and then took ball four. It didn't make for high drama, but it was probably a fitting way to go out, seeing as how I'd walked 1,242 other times in eighteen years, and there was nice symmetry too: I came up with the Pirates, and I was going out against the Pirates. Torborg brought Dicky Schofield in to pinch-run for me so I could get an ovation from the Shea fans. There were only 14,000 people there; when you are twenty-four games out on October 4, even a visit by the first-place Pirates and their 175-pound star left fielder, Barry Bonds, isn't going to bring out your SRO crowds. The fans gave me a nice little acknowledgment as I trotted back to the dugout.

That was it.

An hour or so later, I drove home over the George Washington Bridge, with no press conference or fanfare, no tears or regrets. I am not a big ceremony guy, never have been. I wasn't positive this was the end, but I had a pretty strong hunch it would be. It was an eerie feeling, and kind of bittersweet, thinking that this could be my last trip over the bridge as a player, that almost two decades had passed since I made my debut with the Yankees. Sad? Sure, part of me was sad that I wasn't twenty-one anymore and didn't have it all in front of me. But a much bigger part of me was proud that I'd left it all on the field—done my best and honored the game and honored my family.

Since I had been a young child, I had defined myself in one way: baseball player.

I would never be a baseball player again. It's hard to express how I felt at the moment. It was very, very strange.

Willie Randolph, baseball player, was no more.

I continued driving north, the lights of the bridge receding behind me. The smaller those lights became the more certain I was. It was time. As I drove I couldn't help but think about Billy and how he would have liked my taking a walk in that final at-bat. That was how you were supposed to play the game.

When I learned that Billy had died in that car wreck the day after Christmas in 1989, I was really sad. Truth is, though, and I don't think I'm alone in thinking this way, that seemed like an inevitable conclusion. Over the years Billy and I had become friends. We shared some common interests—hunting and firearms, for example. I'd taken up the hobby of target shooting and enjoyed it. Every now and then I'd receive a package from Billy. Inside would be a gun, usually an older gun, not exactly vintage, but something I'd add to my collection. One of them, a .38 special, must have belonged to a police officer. The curious thing about it was that it had notches carved in its handle.

I guess with my playing days over, I was feeling a bit nostalgic and somewhat melancholy, so those thoughts occupied my mind for a while. Billy was the first big-league manager I played under full-time. People who occupied that kind of position in my life, like a first girlfriend or a first love, were special. I knew that I was going to miss the game, the us-against-the-world approach that I took to the game just as Billy had.

But for a while, it was going to be time to relax, to be that old gunslinger in retirement.

CHAPTER 7

Back with the Yankees

I realize that in recounting my departure from the Yankees, I sounded somewhat bitter. Truth is, I was hurt—both injured and offended. I knew that baseball was a business and all that, but I'd given so many years of my life to that organization. Maybe it was because I had such good experiences in LA, Oakland, Milwaukee, and then back in New York with the Mets that the pain diminished over time. I'd been able to play on the same team with so many other greats in the game. In Milwaukee there was Paul Molitor and Robin Yount, two very classy veterans who eventually made it into the Hall of Fame. I haven't added up the number of Hall of Famers I've played on the same team with, but I bet I'm among the league leaders in that category. With the Dodgers there was Eddie Murray, and with the A's it was Dennis Eckersley. So, if my years away from the Yankees were a kind of farewell tour, then I got to visit some great spots and meet some great people. I was very fortunate in that regard.

In my heart, though, I was a Yankee, and when I got a call in the spring of 1994, asking if I'd like to rejoin the Yankees as the assistant general manager to the GM Gene Michael, I was quite pleased and agreed quickly, but with one provision: I wouldn't start until after the All-Star break. My new job would involve travel, evaluating minor and major league talent, and I wanted some time to spend with Gretchen and the kids. I'd been away from them so much during my playing days. My kids were all pretty good athletes and involved in all kinds of school activities, and it was time to be a bit more of a dad to them. They'd enjoyed being a part of the Yankee family. Andre would come out early for batting practice sometimes, and I remember being stunned by the difference in size and strength between Andre, who'd grow to only five-seven but go on to play a couple of years in the Yankee organization, and Cecil Fielder's son Prince, who was the same age as Andre but was already hitting balls out of the yard even when he was eleven or twelve years old.

The girls enjoyed their time with the Yankees, coming out on Sunday mornings at home for Wiffle-ball games and things like that. None of my kids really enjoyed hanging out in the locker room, but they did enjoy going to the games, meeting the other families, and being a part of what Dad was doing.

I wanted a few months to devote to them, and the Yankees agreed to let me take that time.

If I had any lingering ill feelings toward the Yankees, they were long gone by '93, and I was pleased to read some of the nice things the Boss had to say when asked about my hiring. He told reporters, "Everybody knows that I wanted Willie. I'm very high on his ability and talent." He added, "This is one I've been after for a long time. I can see Willie Randolph being president of the league or commissioner. I don't put anything past him." I can laugh about it now, thinking how much Mr. Steinbrenner would have loved to have an ex-Yankee in charge of the game, but at the time I was flattered. I think he was genuine in his feelings for me. If nothing else, with the exception of those few hours of family leave years before, I don't think I ever gave him any headaches. That may be faint praise, but consider the context.

Looking back on it, I don't know if I was temperamentally suited to be an assistant general manager. I enjoyed seeing some of our young talent play, scouting other teams, and making and renewing connections with other teams and players, but it all felt kind of passive to me. I wanted to be down on the field. I wasn't so far removed from the game that I could sit still and just watch and evaluate. If I saw a middle infielder doing something wrong, it wasn't enough to make note of that player's tendency to not stay on the balls of his feet or to double-tap the ball in the glove before throwing it. I wanted to *fix* those problems, help the guys work through their solutions.

Buck Showalter was the team's manager, a somewhat controversial hire Mr. Steinbrenner had made in 1992. After all, Buck was only thirty-six years old at the time, a year younger than me. Buck had been a Yankee draft choice and spent seven seasons in the minor leagues without ever playing a single game in the majors. His youth, his inexperience in the majors, and a relatively brief tenure in the minor leagues as a manager (five years) all set him apart from most of the other managers whom the Boss had hired. Buck enjoyed the support of Billy Martin. Billy had noticed him during spring training when the minor league staff was around helping out. I can't say that Billy's stamp of approval influenced George, but Buck was on the Yankee coaching staff in 1990 and 1991 before taking over as the manager the year before I returned to the team.

After my initial stint working as a front-office guy, George wanted to know what my next move was going to be. Gene Michael approached me, and I was in a bit of a tough spot. I told Stick that I enjoyed working for him as an assistant GM and learned a hell of a lot. (I sometimes think that Gene doesn't get enough credit for the groundwork he laid to help produce those later great teams. He's one of the smartest baseball men I've ever met.) I felt that I was still a young guy, though, and I liked the idea of being down on the field still sweating and still teaching and interacting with the guys.

The Yankee brass agreed that I'd be a good candidate for a third-base coach since I'd been a good base runner my whole career and had a good feel for the game generally. I got sent down to Tampa to the Instructional League that fall prior to the '94 season. I had no idea how hard it was going to be to coach third—plays developed so quickly, and I had to figure out what angles to position myself at and a whole host of other nuances. Fortunately, Trey Hillman was the manager of the club, and he helped me out a lot. After my quick training session, I told Stick I thought I could handle the job.

What I didn't tell Gene Michael, or anyone else, was that I knew Buck needed to be comfortable with his staff. If that meant I wouldn't be his choice for third-base coach, then that was fine. So, when I got the chance, I spoke with Buck personally. I told him I knew that the perception was that I was George's guy and he had to take me on his staff. I told him that, just between the two of us, if he wasn't comfortable with me as his third-base coach, or if he had someone else in mind for the job, I had enough respect for him and for the team that I'd tell George and Gene that I'd changed my mind and I'd resign. I didn't want George or Gene to think that Buck had rejected their guy and make him pay the price for it down the line. Until now, I've kept that conservation private, and even if Buck had said, "Thanks, and you're right, I want my own guy," I would still have kept my mouth shut. A staff is like a team, and that trust has to be there among the guys. I'm glad that Buck wanted me.

Timing is everything in baseball, and I joined the Yankees at the best and the worst of times. In Buck's first two seasons, the Yankees had experienced gradual improvement, moving from fourth place to second. Much of that was due to the off-season acquisitions, by trade and by free agency, of Wade Boggs, Paul O'Neill, Jim Abbott, and Jimmy Key. Having those last two guys in the rotation was especially important, given the lack of a frontline starter in '92. The staff's improvement in ERA was incremental—going from twelfth in the league (out of fourteen) to ninth with those two additions. Offense wasn't as much of a problem, but with Boggs and O'Neill in the lineup, the team improved from seventh in runs and fifth in hits in '92 to fourth and first, respectively.

Understandably, there was a lot of optimism surrounding the '94 season, and with the exception of a couple of minor deals, the team stood pat. That confidence was rewarded when the team went on a hot streak once the weather improved. On May 4, we were three and a half games behind the Red Sox and the Orioles with a record of 16-10. By June 4, we were two and a half games up with a 33-18 record. By August 4, we were 68-38, a remarkable thirty games above .500

and ten games out in front of the Orioles. A week later, on August 11, the season was over.

The 1994 players' strike was tough on everybody. I was no longer a player, but given what had happened to me over the course of my long playing career, my allegiance was, to be honest, with the players, not with my employers. I don't want to get into all the aspects of it, but I believed that the players were in the right. Neither side trusted the other, but the owners had been found guilty of collusion: I couldn't believe it, but they withheld a required $7.8 million payment to the players' pension and benefit plans. I've talked about being a student of the history of the game. The players' strike showed me that all those veterans who never benefited from free agency, television revenues, and everything else that contributed to rising salaries could have become collateral damage in the war of stupidity.

Still, I didn't want to see the strike go forward, and I never thought that the rest of the season was going to be wiped out, but as time went on and things kept looking so bleak, I felt really bad for all the Yankee fans who'd suffered since 1981. It looked like we were going to win 100 games, Paul O'Neill was having a huge season leading the league with a .359 average, Jimmy Key was lights-out as he won 17 games through early August, and Don Mattingly looked like he was finally going to arrive safely in the promised land of the playoffs.

Of all the teammates I ever had, Donnie is the guy I feel the worst for about not winning. I was sure 1994 was going to be the year. Then it all got taken away from us, all of us—players, owners, on-field and off-field management, and fans. The game I loved was being destroyed. I was in the fortunate position myself of being financially secure, but still, my heart was broken. From August until the '95 season opened in late April in Texas, I walked around with a sick feeling in my gut. I had to do what I was being paid to do, but the idea of having replacement players come into spring training was tough for me to deal with. I didn't want to see the game's standing diminished any more than it already had been by the strike. A rock and a hard place doesn't begin to describe what it was like for everybody.

Just to show you what kind of guy Donnie is, he never once complained about how the '94 season unraveled. That's why he was Donnie Baseball. He went out there and did his job and worked his tail off doing it. I asked him a few times about his back and the strike, and I always got the same answer. *That's the way things go sometimes. You move on. It's all part of the game.* I don't think he was avoiding telling me how he really felt. He's a stand-up guy, and he knew there was no sense in whining or complaining—that wasn't going to change the outcome.

THE FOLLOWING YEAR THE team looked very similar to the one we'd been winning with before the strike. In the lead-up to the 1995 season, we did make one major off-season move, getting Jack McDowell from the White Sox. In the two seasons prior to strike-shortened '94, he'd won twenty and then twenty-two games with Chicago, finishing second and then first in the Cy Young Award voting. Later on we'd get David Cone, and the two of them complemented the young Andy Pettitte in the rotation. Jimmy Key had season-ending rotator cuff surgery after going on the disabled list in late May.

We were the wild-card team, and even though we were only 79-65 in the strike-shortened season, with the way we finished the year—we were 22-6 in the last month—I didn't think anyone could stop us. When we went up 2–0 on Seattle in the Divisional Series, I was even more sure. Then Randy Johnson beat us in game 3, and we blew a 5–0 lead in game 4. We were up 4–2 with five outs to go and David Cone on the mound when things went all wrong. Ken Griffey Jr. hit a massive, upper-deck homer, and then Coney, on his way to throwing 147 pitches, lost the plate. He walked three guys to tie the game in the bottom of the eighth. The tying run was scored by a pinch runner named Alex Rodriguez.

Still, we kept fighting. Randy Velarde had a huge RBI single against Johnson in the top of the eleventh, and now we were just three outs away from a 5–4 victory, and the ALCS. Joey Cora was set to lead off against our starter-turned-reliever, Jack McDowell. A little, switch-hitting second baseman, Cora had already bunted in the game, he had two bunt singles in the last two days, and I had a strong feeling he might try it again. I was in charge of the infield defensive alignment and sitting in the Kingdome dugout, next to manager Buck Showalter.

"Donnie!" I hollered. McDowell threw ball one. "Donnie! Donnie!" I tried again. With the roar of the crowd, I couldn't get Mattingly's attention at first base. McDowell threw ball two. Donnie was always good about studying the scouting reports and knowing the hitters. He wasn't playing deep, wasn't terribly out of position. Given the circumstances, he just wasn't as tight as I preferred him to be, to guard against the bunt. Cora took a strike to make it 2-1. I looked again at Donnie, hoping to make eye contact. "Donnie!" I tried once more. McDowell wound and fired. Cora shortened up, came up in the box.

It was too late.

Cora dragged a good bunt toward first and got out of the box well. Donnie reacted quickly, came in, and grabbed it. Cora raced down the line. Donnie lunged for him but couldn't get a tag on him. The Mariners had the leadoff man on. I shook my head in disgust. My second-guessing began immediately. Griffey singled up the middle, Cora racing to third. Up came Edgar Martínez, Mr. DH himself, the worst possible guy to have in the box. He'd been wearing us out the whole series, going 11-for-20 with eight RBI to that point. I had a terrible feeling about this.

On McDowell's 0-1 pitch he came inside, and Martinez turned and ripped it down the left-field line. Cora scored, and Griffey slid in behind him as the Kingdome shook from all the noise and the Mariners celebrated at home plate. My stomach was knotted in angst and regret. The season was over, and so was Don Mattingly's big-league career.

For a long time afterward, the tape kept running in my head, *Damn, what if I had gotten Donnie's attention and moved him in a step or two?* Would it have made a difference? Would it have kept Joey Cora off of first base? I don't know. Nobody knows. But maybe it would have. I felt responsible for the loss. The game can make you crazy sometimes.

I can still see that ball rattling around that corner and that turf in the Kingdome and Ken Griffey Jr. coming around third base and Gerald Williams picking up the ball in left field and throwing the relay to Tony Fernández, and then bang, bang, play, scores. Games like that haunt you for the rest of your life.

I never talked with Buck about it, but that game had to haunt him as well. The flight home was one of the quietest I'd ever experienced in my time in the big leagues, as a player or as a coach. It seemed like the loss hadn't even fully set in when the Boss spun the managerial wheel of fortune once again, firing Buck. Bob Watson was just joining the team as the general manager, and George wanted him to get acclimated before taking on the task of finding the next manager. Rumors were circulating that my name was in the mix of candidates, and I have to say that I was flattered to be thought of that way. At the time the decision to fire Buck was easy to question. Later on, given how Joe Torre succeeded, it seemed like a no-brainer. That's not to say that Buck's not a great manager, but Joe had the touch with that particular group of guys that allowed the D-word—*dynasty*—to come into play.

I'd seen so many managers come and go during my tenure with the Yankees that the word *surprised* seldom applied to my reaction. Buck was a very knowledgeable baseball man, still is, but he wasn't a name manager. Mr. Steinbrenner liked players and managers who had big names and big reputations. If anything, I was surprised that Buck was hired in the first place, not that he didn't deserve it, but because he didn't fit the pattern of typical Yankee hires. When he was let go, I suppose I was so calloused by that time that I didn't respond the way that I had when Yogi was fired. A lot of managerial water had gone under the bridge by the time Buck's run came to an end.

As it turned out, I almost wasn't a part of that mix contributing to that great Yankee run. Just as I had recognized how tough a spot Buck was being put in when I initially became the Yankees' third-base coach, that was the case when Joe was hired. I was the only holdover from the previous staff, and I knew that the perception out there was that I was, depending on your point of view, George's guy or George's spy. I didn't think of resigning or having the same conversation with Joe that I did with Buck. I thought I'd demonstrated my skills and value to the team at that point. That's not to say I didn't still have a lot to learn, but I liked the job and wanted to continue in the game. And frankly, being in New York was something I also really enjoyed.

Understandably, Joe had some reservations about keeping me around. I didn't blame him. Managers like to have their own guys around, and I'd heard that Joe wanted to bring aboard Dal Maxvill, a former teammate and one of Joe's trusted lieutenants on previous staffs. I also heard down the line that I was retained because George told Joe that if he wanted me gone, he'd have to do it himself. George wasn't going to let me go.

Let me add this. George was a loyal guy who supported me, but I wasn't in his pocket. I never reported to him or went behind the back of the manager. When I was a player, I didn't have the kind of relationship with George that some of my other former teammates did. I wasn't the kind of guy to even speak to him unless he approached me. That was how I handled things as a coach as well.

With Joe, I also knew that trust was important, and while I could tell Joe he could trust me, that wasn't worth a thing—I had to show him by conducting myself the same way as I always had. I worked hard. I did the right things. I had to prove to Joe that I wasn't a pipeline guy—the one providing intelligence to the front office. That was easy because I went home after games; I wasn't ever the kind of guy who got in the elevator and headed up to the offices immediately after the last out. Over time Joe saw that was the case, and we became quite close. I didn't blame him for being suspicious initially; after all, the only way to earn trust is through time and experiences together. I think the fact that Joe asked me to be a part of the staff for the 2013 USA team that participated in the World Baseball Classic speaks volumes about the relationship the two of us have. He didn't have to make that offer, but he did.

I can't say how much of a privilege it was to be on those Yankee coaching staffs. It was like being a part of a premier baseball think tank, sitting with and participating in discussions about the finer points with Mel Stottlemyre and Don Zimmer. It was also incredibly entertaining.

I began to store some valuable lessons in how to handle a ball club. It is true that Buck Showalter was a very intense guy, a stickler for detail, and that he could sometimes come across a little gruff. Joe Torre, on the other hand, epitomized calm under pressure. He really was as unflappable as he's been portrayed over the years. He wasn't cold and indifferent, and he wanted to win with a passion, but he had a way about him that projected confidence and assurance. Of course, it helped that he had some great players to work with, but Joe understood better than anyone I'd ever seen that it was his job to put people in a position to succeed and then not do anything to get in the way of their doing that. How a player got to the point where he was maximizing his abilities was important to Joe, but he believed that players needed the freedom to do what was best for them. If they didn't, and they weren't producing results, Joe would get on them, but mostly with a gentle reminder and not a swift kick in the ass. He respected the guys, and that was reciprocated.

WHILE '95 HADN'T ENDED the way we'd wanted it to, it did bode well for the future of the team. Of course, you would have had to put on multiple pairs of rose-colored glasses to see just how vast a difference there can be between a major league debut and a subsequent Hall of Fame–caliber career. In other words, you can't take much stock in a player's early performances in major league games. There's a lot of truth to the idea that it's not how you start but how you finish. On more than one level, that was particularly true of one of the greatest pitchers in Yankee history.

On May 23, 1995, Mariano Rivera started against the California Angels in Anaheim. He struck out the first two hitters before surrendering a single and a double. He got out of the inning with no damage.

That wasn't true of the next two and a third innings. He gave up six more hits and walked three, and five runs crossed the plate. I'd seen him pitch before and was impressed by his smooth delivery and how the ball seemed to jump out of his hand. It also jumped off those Angels bats. Six days later, Derek Jeter started at shortstop. Playing in his first major league game, he went 0-for-5. He appeared in fifteen games and hit a respectable .250.

Neither of those two opening nights could have prepared us for what was to come.

Meanwhile, Bernie Williams solidly established himself as the team's center fielder in '95, hitting .307 for the year and putting on that graceful display of covering so much ground. Still, he was very much a work in progress in my mind—it was clear there was much more he was capable of.

I would have liked to have the chance to mold that homegrown talent myself, but at the time I wasn't really sure that I was ready to manage full-time. I'd been a coach for only two abbreviated seasons. Still, I had no idea how long I'd have to wait to get my shot. I also knew that these three guys, along with Andy Pettitte, had a chance to be special. Whether they'd make the most of their abundant talent, avoid injuries, and love to compete at the highest level was something we'd all have to wait to see.

Even though we didn't know exactly what it was we had on our hands, we knew we had a group of special guys who'd come up through the Yankee system. That alone brought a different energy to the club. Sure, the team had guys like Boggs and O'Neill whose experience in the field and at the plate was essential, but this team had the kind of energy that can only come from young talent. And it had been a long time since New York baseball fans had been thrilled by the feats of homegrown talent.

As it turned out, the last time New York City had seen a concentration of young talent like this was on a Mets team, not a Yankees team—especially two players who by '96 had switched boroughs to become a part of our organization.

Ballplayers are like anyone in any business: we keep track of what's going on with our direct competitors as well as what's going on in the industry and in the economy generally. In other words, we're fans and we keep up with what's going on in both leagues. When I was playing with the Yankees in 1983, we couldn't help but hear about what was taking place in Queens. A young outfielder by the name of Darryl Strawberry was in the middle of a Rookie of the Year season. The kid just had a look about him. He was six feet six inches tall and weighed less than 200 pounds. He had a long stroke, which was natural considering how long his arms were, but the bat seemed to just lash through the zone with incredible force. Almost like a bullwhip, his swing was one that was meant to punish baseballs. In 122 games that year, he hit 26 home runs, drove in 74, stole 19 bases, and had an impressive slugging percentage of .512. Not only that, he seemed very charismatic, with his wide smile and engaging personality. He was part of the turnaround that saw the Mets go from 68-94 in his rookie season to 90-72 the following year.

So many other things happened to Darryl during his career that it's easy to forget that the guy was diagnosed with colon cancer in 1998, had surgery, and underwent chemotherapy. In 2000 the cancer recurred, and he once again went under the knife, to remove a tumor and a kidney. He was in and out of jail and drug treatment facilities and was so despondent at one point that he stopped his chemotherapy treatments.

One of the other contributors to that turnaround was a nineteen-year-old rookie pitcher who just dazzled everybody with his over-the-top delivery and a nasty yakker (aka curveball) that just froze hitters. We called curveballs "Uncle Charlie," but Dwight Gooden's was such a step above the ordinary pitch that it was nicknamed "Lord Charles." The first time I saw highlights of a "Doc" Gooden game, I was grateful that I wouldn't have to face him. He wasn't nearly as tall as Darryl, but he had that same long, lean athletic build that generated a lot of power for a fluid delivery that was all high leg kick. In his major league debut in April 1984, just two years out of high school, he allowed one run on five hits. That was just the start. He'd wind up going 17-9 with a 2.60 ERA, 3 shutouts, and 276 strikeouts. That last number is pretty astounding. He averaged 11.4 strikeouts per nine innings. That's more than one per inning. He was named to the All-Star squad, finished second in the Cy Young balloting, got some Most Valuable Player votes, and was the Rookie of the Year.

If you hadn't seen Dwight Gooden or heard much about him, the All-Star Game in 1984 was all you needed to get you up to speed. He was the youngest player to ever participate, and showing off his high heat, he struck out the side in his first inning of work. That wasn't surprising, considering he was leading the NL in strikeouts at that point, but I remember watching the game on TV and being amazed by how calm and composed he was.

Nothing could have prepared anyone for what Doc did in 1985. I don't know if anyone will ever have as dominating a year as that young man did. He led the majors with 24 wins, 268 strikeouts, and an ERA of 1.53. That's the triple crown of pitching. He also had an astounding 16 complete games. He could have had an even more dominant year in terms of stats: in September he pitched consecutive nine-inning games in which he didn't allow a run but had a no-decision.

Doc and Darryl seemed to have everything they could have dreamed of. They were stars in major league baseball in one of the greatest cities in the world. Doc was the toast of the town. Enormous photos and murals of him in Times Square and Pennsylvania Station were reminders of just how big a deal he was, and he was still only twenty years old. I couldn't imagine what that must have been like—the adulation, the demands on his time, and all the rest that goes with being a breakout star of that dimension.

I'm not sure what role the larger environment played in the eventual descent of both of these young men into drug and alcohol abuse. I've heard Doc talk about his long and tortured ordeal with substance abuse. He's mentioned how, like most players, he took advantage of the alcohol that was available in the clubhouse after games. Even though he wasn't of legal drinking age, he would have a few beers, or hard alcohol, after the game. He specifically mentioned day games as an opportunity for what I would characterize as "casual" drinking. Guys knew that the rush-hour traffic around New York City was horrendous, so they'd hang out for a while and have a few drinks, rehash the game, enjoy the camaraderie that you really miss once you stop playing the game.

Doc also has said that he was a "people pleaser" and that got him into even more trouble, particularly with his use of cocaine. He so wanted to fit in that peer pressure played a role in his addictive behaviors. Just as we talk about there being a steroid era and a dead ball era in baseball, I don't think it's a great revelation to tell you that there was a cocaine era in the game. If baseball reflects what's going on in society—and in this case it really does—during the 1980s the ready availability of cocaine crossed all kinds of boundaries. Cocaine was expensive compared to other drugs and alcohol, and it came to be associated with the young, the wealthy, and the powerful.

I don't think the problem was more prevalent in New York. You could probably have gotten access to cocaine in Seattle as easily as you could in SoHo. I also don't think that the pressures of playing in New York contributed a great deal to Doc's and Darryl's issues. I do know this: if Doc had issues with wanting to fit in and please people, then the Mets teams of that vintage were not the best places he could have been. Both Doc and Darryl, as well as others, have been forthcoming about what those years were like in that clubhouse—the drinking, the using, the womanizing were legendary. I wasn't there, and I'm sure there were some guys who thought that some of that behavior should have been reined in, that there was going to be a price to pay somewhere down the line. The Mets teams of that era were so talented that it's hard to believe that they only won that one title in '86. That had to be a disappointment to them, and I know it was to their fans. I also know the feeling that comes from failed expectations, but maybe some of the guys were just too numb to it all to really feel it? I also don't know if anyone could have stepped into that environment and talked some sense into those guys.

It may have been because of where and how I grew up, but I didn't have that same sense of youthful invincibility, the feeling that nothing could touch me, that's common among all young people, not just ballplayers.

I know that I was very fortunate to have people looking out for my best interests. Growing up in the projects, I saw drug use all around me and its devastating effects on individuals, families, and the community at large. When I had any money on me, even just a dollar or two, I'd run even faster. The regular thugs were bad, but the drug dealers were the worst. If they weren't strung out, their customers were, and you never knew what either group might do to you to keep the high going. The dealers had their fancy cars and their evil wares, and they were always looking for new customers, just as the old customers were always looking for easy money. It added up to big danger.

By the late 1960s, my neighborhood felt like a drug-infested war zone, and I'll never forget the night my father went into battle. There was this one dealer who was really bad, always hanging out near our building. My father usually ignored him, but not this night. My father's not an especially big guy, but he is sinewy and tough, a no-nonsense man, and when he has had enough of something, he has had enough. Trust me on that. He wouldn't have cared if the dealer had a militia behind him. In the courtyard near the lobby of our building, he got into this dealer's face. He jabbed his finger at him, and then he went right at him. "You stay away from my kids, you hear? Because if you don't, I'm going to come looking for you, and I'm going to find you, you understand? Now get the hell out of here."

My father has never been a demonstrative man, somebody comfortable showing emotion or affection. He worked hard and was hard, even at home. He was almost never playful. His life never taught him about being playful. I can count on a couple of fingers the times I had played catch with him. My dad showed his love by providing and protecting. I don't think I ever felt more protected than I did that day. He was a tough man in a tough place, and man, did I admire his courage.

Seeing my father take on that man let me know something else. Drugs were not something to mess with. If my father was willing to put himself on the line like that, the risk-reward balance to using must have been tipped pretty heavily in one direction. I did my share of drinking, within reason, but fortunately for me, I never was tempted by cocaine or the other substances that were readily available to big-league ballplayers and others with the cash and the cachet to socialize in those circles where doing lines was as acceptable as having a drink.

I remember when I first heard about Doc and Darryl and the fight each one was having with addiction. My first instinct was to get in touch with them to talk to them. I don't know exactly why it was that I thought I might have something useful to say, but I knew that I was grateful that I didn't have the disease. I was also even more grateful than ever that I had two parents who instilled in me values that kept me out of trouble. Back then, my parents' tools of persuasion, the Belt and the Bible, weren't my favorite items in the world. I never engaged in all-out rebellion against my parents or anyone else who used these tools, but I was like any kid and hated to have my independence infringed upon.

These tools combined, however, kept me in line.

I'm sorry to say that I never did reach out to Doc or Darryl. I didn't think it was my place to do so. I wasn't some kind of expert, and since I didn't suffer from the same disease, hadn't walked the walk that they had, I might not have had anything valuable to say to them. In those imaginary conversations I did have with them, I just wanted to listen to them, to lend a friendly, nonjudgmental ear. I came up to the big leagues at about the same age they did, and I knew what it was like from a very different perspective as a husband and a father. I wouldn't have preached to them, but I would have told them that you can have your fun on and off the field, but there comes a time when you have to put away those adolescent pleasures and find deeper and more meaningful ones.

Knowing that addiction is a disease, I realize that my words would have been far too simplistic to change anything for them. That's not what I was hoping to do, though. Just letting them know that there was another way they could fit in, that another man who came from a similar background, someone relatively close to their age, had made different choices and had things turn out well—that was the message I'd have delivered.

By the time Darryl and Doc joined the Yankees in 1995 and 1996, respectively, they were long past their glory years. They had some of their troubles behind them, though, and were still beloved in New York.

I know that a lot has been said and written about George Steinbrenner, and that signing marquee players was one of his famous habits. What sometimes gets lost was that he really believed that people deserved second chances, and sometimes third and fourth ones. To me that generosity had a lot to do with his motivation when he was signing Darryl and Doc. Sure, he liked the headline attention, the gate receipts they might generate (and did), and all the rest that went with the great story, but he also wanted to give these guys another opportunity to do what they did best—hit and pitch.

Mostly because I was in charge of infielders as a coach, I didn't spend much time with Doc. Pitchers exist in their own little bubble, and I wasn't about to intrude on that—except one time. When I was thirty-five and playing with the Dodgers in 1990, I got hit by Dwight Gooden not long after I had a key hit in a Dodger victory. In my first at-bat against Gooden, I lined a single to center, stole second, and went to third on an error. The next time up Doc drilled me. You develop a pretty keen instinct for knowing when somebody wants to hit you and when the ball truly just got away. In this case I had no doubt. Doc struck out fifteen that day and walked one. Wildness was not a problem. I brought the subject up with him when he came over to the Yankees.

"Oh no, I wasn't throwing at you," Dwight said. "That pitch just got away from me." His sheepish look, and his reluctance to look me in the eye, said otherwise.

Doc and I talked and were cordial, but there was also the management-worker divide that exists between coaches and players. We'd joke around and all that, but there's always going to be a bit of distance between a coach and a player. The same was true to a certain extent with Darryl. For some reason, though, he and I had a better relationship than I did with Doc. Darryl came to us late in the '95 season for the stretch run, got released, and played in an independent league, hoping to get another shot. In July '96, he was back with the Yankees. In August of that year, we were all teleported back to 1985. In his first three at-bats, Darryl hit line-drive home runs deep into the right-field bleachers at the Stadium, the kind of "see ya" shots that send a thrill up your spine just watching them.

Being in the third-base coaching box, I had a pretty good view of them, and as Darryl came trotting around the base paths, he seemed to have regressed in age, his expression going from "take that" satisfaction to peace to "I can't really believe this" joy. He was a big part of our ALCS success in '96 against the Orioles, hitting 3 home runs and driving in 5 while hitting .417 in those 4 games. With Doc and David Cone also on the team, the ex-Met factor was pretty high and more than welcome. Darryl had that down year in '97, but came back from cancer to play more than 100 games in '98, for the first time since 1991. His twenty-four home runs were a big contribution to our World Series–winning effort.

Darryl and I still keep in touch. His faith has helped him turn his life around, and his ministering to and testifying before others, as well as his charity work, are a testament to his spirit. He was considered a great postseason clutch hitter, but I think it's his postcareer work that shows how clutch he really is.

Both Doc and Darryl are still loved in New York. I think that's a testament to the city and its fans as well as the two guys. As tough as New Yorkers can sometimes be, they've also got big hearts. I think that even more so than Reggie and Derek and some of the other Yankee greats, Doc and Darryl really embody what New York is all about. Those guys hit the highest of the highs and the lowest of the lows. But

My mother and father worked as sharecroppers in South Carolina. Their work ethic and commitment stuck with me through the years. I never let the major leagues get to my head.

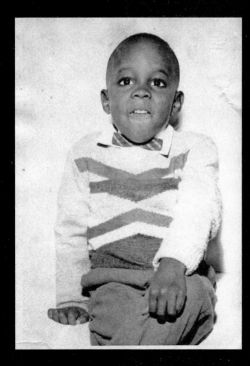

I don't think my parents ever imagined I'd grow up to be an All-Star player. I'm so blessed to make a life and living off the game I love.

I loved the game so much it didn't matter if I was playing in the sandlots of Prospect Park or Yankee Stadium.

My high school coach, Herb Abramowicz, was a father figure to me on and off the field. He helped me manage the scouts my last year and eventually delivered the news that I was drafted to the Pittsburgh Pirates.

I have my trainers, Gene and Steve, to thank for keeping me healthy and on the field all those years.

Reggie Jackson was famous for his swagger and confidence on the field. After

Dock Ellis's unpredictable temper prepared me for the rowdy Bronx Zoo years. I learned that wanting to play was one thing, but complaining about not getting to play is another.

Bobby Murcer was probably Thurman Munson's best friend on the team. In our first game after Thurman's death, Bobby contributed five runs and won us the game. It was a difficult day on the field, but that storybook ending was exactly what the team needed after losing its captain and friend.

John Milton "Mickey" Rivers was always doing something to get the team revved up.

Ron Guidry, Graig Nettles, and Goose Gossage are some of the best players I had the chance to play with, all Yankee legends.

Ron Guidry had the single most impressive season I've seen to this day. In 1978, he was just about unhittable. Ron reminds me of Mo in a lot of ways. They both made throwing those devastating pitches seem effortless.

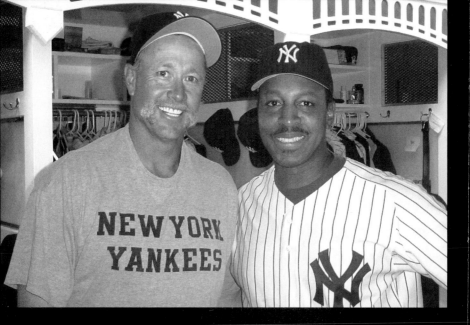

Goose Gossage was as intimidating a presence as you could get on the mound, but he was also one of the nicest guys I ever met.

Mel Stottlemyre was part of the veteran coaching staff that helped the Core Four come into their own under Joe's management.

Don Mattingly (*right*), pictured here with Wade Boggs, was a Yankee through and through. I was always so disappointed that he never won a World Series, but he was a stand-up kind of guy and never once complained about it.

Wade Boggs, David Cone, and David Wells were some of the great players I coached.

When Mariano Rivera retired in 2013, he was universally respected in an exceptional way. He was a once-in-a-lifetime kind of player.

Jorge Posada was never a vocal guy, but he sure was a fiery player. He's in the running for one of the best catchers of his generation.

I can't say enough about Derek Jeter as a player and a man. Besides being one of the best shortstops I've encountered, he also embodies the Yankee Way. He was born with that old-soul coolness that makes him impossible not to admire.

Dwight "Doc" Gooden was one of the most impressive rookie pitchers I've ever seen. He went on in 1984 to be the youngest player ever in an All-Star game. The no-hitter he threw in '96 was the highlight of the season.

This picture was taken right after Aaron Boone won the series by hitting Tim Wakefield's first pitch into the stands for a series-winning homer. He was my pick to click and I sure was right!

From my earliest days with the organization, I was welcomed into the fraternity of Yankees, and Yogi Berra was instrumental in introducing me to greats like Whitey Ford (pictured here), which gave me a strong connection to the team and its history.

Roy White (*left*), pictured here with Rickey Henderson and Hector Lopez, was a hero and mentor of mine. Roy's cool demeanor taught me how to remain calm on and off the field and inspired me to follow in his footsteps and take up martial arts.

Whitey Ford, Phil Rizzuto, and Yogi Berra, three legendary Yankees.

Yogi was a down-to-earth guy and a real pleasure to work with. He had so much respect for the game and exemplified the Yankee Way. As a manager and a player, he meant a lot to the franchise

When Joe took over the team, I was the only holdover from the previous coaching staff, but that didn't stop Joe from trusting me.

Coaching my All-Star infield in 2002 (*left to right*): Jason Giambi, me, Derek Jeter, Robin Ventura, and Alfonso Soriano.

This photo of Bobby Richardson, Alfonso Soriano, and Horace Clarke always reminds me of the legacy of Yankee second basemen.

This was one of my proudest moments. My daughter Ciara graduated from Fordham University and I was honored to deliver the commencement speech.

My son Andre went on to play the game and even spent some time in the Yankees' organization. Recently, he attended Mariano Rivera's retirement ceremony with me.

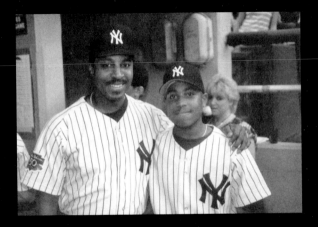

Becoming the Mets' manager was one of my life goals and I was proud to share that moment with my entire family.

the thing is, they came back from those rough periods, just as the city has done time and time again. There's very little that is small about New York, and if you're going to play on the biggest stage, you might as well put on the grandest drama or the most raucous comedy you can. You've got to leave people with an impression, and that's a hard thing to do when there're so many people around and so many distractions. Darryl and Doc managed to rivet the attention of an entire city and provide us with some great memories.

FOR A LOT OF Yankee fans, the '96 season is a rich deposit of memories. What I remember isn't so much the highlights, like Doc Gooden's no-hitter, Andy Pettitte's breakout 21-8 season, or Bernie Williams hitting 29 home runs, driving in more than 100, hitting over .300, and entering into the MVP conversation. No, what I remember most is how fundamentally sound that club was.

When Joe Torre was hired, one of the papers ran the banner headline "Clueless Joe." Well, Joe may not have had great success as a manager prior to coming to the Yankees, but he instilled in the team—the entire staff instilled in that team—the need to do their jobs the right way and take care of the little things. He brought a National League mentality to the Yankees. Sure, we had the designated hitter, and we had to make some moves in the season, and our "small ball" philosophy changed a bit with the acquisition of Darryl Strawberry and Cecil Fielder, who were slower, more station-to-station kinds of guys. But early in the season Joe had us put on a clinic with our two middle infielders, Derek Jeter and Mariano Duncan, who helped lead the way. Given what happened in subsequent years, it's easy to forget what Mariano meant to that '96 team. He was a versatile guy, a veteran, and maybe I'm prone to look at second base as a key position, but you can't deny that the man hit .340 for us in 109 games. I also mention him because he was an important part of that team's nice balance of veterans and young players, and that's always a good thing to have.

We were probably deepest at the pitching position. In addition to Andy's great year, John Wetteland led the league in saves with 43, and Mariano, in a setup role, was outstanding. Rivera gave up only 73 hits in 108 innings, and with a record of 8-3 and a 2.09 ERA, he finished third in the Cy Young balloting that year, while Andy finished second. Anytime you have that kind of deep pitching, you're going to do well. It seemed like all we needed to do was to get to the sixth or seventh inning, turn the game over to those two guys, and we were golden. And it was confidence-inspiring for the starters, who knew they could go as hard as possible from the get-go and then turn things over to that pen.

For a long time, the Yankee organization didn't have many home-grown pitchers succeeding at the big-league level. We brought in a lot of free agents, but with Mariano and Andy, we had something special. Our scouts deserve some of the credit there; Mariano was an undrafted free agent and Andy was selected in the twenty-second round. With lots of veterans in the rotation, it was going to take a lot to become a starter. Andy had the advantage of being a lefthander, and Mo had the disadvantage of having had an arm injury early in his career. The decision to make Mo a reliever wasn't one I was consulted on, of course, but his evolution into a closer was something I saw as inevitable in a way. Mo snuck up on me. He was so quiet and unassuming and that was kind of how his early days with the Yankees progressed. Eventually, when I saw how he was "Mo-ing" down hitters in his setup man role, I kept thinking, *Leave the guy in there.* Eventually, he took over in that capacity, and to his credit, John Wetteland never raised any kind of fuss about it.

The bottom line is that we got contributions from all over the place. David Cone went down with an arm aneurysm that required surgery, and Dwight helped pick up the slack. Kenny Rogers won twelve. Jimmy Key came back from injury and won twelve. Wade Boggs continued his relentless hitting. Tino Martinez, who had the unenviable task of trying to replace fan favorite Don Mattingly, struggled early on, but battled through it and led the team in RBI and finished second in home runs while playing great at first base.

I think the World Series really encapsulated what that ball club was made of.

The Stadium is supercharged with the first World Series game there since 1981. Game 1, our ace is on the mound. He gets the tough Atlanta Braves out 1-2-3. We come back in the dugout and can feel the walls and floor pulsating with excitement. At the end of the day, we get our heads handed to us, 12–1. Okay, bad day at the ballpark. We'll get them the next time. The masterful Greg Maddux shuts us out 4–0. Two games. Sixteen runs surrendered. One scored. Two home games lost. That's a big hill to climb, and it seems even bigger when, in Game 3, we're clinging to a 2–1 lead behind a gutsy performance by David Cone. Derek leads off the eighth with a single, and Bernie follows that with a big home run, driving in his second and third runs of the game. We add another and go on to win 5–2, with Graeme Lloyd stepping in to help out Mariano and get us to Wetteland in the ninth.

Game 4 was also a microcosm of that season. Going into the top of the sixth, we're down 6–0. We've only gotten two hits off Denny Neagle, and though he's walked a few, we've failed to take advantage. Facing the very real possibility that we could be down in the Series 3–1, we battle back. You know, every team will say in that situation, "A lot of ball game left." They'll say it, but a lot of them won't really believe it. This team believes it and produces. Three runs in the sixth to halve the lead. No runs in the seventh. Six outs to get at least three runs. In the eighth, we scratch out a couple of hits, with Charlie Hayes and Darryl Strawberry getting on. Jim Leyritz steps up and yards one. Tie game. Talk about clutch. Here's a guy who's played in only eighty-eight games for us, who's had only eight at-bats in the World Series, but what a contribution.

The tenth inning, to a baseball purist, results in an anticlimactic finish not in keeping with the comeback. With two out, we score two runs with the aid of only one hit, three walks, and a costly error. Still, a win is a win.

The measure of a player and a team is what they do after they've been knocked down. Andy Pettitte was down and out in Game 1. He'd be the first to tell you that he was terrible in Game 1. So what did he do? He bounced back and pitched eight innings of shutout ball in Game 5, and we won 1–0, beating a dominating John Smoltz—who to that point had been 4-0 in the playoffs, mind you—to take a 3–2 lead in the Series.

Let's be real here. How many of you Yankee fans liked our chances going into Game 6? Greg Maddux versus Jimmy Key. Sure, Maddux hadn't had his best year—he was 15-11 in the regular season and 3-1 to that point in the postseason—but he was in his prime. Jimmy was coming back from a '95 season in which he appeared in only three games before being shelved.

In Game 6, he outdueled the perennial Cy Young candidate 3–2.

If I'd been Mickey Rivers and betting on our chances, I can't say that we were a long shot, but I do know that when you looked at the two teams, the Braves' regular-season performance, combined with that rotation of Smoltz, Maddux, and Glavine, would seem to have given them the edge, especially after they got out of the gate up 2–0. But I had some insider's knowledge: I knew firsthand the kind of hearts that beat inside the guys in our clubhouse. I saw how they responded to those losses, how they took it personally and didn't doubt themselves.

It was interesting to see how guys revealed themselves that year. Leyritz was a professional hitter, a thirty-two-year-old veteran of seven seasons with the Yankees. While in some ways his home run was unexpected, you need contributions from guys like him to win it all. You also need some of your young guys to step up when the pressure's on, and that's exactly what a young man out of Kalamazoo, Michigan, did that whole year from start to finish.

It was clear to us that the kid was talented when he first came to spring training in 1996. I didn't even have to see him play to know that. After all, Derek Jeter was a first-round selection, the sixth pick overall, so you knew he had some skills. He certainly had the physical aptitude to play the game. Again, the game had changed by the time Derek arrived on the scene, so a shortstop who was six-three wasn't so unusual at that point. The amazing Cal Ripken Jr. was one of the guys responsible for breaking that old mold of the compact middle infielder. Drafted in '92, Derek moved through the organization pretty quickly. He paid his dues in the Rookie League and A-ball in '92–'93, progressing from A to AA to AAA in '94 before getting a late-season call-up in '95.

He's earned the nickname "Captain Clutch." He seems to rise to the occasion with a regularity typical of the true greats of the game. More than that, Derek has a "cool factor," and he had it from day one. I'm not talking about arrogance, which will earn you disdain from teammates and opponents alike. Derek's cool suggested a kind of knowingness, an "old soul" quality that I remember my mother and father and other relatives talking about to describe young people who seem fully in possession of who they are and what they're meant to be about even at a very early age. Call it maturity or whatever else you want, but Derek Jeter had all that right out of the box, no assembly required.

He was Rookie of the Year in '96, his first full season with us, and the only criticism I could level at him at the time was that he struck out too much—102 times that year, with 48 walks. I can't say that he was an undisciplined hitter, but for a guy hitting in the top third of the order, I'd have liked to see more of an emphasis on contact with two strikes. So, okay, he was a kid, and he also hit .314, so that gives you some idea of how much of a stretch it is to find something he needed to work on. I suppose that I needed to work on accepting the fact that hitters of this vintage didn't think that 100 strikeouts was anything to hang their heads about. For his career, Derek has averaged 109 strikeouts per 162 games, and he's done okay for himself.

The true test of his coolness under pressure came in his first postseason appearances. It's easy to get caught up in the hoopla, and the intensity of those games can make you press, but Derek hit .412 when we beat the Rangers in four games, going 3-for-5 in game 2, which was really a must-win game since we had dropped the opener. Leading off the bottom of the twelfth, with us down 1–2, Derek turned around a Mike Stanton pitch and drove a line drive to center field. Not trying to do too much, he just made really solid contact and got on to set up a heartbreaking loss for the Rangers when Charlie Hayes dropped down a bunt after a Tim Raines walk. Dean Palmer fielded it but threw it away, and I waved Derek around to score.

When most people think about the 1996 ALCS against the Orioles, they remember the home-run-that-wasn't in game 1—a kid named Jeffrey Maier reaching down his glove to snag a ball (and an out) away from Orioles outfielder Tony Tarasco, enabling the Yankees to tie the game. What I remember is Jeter, going 4-for-5 in that game and hitting .417 in the series. I remember him going the other way against a tough pitcher, Armando Benítez, and hitting the ball to the top of the wall when we were in desperate need of some late-inning magic. If an over-exuberant twelve-year-old and some divine intervention helped, well, we weren't going to complain.

Derek cooled off a bit against the stellar Braves pitching staff, hitting .250. Anybody who can hit .250 against the likes of Smoltz, Maddux, Glavine, and Neagle is doing something right. And he continued to do it right in the postseason throughout his career. Can you imagine this? Derek Jeter has competed in 158 postseason games in his career. That's nearly a full regular season. And he's hit .308 overall (.321 in his seven World Series) with 20 homers, 62 RBI, and 18 stolen bases. Yes, that .308 is lower by four points than his career batting average, but I think I'll give him a break on that one.

I was fortunate to be involved in drought-breaking World Series victories, and I believe that what happened in '77–'78 had a greater impact on the city of New York than the one in '96. Part of that had to do with the political and social climate in New York in the late seventies. The city had been on its heels for a while, and that victory really gave people something to rally around. The '96 win felt like it was more a part of a progression. We'd taken baby steps in both '94 and '95, and though Joe was a question mark in many people's minds, he took such firm control of things that it almost felt like a foregone conclusion that we'd get there. Notice I said *almost;* you can't take anything for granted in this game. The city's fortunes by '96 seemed to be in a much better place, and that was the case with the Yankees as well. Anything seemed possible, and I know that I certainly liked that feeling.

CHAPTER 8

Dynasty

The word *dynasty* gets thrown around a lot in discussions of sports teams, and in particular the Yankees. When you have sustained success over a period of years, that's inevitable. When I think of dynasties, I think of the Chicago Bulls and Michael Jordan's run of championships. People sometimes forget what it took for Bulls management to surround that epically talented young man with a "supporting cast" that could help him win. Basketball is a game of matchups and guys having to accept their roles. In baseball, while you have that direct matchup of one-on-one with the hitter versus the pitcher, you really don't have to have guys who are willing to step aside on the field and let someone else score, and this was as true for the Yankees as for any other baseball team. Sure, ballplayers have to do that when it comes to media attention and those kinds of things, but you can't reach the highest levels of anything without a good bit of ego. The Yankee squads Joe directed in the '90s and beyond certainly didn't play like a bunch of Buddhist monks offering up their sacrifices and doing no harm to one another—or the opposition—but that being said, it was also true that the Yankees of this era were about as egoless as a major sports team can be.

And boy, did they love to get after it on the field. As a coach, you don't spend a lot of time in the clubhouse with the players. In fact, you spend very, very little time there, but you hear things eventually, and for nearly every bit of our great run I didn't hear about any real squabbles like I experienced back in the late '70s and early '80s. We had a couple of guys with a fiery temperament and other guys who were real characters, but maybe because I wasn't in the thick of it, I got the sense that, unlike during my playing days, nobody actively disliked, resented, or was jealous of a teammate.

During the run of championships during the '90s, it seemed like a new Yankee way was being developed. A lot of the credit for that goes to Joe. He was the one who came in with such a professional approach, and his quiet leadership really set the tone for the guys. One of Joe's other strengths was his clarity about the guys and their roles. That helped to keep the grumbling to a minimum—as did all the winning. But the front office seemed to have decided that instead of acquiring the biggest names it was important to bring in guys who, instead of being characters, were what is now called "character guys," good solid citizens who weren't going to stir things up. Scott Brosius, Paul O'Neill, Bernie Williams, Mike Mussina, Jason Giambi, and others fit that description. Sure, we still brought in guys who had reputations for being a little hard to deal with and who might not seem to fit in with this new model of Yankee ball clubs, but because they were the exception rather than the rule, they fell in line for the most part.

In Joe's first years, he did have to step in a few times, or he'd talk to one of the Core Four about an issue that he thought needed to be addressed. Eventually, though, because the expectations were made clear, the guys policed themselves. As a manager, that's how you want it to be. It took some time for Derek to grow into his role as captain, but when he did, as a staff, we kept an eye on things, but we knew we didn't have to be hypervigilant. I also can't say enough about how having a veteran coaching staff really helped those teams—Mel Stottlemeyer, Chris Chambliss, Jose Cardinale, and Don Zimmer. Add Joe and me into that mix, but I'm not about to add up the total number of years of professional baseball experience that collective had. There wasn't much that we hadn't seen or experienced in the game, and that helped us all keep an even keel. It took a while for that '96 team to jell, but the process was put in place and it continued throughout my time as a coach under Joe. Tino Martinez was one of the guys whose buttons could be pushed and he'd respond, but that was part of his competitive nature. Later on, Jorge Posada and Orlando "El Duque" Hernández had their famous dustup, but the biggest difference was that guys wanted to keep any conflicts and their thoughts about them in the clubhouse. I know that's frustrating to journalists and fans who want the inside scoop, but handling matters internally was the healthiest way to go about things. Too many "he said, he said" conflicts can just wear on you.

Joe set the tone for that by never making any kind of negative statements about the players in the media. If he had something to say, he'd do so privately. He'd deal with every matter as soon as he became aware of it, and that created as professional an environment as any I'd ever been around. I also think that leading us to a World Series title, in the face of that initial media doubt, cemented his relationship with George Steinbrenner. That '96 title was a kind of "I told you so," for both of them. Even though we lost to Cleveland in the '97 ALDS and didn't repeat, it wasn't like our performance suffered greatly. In fact, in most statistical categories, particularly in pitching, we had a better year. A big reason—in every sense of the word—for that pitching improvement was our acquisition of David Wells in 1997.

I'm not saying anything original here, but David would have fit in well with those Bronx Zoo teams. Any guy who breaks his hand in a street fight before reporting to spring training is going to have some baggage. When he also reports with the kind of flesh baggage that was hanging off Wells and lets the media know that his appetites for food and drink and his battles with gout are all just a part of the package, you've got a guy who clearly was flying—well, trying to fly—in the face of the modern athlete's fitness regimen and discipline. David's appetites endeared him to many fans and some members of the media. It seemed like David was one of those guys who aren't bothered by playing in New York. They walk out onto the biggest stage, welcome the spotlight, and put on one hell of a show.

David pitched well enough in 1997, but the 1998 season was when he came into his role on the team—as did everyone else. We'd been good before then, but '98 made us great.

Oddly enough, for a season as successful as that one, we began poorly, going 1-4 out of the gate. On April 6, we lost to the Mariners, 8–0, and we started to hear some things about no team in history ever going 1-5 to start and then winning the World Series. Things had been calm with the Boss, but that ALDS loss to Cleveland in '97 (which in fact was a huge motivator for everyone on the team) coupled with the slow start in 1998 got the firing speculations going. After the loss to the Mariners, Joe called a team meeting, but he turned it over to the players and let them have their say.

Here's where veteran leadership comes in. We'd struggled against the Mariners since that crushing playoff loss in '95. David pointed out that late in the game, with the Mariners way out in front, Edgar Martínez had swung at a 3-0. As he put it, those guys were trying to have some fun at our expense, and we should take that personally. We won the next day, 13–7, behind David Wells, and then our next seven games after that. We lost one, won six, lost one, won eight, and by May 6 we were 23-6. Good-bye, firing discussions.

That didn't mean that things were smooth sailing the rest of the way. Joe wasn't happy with David Wells, particularly after the May 6 game in Texas. It was a scorcher for early May, with the temperature in the mid-90s. David only lasted two and two-thirds innings, giving up seven runs in that short stint. But Joe was savvy enough to know when to use the media as a motivator. After the game, he publicly questioned David Wells's fitness, and while doing that could have blown up in his face, in the end it didn't. Joe understood a team's needs, and he wanted to light a fire under David. I didn't know this at the time, but I later learned that David had been tempted to go to the press and rip Joe. Instead, David Cone talked him down and suggested that the two of them, Joe and Wells, work it out between themselves in private. That's what happened: their "private" meeting was pretty loud, but things got aired out between them.

It helped that David Wells went on to pitch a perfect game on May 17. I'm not going to suggest a direct cause-and-effect relationship between that meeting and the results of Wells's start on the 17th, but I do know that, as a team, we handled the situation and the guys were absolutely relentless all the way through the season.

We were a deep club, and that helped, but the success of the '98 team was also so much about the determination those guys exhibited all season. You could see and feel that they were focused. With that air about them, a confidence that bordered on arrogance, they just went out there and won and won and won. In lots of ways, that team was the most Yankee-like of any I'd been associated with. I've been around the game a long time, and seeing that '98 team win 114 games during the regular season ranks right up there with some of my fondest memories in the game. Every now and then we'd sit back and shake our heads. The thing is, you can never take winning for granted. That's true of World Series games as well as any individual game.

As with any season, there were bumps along the way, and one of the most memorable that year was with Chuck Knoblauch at second base. Getting comfortable in a new environment, particularly New York, is important.

Chuck Knoblauch was a Gold Glove second baseman in 1997 with the Twins. He came to the Yankees the following year, and that's when things started to go wrong. "Knobby," as we called him, started having problems making the simple throws from second base to first. Routine stuff. Throws he'd done hundreds and hundreds of times in games and thousands and thousands of times in practice. My heart went out to him.

I was so excited when we first acquired him because I saw some similarities between his game and mine. He had a bunch of good years with the Twins and was a great table-setting hitter at the top of the order. We had some pop in the middle of the lineup, and when we had guys who could get on base in front of them, we could just keep that line moving and keep that lineup turning over. And that's what we did. But then Knobby got a case of what golfers call "the yips." I'd never had them, had only really heard about Steve Blass, and so that was a fresh challenge for me. How much of it was the pressure of being a Yankee and having the big contract in the big city, I can't really say. I do know that it wasn't something physically wrong with Knobby. His arm wasn't injured, but something was going on psychologically that led him to commit thirteen errors in '98 and then doubling that total in '99.

Chuck was a good kid, a tough Texan who played at Texas A&M, and a proven major league ballplayer by the time we got him. He'd won the Rookie of the Year Award, was selected as an All-Star, got that Gold Glove and Silver Slugger Awards, and was a very conscientious guy. Truth be told, though, what happened with Knobby wasn't just an overnight thing. When we played Minnesota, I could see some hesitation on his part, some stuttering kind of movements, particularly on double-play balls when he had to make the turn. Nothing too serious, but he wasn't what I'd call "fluid." "Leaky and sputter" might be more like it.

As a player and early on as a coach, I felt more comfortable trying to help guys out with the on-field stuff. As I got more accustomed to my role as a coach and later as a manager, I realized that guys wanted you to work with the whole person, not just the second baseman, and so I began to take a more holistic approach. One of the more difficult things I had to do as a coach was work with someone who unexpectedly developed a problem that has famously tripped up a few guys. In working with Chuck Knoblauch and dealing with his throwing issues, I realized that I'd seen something similar happen earlier in my career, during my short stint with the Pirates.

Steve Blass has the unfortunate distinction of being better known for a syndrome than his on-field performance. I'm sure that other guys before him had to deal with similar issues, but Steve is the Pirates pitcher from the mid-'70s whose name is paired with the concept of "losing it." He was a successful pitcher for a number of years with the Pirates, but suddenly, in 1973, he just lost the ability to throw strikes. After going 19-8 with a 2.59 ERA in '72, he went 3-9 with a 9.85 ERA a year later, issuing 84 walks in 109 innings. The year before he had also walked 84—but in 279 innings. So his walks-per-nine-innings ratio went from 3.5 to 8.5. Astounding. The next year he was out of baseball completely, and he still wonders what went wrong mentally that caused him to so suddenly stop being able to do what he'd done so naturally and so easily since he was a kid. He tried everything from traditional psychotherapy to transcendental meditation, but nothing could help him get back in the groove.

I do think that Chuck's issue was compounded by being in New York. He wanted to do well, and he put more pressure on himself to succeed. With a guy like that who's struggling with a mental issue rather than a physical one, I could beat all the ground balls in the world at him, callousing up my hands till they were as hard as a fungo bat, but that wasn't going to cure what ailed him. The thing was, though, we couldn't go to him and say, "Hey, it's nothing physical or mechanical with your throws. It's something upstairs." You could do that with a guy and his hitting, tell him to relax, maybe give him a day off, work with him in the cage extra to get his confidence back. That approach wouldn't really work with what was going on with Chuck.

Still, that's where you had to start. Deal with the mechanics. Talk with him about arm angle and release point, things you seldom did with position players. To focus on the mental aspect of it from the get-go would have just messed him up even more.

It's like Yogi Berra said: "Ninety percent of this game is mental. The other half is physical."

The way I looked at it was that throwing a baseball is about as unconscious an act as you have in the game. You've been doing it for so long that injecting thoughts into the nearly unconscious process is going to foul up the works. By the time you're a big-league infielder, even getting a good grip on the ball, making sure you're throwing across the seams if you can, is second nature. The temptation is always to come up with a fix, that's why you're a coach, but there's a "throw-22" involved in this: if you try to address it by focusing on it, you're injecting more thoughts, and negative ones, into a place where there might already be too many thoughts jacking things up. But if you don't acknowledge the problem and don't try to solve it, maybe relying on nature instead to work its magic, you've got a lot of fans in the stands in jeopardy. Just ask Keith Olbermann's mom, who got clocked with a Knobby Special that sailed well over Tino Martinez's head and busted her glasses.

That didn't do much for her confidence in him (as Keith Olbermann pointed out in a classic quote), and it did nothing at all for his confidence in himself. As hard as it is to hear all the clichés coming at you in a situation like this ("Hang in there," "Just relax and let it go," "Keep it free and easy"), a far worse blow to the ego is silence. So that was a delicate balancing act we had to accomplish.

Guys have a kind of gallows humor. If a pitcher gets a line drive whistled past his head, you're just as likely to hear somebody on the bench say, "He should ask for the protective screen," as you are to hear, "Thank God that didn't make contact with him." Sometimes your teammates' rips on you can take the sting out of a wound. I don't remember who said it, but once when a pitcher was getting roughed up pretty good, walking a couple of guys and then surrendering back-to-back doubles, I heard a guy on the bench mutter, "He's got two pitches. Balls and doubles. And they're both working tonight." Later, when the pitcher came out of the game looking like he could just take a bite out of the bench, one of the starting pitchers on the bench walked up to him, put his arm around his shoulder, and asked, "How do you grip those doubles?"

That kind of teasing goes on all the time and is a form of acceptance as well as a fine art. Sometimes guys go too far, though or some guys are too sensitive. A former Yankee, whose identity I will protect, was verbally worked over so mercilessly back in the mid-'80s that he was reduced to tears. And don't think that we didn't give him crap about that too.

Teammate jabs, though, were often easy compared to the New York media. Randy Johnson's run-ins with the New York press were well documented, but media types weren't the only targets of his surly demeanor and look—it was an advantage for him as a pitcher too. Anyone who is six-ten and throws as hard as he did, and with as nasty a slider as he possessed, wouldn't seem to need that kind of additional advantage, but that was Randy.

Though the media scrutiny was different when I was a player, you always had to deal with it, and guys struggled back then too. Ed Whitson isn't a name that casual fans of the game or the Yankees will recall when discussing the days of glory. In so many ways, Whitson was the poster boy for all the things that were wrong with how the Yankees operated in the 1980s. The Yankees signed him as a free agent after he had the best year of his career for the Padres, winning fourteen games. Once again, no attention seemed to be paid to how he would fit in in New York, and how suited he was to handling the heat. I actually was optimistic at first. Whitson was twenty-nine, in his prime, and seemed like a badass sort of guy, a tough hombre who would go out and battle you and throw at you, and he seemed as if he really wanted to be here. At his first press conference, he said, "I hope I can contribute to another World Championship here. The Yankees have a great tradition. Like someone told me, when a ballplayer walks down the street, people say, 'There goes a major league ballplayer.' When a Yankee walks down the street, they say, 'There goes a Yankee.' That's the difference."

When I heard that, I thought, *Wow, this guy gets it.* Then the games began, and I saw Eddie Lee Whitson get as rough a going-over from the fans, and get more stressed out because of it, than any player I ever saw.

Whitson began the year by straining his back when he was pulling on his stirrups before his first start, and it just spiraled down from there. He went 1-6 in his first eleven starts, with a 6.23 ERA. The fans started getting on him, and when they saw that Whitson, an emotional, high-strung guy, was affected by it, they got on him even worse. Whitson got himself straightened out, threw a couple of shutouts, and put together a fine stretch of pitching for a month or two, but by then Billy Martin had long since made up his mind: Whitson was so far in the doghouse that he wasn't ever going to get out. That's how Billy was. If you were one of his guys, he'd do anything for you. If you weren't, he'd bury you.

Billy hated players who showed any fear or fragility. He and Whitson weren't going to be a good fit anyway, but once Billy saw what he
perceived as weakness, that was it. We trailed the Toronto Blue Jays by
two and a half games in September when Whitson blew a big game,
giving up four runs in two innings against the Jays. Not long after
that, we went to Baltimore for a three-game series. Martin told Whitson he wouldn't pitch. They got into a fight at a hotel bar. Luckily, the
two got separated and pushed into different elevators. But Billy was
waiting for Eddie at the end of the elevator trip, and they fought some
more. Billy broke an ulna in his right arm. Whitson suffered a cracked
rib and split lip. His year was over.

By the time the next year came around, the manager had changed—
Lou Piniella replaced Billy—but not much else was different. Whitson
was a wreck. It was so sad. It really was. Before games he was pitching,
he'd be all jittery and jumpy, his nerves overwhelming him. I remember
visiting the mound one time, hoping to get him to relax after he put a
couple of guys on base and the fans were starting up.

"C'mon, bro, we'll get out of this," I said. "You got good stuff. Just
trust it. Calm down, we'll get a couple of outs, and we'll go get you some."

I looked in Eddie's eyes. They were wide with fear, and darting
all over the place. I could feel the anxiety just pouring out of the
mound. I could see him overthrowing on every pitch, trying to throw
150-mile-per-hour fastballs and perfect curveballs. Nobody can pitch
that way. Nobody.

The fans had him so terrified that he mapped his routine around
avoiding them. He'd wear his warm-up jacket in batting practice, hoping nobody would recognize him. When it was time to go to the bullpen, he would walk under the stands so nobody could boo him. He'd
leave the Stadium through the bleachers and walk the long way around
to the players' parking lot—again, so he wouldn't be hounded by the
gauntlet of fans who waited outside the players' gate.

His precautions didn't eliminate the problem, unfortunately. A
fan followed him home to New Jersey one night, he said. Another

time somebody left nails in his driveway. Death threats supposedly were made, and people were harassing his wife and kids. Even before Lou decided not to start Whitson at the Stadium anymore, Eddie had moved his family back to Ohio, where they would be safe.

"I didn't guarantee them that I'd be another Sandy Koufax or Whitey Ford," Whitson told a reporter after another poor outing. "All I can do is hope for the best and give them my best."

It's a helpless feeling when a teammate is going through something like this. You want to try to take it away, insulate him somehow, but there's really nothing you can do except let him know that you are there in good times and bad, and that you believe in him.

The melodrama lasted until July 9, 1986, a Wednesday. We were in Arlington, Texas, to play the Rangers. It was one of the best days of Eddie Lee Whitson's life, not because we beat the Rangers, 5–4, but because he found out he'd been traded back to San Diego. We picked up Tim Stoddard in return, and the truth is, we would've been lucky to get a basket of used resin bags for Whitson, because he wasn't pitching well and the whole world knew he wanted out.

Whitson left the Bronx with an overall record of 15-10, a 5.38 ERA, and no desire to see the George Washington Bridge ever again. In the four seasons that followed, from 1987 to 1990, he won 53 games with the Padres and was a frontline starter. It just goes to show you how important confidence is, and how important it is that your manager and teammates believe in you. That's especially true in New York. Whether you've played for the Mets or the Yankees or you're one of the Fabulous 117—guys who played for both teams—you've had some unique experiences.

ASIDE FROM KNOBLAUCH'S STRUGGLES, there wasn't much— not even the bright lights of the Big Apple—that could phase that '98 team. We cruised through the playoffs and won the World Series hand- ily. After the regular season we'd had, the whole thing went just the way we'd hoped it would. No one took a thing for granted, but still, that was when it started to seem like the big D-word just might have a place in our team's vocabulary.

If '98 introduced that word, '99 defined it for us. Perhaps the biggest change between seasons had been the addition of Roger Clemens, who came over from the Blue Jays in a trade for David Wells before the season began. Before becoming a Yankee, he was about as popular in our locker room as a urine test. We couldn't stand the guy, and we had our reasons.

He hit Jeter in spring training one time when Derek was just getting started, and there was no doubt in my mind about why. Clemens wanted to get into Derek's head right away, knowing that he was going to be a star player for a long time. Clemens did the same thing to another promising young Yankee, Bernie Williams. It was a night game in Boston in mid-August of 1993. We scored four times in the top of the first. The big hit was a two-run single that Bernie ripped to center off Clemens. Roger was getting outpitched by soft-tossing Jimmy Key and wasn't too pleased about that. Bernie's next time up Clemens beaned him. That's the way the man did business. He burned as hot as anybody I've seen on a mound. I got to see that up close once and was happy to help him burn even hotter . . . so hot that he got tossed out of a playoff game.

It was game 4 of the 1990 ALCS between the A's and the Red Sox, in the Oakland Coliseum. I was playing second and batting eighth for the A's, right behind Mark McGwire. Roger had already gotten outdueled in game 1 by Dave Stewart, and the Sox were down three games to none. We had two guys on and a run in in the top of the second when I came up. There were two outs. Roger had gone to a full count and to 2-2 on the previous two hitters, and he looked agitated, without his usual command, so I was going to be plenty patient. After Clemens threw ball one, he barked at plate umpire Terry Cooney.

"Do you hear that? You hear what he just said?" I said to Cooney, quite innocently.

Clemens threw another ball, to fall behind 2-1, and chirped again, hollering, if I recall correctly, "Where the ——— was that?"

"You can't take that. He's showing you up," I said to Cooney, just trying to be helpful.

After pretty much every pitch Clemens was bitching and moaning, and after every pitch I pointed out to Cooney that he was being shown up and that no self-respecting umpire should allow that to happen.

On 3-1, Clemens wound and fired again, a fastball. It could've had some of the plate, but I thought it was outside. I wasn't sure, so I let it go. Cooney called ball four. I went to first. Clemens went ballistic. Really let Cooney have it. Clemens said he spoke a single profanity, but in our dugout Stewart, who said he heard the whole thing, reported that Clemens told Cooney, "You get your big fat [bleeping] ass back behind the plate and call the [bleeping] balls and strikes." Cooney asked him what he said, and Clemens repeated it.

Cooney ran him, Clemens's day was done after an inning and two-thirds and thirty-eight pitches, and then all hell broke loose—fifteen minutes of arguments and tantrums and Gatorade-bucket throwing. I stood on first base and watched the mayhem unfold, quietly pleased that I had contributed to the A's cause with my innocent and helpful comments.

I'm sure Roger never knew what I said and probably wouldn't have cared anyway. There was no reason to bring it up when he showed up at Legends Field for the first time. He had much larger issues to deal with, such as becoming a Yankee. The first time he got on the mound, Jeter and Chuck Knoblauch tried to lighten things up and help the adjustment process along by going up to bat wearing a full set of catcher's gear. Everybody got a big laugh out of it, even Clemens, who, quite honestly, is not a big laugher. Hijinks or not, make no mistake: Clemens was not one of us yet. Not by a long shot. How could he be, with that sort of history?

I mean, just a few months before, Clemens, as a Blue Jay, had drilled Scott Brosius in the back. Torre was fuming—we all were. A half-inning later, Hideki Irabu got some payback by hitting Shannon Stewart, and the brawl was on. There were guys all over the field, and I can still see Chad Curtis, our outfielder, running over to the railing of the Blue Jay dugout, calling Clemens out. Clemens is a big, strong Texan, but when that brawl started he was up that runway faster than you can spell "Rocket Man." (I'm not saying he was afraid; I don't know that. But I do know this: he seemed to want no part of Chad.)

"It was so blatant that Clemens threw at Brosius," Joe Torre said afterward. "[He] gets away with things that get other people thrown out of games. As long as they let him get away with it, it's going to continue."

When Roger came over to the Yankees, Joe revised his opinion of the man, but we couldn't just magically forget all those years of him dusting guys, trying to intimidate us, any more than Roger was going to propose a group hug. It's hard to say how a player, who has been your opponent for so long and then comes to your team, actually becomes a part of the team. Some guys mesh right away. Others take years to fit in. Joining a team—especially a close-knit group like those Yankee teams of the late '90s—is an art, not a science. And when there's history between the guys, it becomes even more complicated. Roger made an earnest effort to try to connect with us. When we played in Texas, he had us over to his house for a barbecue and to meet his family. I'd say it took a full four or five months before the team really warmed up to him. I can't tell you what the turning point was when he became one of us, but in time he did.

Though it took us all some time to warm up to the concept, Clemens, as he always does, worked hard and became a crucial part of that team. Never afraid to throw choice words along with his fastball, Clemens remained a character, but the things that made him hard to play against were now working in our favor. He was one of the toughest competitors out there, and having a guy like that on your staff can be a big boost to the club. And he was a great teammate because you knew that he had your back. As a hitter, you want to have a pitcher who isn't afraid to throw inside. If one of their pitchers buzzed you or hit you,

you could at least take some comfort in knowing that Roger was going to even the score, and sometimes go ahead.

Over the course of the season he grew into a teammate and an important addition to the rotation. He proved to be effective in a lineup whose history seemed to grow with each passing year, and by the time we swept the Braves in the '99 World Series, it had become official: Roger Clemens was a Yankee.

CHAPTER 9

New York, New York

When you have a run of success like I did and the Yankees did in the late '90s, you'd think I'd have fond memories of the victories, the series clinchers, and all of that. But the truth is, and maybe this is my competitive nature, losing hurts a lot worse than winning feels good. Losing also produces a sensation that lasts a lot longer than the satisfaction that comes from winning. Maybe that will change over time, after I've been away from the game for a decade or two, but I bet if you asked any of the guys they'd tell you the same thing. I don't think any of us ever woke up in the middle of the night after flashing back on a win, but we sure did have some nights of sleep interrupted by those losses and all the what-ifs that come with them.

I'd also be willing to bet that Yankee fans have that same experience. That's human nature, I guess, but after winning eight straight World Series games in 1998 and 1999 to beat the Padres and the Braves, we faced a potentially nightmarish situation in 2000 when we squared off against the Mets in the World Series.

You can't play ball in New York without experiencing the tension between the two clubs there, and over the course of my career as a player, coach, and manager, I was lucky enough to experience that in many different ways. As a baseball player in a city with two teams, and as a kid who grew up admiring one of them, I was very aware that the Mets were the redheaded stepchild compared to the much-favored

Yankees. That was understandable: the Yankees had been around for a heck of a lot longer than the Mets, and they had won a lot more championships.

As a player, regardless of which team you played for, some of the effects were the same—media scrutiny, fan intensity, and access to all that New York City has to offer. I can't say that as a Yankee I felt like I was competing with the Mets players for attention, endorsement opportunities, or anything like that. Call it part of what some think of as the Yankees' arrogance, or just simply the fact that we played in different leagues and I played at a time when there was no interleague play, but in a lot of people's minds the Mets were a kind of distant moon orbiting around the Yankee planet.

Personally, I've never agreed with that. Despite the intense interest the Yankees generate, New York is a National League town historically, and there has been interest in the so-called Senior Circuit since before the Yankees existed. The New York Giants and the Brooklyn Dodgers were both NL teams. I don't know if it's the history, the fact that there's no designated hitter in the NL, or what, but the Mets buzz is different than the Yankees. When they are winning, as they were in 2000, it's not like when the Yankees are winning. Maybe Yankee fans are so accustomed to success that they don't get as hyped up about the regular season as the Mets fans do. Maybe the Mets' success, being a rarer commodity, is more valuable.

For whatever reason, every now and then the Mets moon would eclipse the Yankees planet in terms of attention and focus. Good examples are 1969 and 1986. The Mets won the World Series both those years, and in '86 the Mets also outdrew the Yankees by about 500,000 fans. That came in the middle of a streak of years from about 1984 to 1990 when the Mets outperformed the Yankees on the field and in attendance. The fact that the two teams combined for more than 5 million in attendance is a testament to how large the city is, but even more to how fanatical the fans are. And all of those fans were ready for the entire World Series, not just one half of it, to be played in their hometown.

I can't tell you how many anxious nights I spent during that span of six days. On paper, we came into the playoffs that year arguably the weakest of the four American League qualifiers. The White Sox, the Mariners, and the A's all won between four and eight games more than us. Our eighty-seven wins that year were the lowest number during Joe's tenure with the club, when the team averaged ninety-eight wins per season. We lost fifteen out of eighteen to close the season and saw our division lead dwindle from nine games to two and a half. Not exactly how you want to go into the playoffs, but those guys produced when it mattered.

The truth, though, is that as a staff we weren't nearly as concerned as a lot of Yankee fans were about that poor finish to the season. We sat in a meeting and agreed that the late-season slide was probably going to turn out to be a blessing in disguise. It was like the "scared straight" programs some young people get exposed to. Youth offenders are taken to a prison, where inmates talk to them and give them a not very subtle message: if you don't shape up, this could happen to you. I think that's what happened in 2000. The guys saw how hard it was to win consistently, and that slump was both a wake-up call and a humbling reminder of just how easily it could all slip away. I never got a sense that the guys were cocky, but like a lot of athletes, they were letting their vision get too far out in front of them. The season was long, they knew they were good, they knew that it was what they did in the postseason that mattered, and they wanted to accelerate the pace a bit. *Let's just get this over with,* they were thinking, *and get on to the important thing—the playoffs.* Well, once you start to lose focus on the here-and-now, you lose a few games. Then you start to want to make up for that small slide. Some guys try to do too much. The next thing you know you've lost fifteen out of eighteen. Fortunately, the guys pulled it together.

As was his practice, Joe didn't hold any team meetings to rally the troops before the playoffs started. At least not in the usual sense. Joe's get-togethers were almost always positive reinforcement sessions, reminders of how good the guys had been and simple statements like,

"Let's get back to being who we are." One of the things that always amused me and the rest of the guys was Joe's habit of wrapping up meetings by calling on one of the less vocal guys to add his input. He'd frequently ask Jorge Posada, a fiery but not particularly vocal guy, "Hey, Jorgie. You have any words of wisdom you want to add?"

Jorgie would frown and then stand up, his brow furrowed, and then mutter, "Yeah. I've got some words of wisdom. Let's go out there and f——ing win a game!"

Everyone would bust up laughing, and even more so when Joe would ask Hideki Matsui to do the same. Hideki's "words of wisdom" were similar to Jorge's and got even more laughs. That was the effect Joe was going for. Keep it loose. Don't make the guys think they need to do too much to win.

Having a World Series played exclusively in one city, and particularly in New York City, intensified the fever pitch. The Mets, like us, hadn't exactly set the league on fire in September, going 14-14 after a sizzling 20-9 August. Like a lot of wild-card teams, they got hot at the right moment in the playoffs. They were a solid club anchored by Mike Piazza, who had a monster year, hitting .324 with 38 home runs while driving in 113. Somehow, Jeff Kent and Barry Bonds finished ahead of him in the MVP voting, but the Mets got the best of the Giants in a 3–1 NLDS win.

The Mets' pitching staff was deep and somewhat overlooked. Mike Hampton and Al Leiter won thirty-one games between them, and Armando Benítez, as big and intimidating a closer as there was in the game, saved forty-one. Overall, their staff finished third in the league in ERA. Our staff allowed a half-run per game more, and with David Cone struggling to a 4-14 regular season, Orlando Hernández only going 12-13, and Roger Clemens finishing with an un-Clemens-like 13-8 record, we weren't exactly dominating folks. Fortunately, none of that mattered with the slate being wiped clean in the postseason. Some guys can rise to the occasion and make up for a down year, and others just let the trend continue or suffer a downfall. No matter which, what you do in the playoffs is magnified.

The same was true of the fans' intensity. It was every New York fan's dream to have a Subway Series like this one. It was somewhat harder on the players, because the normal routine was upset. Usually, when you're on the road, you have a different routine than you do at home. When you're playing both home and away games in the same city, your routines get out of whack. Some guys chose to dress at the Stadium and then ride the bus in uniform to Shea. Others used the locker room at Shea. That might not sound like a big deal, but it was kind of weird to be riding the bus from the Bronx and crossing the Triborough Bridge into Queens, with some of the guys reenacting their high school or minor league days.

I can say this. I never felt as much pressure to succeed as I did in that Series. I've told people that I would have given up two of my championship rings in order to beat the Mets. As a hometown guy, it would have been tough, maybe even impossible, to show my face anywhere in the city if we had lost that Series. If you know anything about African American culture, then you know that beauty shops and barbershops are the hub of gossip and much else besides cuts, braids, and manicures. I knew that if the Mets bested us, I'd need to wear a suit of armor when I went to get my hair cut at my uncle George's place in Brooklyn. The verbal barbs would be sharp and the aim deadly.

Thankfully, a few years later, when I found myself being introduced as the manager of the Mets, this Series was the furthest thing from my mind. To this day, one of my most deeply felt moments of pride came when I was first announced as the manager of the Mets. I always thought it was important to carry on the legacy of the people who came before me. That's why I am a Negro League historian. My office in Shea Stadium was covered with photos of great black ballplayers—guys like Josh Gibson and Cool Papa Bell. Before Double Duty Radcliffe, the pitcher-catcher and longtime battery mate of Satchel Paige, died at 103 years old a few years back, he told me how proud he was of me.

"What are you talking about, Duty? I'm proud of *you*," I replied. "You are the guy who went through the hard stuff. You are the one who helped keep the Negro Leagues going, who made it possible for all of us." George Steinbrenner and Yogi Berra left me very nice messages after I got the Mets job, but the message that meant the most came from a Hall of Famer and another Negro League legend. I kept saving it on my phone every twenty-one days, right up until the time I got fired and had to give the phone back to the Mets. Every time I heard it, it just filled me up with a good feeling.

"Hi, Skipper, this is Buck O'Neil," the message began. "Willie Randolph—the first African American manager in New York City. I hope we get to talk to you soon, but we just want to let you know how proud we are of you."

Every day of my three and a half years with the Mets, I thought of people like Buck O'Neil and Double Duty Radcliffe and tried to carry myself in a way that would make my baseball ancestors proud. I wanted them to know that I never would've had the baseball life I've had without them. I wanted them to know the connection I felt to them, and how honored I felt to be following in their cleat steps, because the stark truth is that if I'd been born a few decades earlier, it would've been me playing in the Negro Leagues, sleeping in colored-only hotels. It would've been me making next to nothing.

It would have meant a very different life for me, and a very different future for my children.

It still seems strange to me that it took until 2004 for the nation's biggest city, a city where baseball segregation ended sixty years ago, to have a manager of color. And I guess it's a little ironic that my tenure with the Mets ended the same year the ultimate barrier breaking occurred: the election of Barack Obama as president of the United States.

I never thought I would see a black man in the White House in my lifetime. Even when I watched the returns come in on election night, part of me just couldn't believe this was happening. I kept waiting for something to get screwed up. My skepticism turned out to be unfounded, and watching President Obama's inauguration was one of the most remarkable experiences of my life. Gretchen and I were riveted to the TV. When we saw the Obamas walk down Pennsylvania Avenue, my eyes welled up. I had goose bumps on my arms most of the day. Of course, one election doesn't make racial prejudice disappear, and it can't erase history. But how could you not have been moved by the power and symbolism of that moment? How could it not have filled you with great hope?

And how could I look at Barack and Michelle Obama, the president and first lady of the United States of America, and not think, *My mom was right. Anything is possible if you dream big and work hard.*

After I became the Mets manager, I couldn't think of a better way to give back to the game and the city that had meant so much to me than to manage the Mets. If you didn't grow up in New York City, it's pretty easy to imagine that kids from all over go to Central Park to hang out and later skate at Wollman Rink or go to Times Square to be dazzled by the lights. Truth is, back in the day a lot of us would have never left our neighborhood, let alone our borough, if it weren't for sports. Neighborhood affiliations were everything, and so was access to cash. My dad worked hard, but the island of Manhattan might as well have been an island in the South Pacific as far as we were concerned. If there was a parade down Central Park West to Thirty-Fourth Street and Macy's, I didn't know much at all about it, let alone see it. The only inflated bags of gas we saw were the wind-whipped paper and plastic bags that found their final resting place in the trees and street gutters. I didn't know what I was missing, so I didn't mind.

I received a different kind of education and cultural exposure, one that served me very well as a player, coach, and manager. Baseball was very good to me from early on, and it showed me that there was another way to live. In July 1965, a unique opportunity came my way. I had just turned twelve years old when I was selected to be a part of an all-star squad that was going to travel to Puerto Rico for a series of games against local teams. I can't tell you how thrilled I was. I loved Latin food—Dominican, Puerto Rican, Mexican, or from wherever. I was raised on a lot of rice and beans and food like that since my people were from South Carolina. I never met a Dominican *empanadita* that I didn't like, and Puerto Rican *aroz con dulce* satisfied my sweet tooth.

It was more than the food that appealed to me. I played some drums back in the day in the old neighborhood. On a hot evening in the summer, when everybody was out hanging out, we'd bring out the *congueros,* the bongos. That's how I got exposed to salsa music and other Latin music like *merengue.* It was so cool on a nice night to have a group of people out in the park playing those various drums (sometimes nothing more than an overturned plastic bucket) with whoever wanted joining in while other folks were dancing away.

I had Fourteen Brothers to thank for the opportunity and the exposure to the cuisine and the culture. Fourteen Brothers was a restaurant that sponsored the trip and a local youth baseball team that I played for. When you first set foot in the place, you were greeted by an enormous glass-and-wood display case, with all the trophies the teams had won going all the way back to the '50s.

With the exception of car trips to South Carolina to visit family, I'd never been anywhere but the city of New York. That trip was the first time I packed a suitcase, a cracked leather thing that had to be older than my grandmother and grandfather. It reminded me of a well-worn baseball glove. We flew out of JFK airport, and seeing those TWA jets, with their red letters leaning forward like a runner taking a one-way lead off of first base, set my heart pounding with excitement. Later on, of course, air travel became a routine, if not boring, part of my life, but taking off and watching the world grow small beneath me for the first time was unforgettable.

We arrived in San Juan and were met by a small contingent of local men who loaded us into a couple of station wagons and brought us to the various host families with whom we were going to stay. We were the guests at a big party, and for the first time in my life I saw an entire pig being roasted. I was a bit bug-eyed about that, seeing the head and all, but the pig seemed to have this big grin on its face, and I imitated that expression when I bit into that juicy flesh flavored with things that tantalized my tongue.

We played a game a day, traveling from San Juan to Ponce and then to Caguas and Mayagüez. For a kid from the inner city, this was like being in a jungle paradise, seeing all the palm trees and other low-slung trees that were bursting with red and sometimes purple flowers. The place didn't smell like dust and car exhaust either—the fresh ocean breezes and the sunlight seemed to perfume the air. Mostly, though, I remember the ball fields. Even the dirt—a rich, earthy, reddish powder that stood out against the deep, deep green of the grass—seemed tropical.

I've long since forgotten how we did in those games, but I've never forgotten how it felt to be immersed in that culture. I lived in a concrete-and-brick monstrosity my entire childhood and adolescence, so sleeping in a house with windows that pivoted up and away from the walls, bringing the outside inside, was a revelation.

I was also introduced to the *mosquitero,* the tentlike netting draped from a frame over and around the beds. I wasn't sure of the proper use of the device, so the first night I lay in bed and saw the mosquitoes gathering on the fabric, and I did what I always did when I saw a mosquito. I slapped it between my hands to kill it. The sounds of my hands coming together must have alerted the host mother. She came into the room, saw her *mosquitero* freckled with bug guts and blood, and waggled her finger at me. I think I heard a couple of curse words, but mostly I heard and understood the word *no.*

There's no doubt that the rise of Latin ballplayers in major league baseball has been an ongoing trend. Maybe it's not the most politically correct thing to say, but many Latin players do play the game with a different flair than non-Latins. Some of that may come from the fact that they have to compete for attention, and some of it is simply cultural. When you compare the food and music that are native to those regions with what we have traditionally in the United States, there's just something more vibrant about Latin culture. I know this is a broad generalization, but I also know that there's some truth behind it.

If you try to treat everybody alike and don't acknowledge their individual or cultural differences, you're not going to be very effective as a leader. Yasiel Puig, a Cuban who played for the Dodgers in the 2013 NLCS, got into some hot water for showing up the umpires when he disagreed with ball and strike calls. I don't agree with doing that, but I also understand this. He's a young and inexperienced kid. He didn't go through a traditional apprenticeship program in the minor leagues in the United States. He's also an electrifying talent and personality. What some might call his antics in celebrating his on-field achievements don't always fit into the mold of a classic major league player. But he'll learn over time where the boundaries are.

NATIONAL LEAGUE TOWN OR not, when the Subway Series began, we felt good about where we were as a team. You never know who's going to step up in any particular game—the extra-inning thriller that was Game 1 ended with our second baseman, José Vizcaíno, getting four hits in six at-bats. It was a great pitchers' duel, with neither team scoring through the first five. We threw a runner out at the plate to end the top of the sixth and then scored two of our own against Leiter. Unfortunately, the Mets battled back with three in the top of the seventh. We went into the ninth trailing by a run, and that eight-game World Series winning streak was in serious jeopardy with Benítez on to start the ninth.

We were known as a team that was patient at the plate and worked deep into counts. Paul O'Neill worked to a 3-2 count before walking. Luis Polonia and Vizcaíno both singled, and we had to hold Polonia at third on a sharply hit ball to left. As tempting as it is to make an outfielder deliver a good throw in that situation, we still only had one out. Knoblauch delivered, and the Stadium erupted in delight and anticipation. Derek strode to the plate, but this turned out to be one of the rare occasions when he couldn't deliver.

I really thought we were going to win it in the tenth, and should have, but after two walks to start the inning and then a wild pitch to advance the runners to second and third with no outs, Glendon Rusch came in and shut us down on a pop-up, an intentional walk to load the bases, and then a double play. Bobby Valentine's moves paid off in a big way for him. Turk Wendell nearly worked his way out of another bases-loaded situation in the twelfth, but Mr. Vizcaíno capped off a terrific night with a walk-off single to send us all home for a peaceful night's sleep.

The next night, Game 2, was one that went down in the books, but not for the reasons that any of us wanted.

We had Clemens on the mound, and he was his fiery, competitive self, but that night he did cross the line. I know that guys get amped up during crucial games, and especially in the postseason, but I could see from the dugout that Roger was surprised to have to field the shattered barrel of the bat after Piazza fouled off. Throwing it in the direction of Piazza was a rash reaction. Claiming that he thought it was the ball was probably an even weaker response.

So much else has been written and said about the incident—that Roger cried between innings, that Mike took martial arts classes in case he fought Clemens in the future, that Clemens hit Mike in the head because he couldn't get him out consistently and needed the psychological edge, and all the rest—that it has become the stuff of legend. Clemens was fined, as he should have been, but he wasn't tossed from the game, a decision I also agree with.

In spite of the Piazza drama that night, Clemens was his bulldog best, shutting out the Mets on two hits through eight innings. And that was when the game went from peaceful to gut-wrenching in the top of the ninth. Ahead 6–0, Joe chose to go with the setup man Jeff Nelson to close out what should have been an easy victory. Three batters later, he was out of the game, Mo came in with a runner on and two runners in, and then put on the kind of performance that had managers everywhere reaching for the Maalox, their rosaries, the therapist's emergency phone number, or whatever other source of relief, salvation, or sanity they could find.

Joe was legendarily calm, but after a while, like you can do with some poker players, I detected what I thought was his "tell." Joe didn't cough because his throat was tickling him, it was a nervous reflex, a way of expelling whatever negative emotion was churning inside him when things weren't going the way he hoped they would.

There was an added sound to that cough, a kind of yip a little dog might make along with its bark, high-pitched and soft, and only audible to those sitting near him. More than a few coughs got emitted that inning. We hung on for a 6–5 win, but I know I aged a couple of years during that very long and very stressful inning.

We failed to hold a slim lead in Game 3 and the Mets beat us 4–2, with Piazza and Todd Zeile, their two best hitters, leading the way. Game 4 was a taut 3–2, with both teams scoring early, the bullpens coming in and shutting the door, and Mariano going two full innings for the save. That move could have backfired, but we put the Mets away in the fifth game, with Mike Stanton getting his third win of the postseason and Mariano preserving the win in the ninth for his sixth postseason save. Roger was the only starter to earn a win for us in the five games, and that doesn't say as much about our starters as it does about the depth of our bullpen. The games were all tight, and I think Joe's experience playing and managing in the National League helped us with strategic moves such as double switches and all the rest that goes with not having the designated hitter. We celebrated another World Series victory, and I was able to show my face—and hair—around my uncle George's barbershop.

AS THE 2001 SEASON drew to its end, I don't think that anyone could have anticipated what was going to dominate the conversation at Uncle George's and everywhere else in this country. The events of September 11, 2001, unfolded with all the elements of a waking nightmare. On Sunday, September 9, we finished a sweep of the Boston Red Sox at home. We had a thirteen-game lead in our division. We had Monday off, and a midafternoon flight to Chicago was scheduled for Tuesday, the 11th.

The first I heard of the attacks on the World Trade Center was my wife waking me up to tell me that a plane had hit one of the towers. Like a lot of people, I initially thought that a small plane had wandered off course. I'd spent enough time on flights to know how rigorous the rules were for getting into and out of New York City's airspace. Something didn't sit right with me, and I made the next jump in logic. Somebody had intentionally flown a small plane into the building, in some bizarre suicide attempt.

Of course, as events unfolded and the reality hit home, my feelings of confusion were transformed into anger. This was an attack on my city, and I couldn't believe that anyone would do something like that. I also had some direct concerns. My wife's niece worked in one of the towers, and I knew of several other people in the Yankee family who had friends and relatives there. Fortunately, my niece made it out, but that did nothing to diminish my feelings of anger and helplessness. I really felt like someone had come into my own home and violated the safety and security that I'd worked so hard to provide for my family. Like most Americans, I spent the first few hours and much of the next two days riveted to my television screen.

Fortunately, I could find an outlet for my feelings and my desire to do something to help. I'll never forget walking into the Armory and the Javits Center and seeing all the people gathered there, some of whom had lost loved ones, others being members of the first responders' teams. I saw supplies stacked up and thought that this must be what it's like to be at war. I felt awkward being there, not knowing what it was I could say in the face of such an immense tragedy. Seeing Bernie Williams at one point consoling someone and breaking down in tears set an example for me. People didn't want our words of wisdom, they just needed our presence, a smile, a handshake, an autograph.

Being a New Yorker, I knew the Yankees' place in the city's history and hearts, but I'd never fully understood how deep those roots go until we spent time with the fans during those six days that transpired before the commissioner said that baseball would begin again. We all had different levels of emotions and different opinions, but seeing those people in those first days after the attacks helped me understand that perhaps playing was the right move. That said, if the decision had gone the other way—to cancel the season—I would have supported that as well. I wanted what was best for the city and the nation, and I was willing to set aside whatever I thought was best for me or for the Yankees or for the game to ensure that the larger interests were best served.

One of the things that impressed me about Mayor Rudolph Giuliani—and there were a lot of other things as well—was his encouragement and insistence that we carry on our lives in the wake of 9/11. We did that in concluding the season.

Everyone has their own 9/11 story, but I wish that everyone in this country could have experienced what we did when we played our first game in Chicago on the 18th, and especially when we played our first home game on the 25th. I know that New York and the Yankees are frequent targets of a lot of people's anger and resentment. We didn't feel that in Chicago or Baltimore. People set aside their feelings about the Yankees and Mr. Steinbrenner and their perception of the Yankees as buying championships and simply embraced us. They opened their hearts and minds, knowing that we were all hurting, and no one more so than the people of New York City.

The ceremony on the 25th was one of the most moving experiences I've had in my life. To this day I can run images from it through my mind like I'm watching a video of it. In particular, I was moved, as I always am, by the music.

But before that came the silence. I know that logically it's not possible to say that the hush that fell over the Stadium that night was any deeper than any other kind of silence, but we didn't perceive that silence with our ears. We felt it with every nerve ending in our bodies. A somber thing, that silence burrowed into me and made my heart jump in the same way that it had when I'd first seen those horrible images on my television screen. As the silence lingered, though, that moment of fear passed and it became what it was intended to be—a moment of communion and connection.

Looking up and seeing those flags waving against the dark backdrop of the night, I felt proud and hopeful and never more honored to wear the Yankee pinstripes. Then, when Branford Marsalis sent out those first notes of "Taps," I felt tears welling in my eyes. As the program continued I thought about how fortunate I had been in my life. To have grown up in this city in a tough, tough place, and to then be on that field in New York, I knew that I was one of the representatives of what makes this country so amazing. Toward the end, when I heard Ronan Tynan singing "God Bless America," I marveled at that man's pipes and at how, even though I'd moved into the dugout tunnel for pregame throwing and batting practice, I could *feel* that crowd's spirit and energy. A few moments later, I heard another sound—of a ball pounding into a leather glove.

Wondering what was up, I looked over and there was the president of the United States of America warming up before going out to the field to throw out the first pitch. Now, I knew that President Bush had once had an ownership interest in the Texas Rangers, but I had no idea the man possessed the skill and coordination to deliver a decent fastball right to the catcher. I was hoping he wasn't going to leave it in the pen, and he didn't disappoint.

Nor did we, for a while. With the eyes and ears of both our home city and our nation on us, our role was suddenly different. Representing New York had never meant so much, and that was exactly how we played the game. We certainly didn't win every game for the rest of the season, but we played with an urgency and a sense of importance that felt preordained.

Getting to the World Series again, this time against Arizona, was like living out a Hollywood script. We all, to a man, wanted to deliver another victory for the people of New York City. We wanted it so, so bad, but it wasn't to be.

Game 7 seemed to be a perfect expression of the kind of roller coaster of emotion we all felt that year, the incredible highs and lows. I felt every hair on my body stand up when Alfonso Soriano hit his home run off of Curt Schilling to start the top of the eighth and give us a 2–1 lead. You talk about a tough 1-2 punch, Randy Johnson and Curt Shilling sure provided that for the Diamondbacks. To get on top of them with just two innings to go was huge, obviously, and we liked our chances. When Mariano struck out the side to close out the eighth, we very much liked our chances. Then Mariano proved himself to be human. The most puzzling part of that for me was the error. He's such a great athlete and such an intelligent player that seeing him make that throwing error unnerved me and, I think, unnerved him. Watching that ball drop into centerfield was like watching our hopes rise and fall.

Skeptics might say that it was just a game and in comparison to the lives lost and the incredible toll of suffering so many endured, what did it matter? Well, that's all true to an extent. But you give what you can, and that's what we tried to do. The blow of losing a World Series title was softened somewhat by the events that came before it. We were all better able to put things into perspective as a result. Still, after all that New York had suffered, we had wanted to do what we could to help bring some much-needed joy to the city.

CHAPTER 10

Rivals and Revivals

We're all professional baseball players and are paid handsomely to win and to entertain people regardless of circumstances. The 2001 Yankees had failed and we knew it, and while there's no comparison between the kinds of losses that came into our lives that year, we all had to move on.

The next three seasons for the Yankees were marked by the kinds of highs and lows similar to the 2001 World Series Game 7. Our rivalry with the Boston Red Sox had plenty of both. The 2003 American League Championship Series was the epicenter of a series of rumbles that have continued since. There's not much I can add about the intensity of the rivalry between the two teams, but I know that when I look back on those events, I still feel my heart rate climb.

My pulse was racing in Game 3 of that Series when Pedro Martinez hit Karim Garcia. I had a sense that something was about to happen. I had my own history with Pedro. Earlier that season Pedro had hit both Derek Jeter and Alfonso Soriano. I can't read a man's mind and know for certain what was going on there, but I really believed that, if nothing else, Pedro was trying to intimidate two of our good young players. I knew that Derek could handle himself, and we'd had prior conversations about guys pitching inside to him.

Still, my blood was boiling that day, and after the inning was over, as Pedro and I both went toward our respective dugouts, I let him know how I felt. "You're going to get someone hurt out there," I told him. He let fly with a few choice words, never turning to face me, and that was that. Of course, I never forgot that exchange, and I knew that Pedro would try to seize every advantage he could in facing hitters.

What happened next, I couldn't have predicted. I wasn't happy about Pedro hitting Karim, but in contrast to how Don Zimmer was acting, it was as if I was sitting on a quiet beach somewhere enjoying a peaceful sunset. Zim's face was all red, and with that chaw of his going and him yelling, if the situation wasn't so serious, it might have been a little funny. With Soriano at the plate, Karim took off for second, taking out the Red Sox second baseman Todd Walker on a hard slide, and the two of them got into it. We all rushed out of the dugout. The next inning Clemens threw up and in to Manny Ramirez and the benches cleared again. Melees like that are always just a rush of sights and sounds, but when we all saw Pedro throw Zim to the ground, I was completely stunned. *Did he really just do that?* It seemed so implausible that at first I was as confused as I was angry. That bit of confusion was followed by another. Do I go after Pedro or do I go to help Zim? I chose to do the latter, and seeing him lying there on the ground being tended to by Gene Monahan was as surreal a scene as I'd witnessed.

Game 7 had a mix of predictable and surreal as well. Before games, I often threw batting practice for some of the guys. That day I was pitching to Aaron Boone, and I said to him, "You're really swinging the bat well today. You're my pick to click." A lot of guys do this in baseball—before a game you select one player who you think is going to have a good game—he's your pick to click. I always liked Aaron and his approach to the game. He had good speed and he reminded me of another of my favorite Yankees, Chuck Knoblauch.

As it turned out, my sense of who was going to click was correct. Leading off the eleventh inning, Aaron launched Tim Wakefield's first pitch into the stands for a walk-off series-winning homer. (I still have a great photo of Aaron sitting on my lap in the clubhouse later as we celebrated a tremendous victory.) We all poured out of the dugout, and that's when the other surreal scene played out before me. While the rest of the guys were all celebrating on the infield grass, I saw Lee Mazzilli, one of our other coaches, standing over someone on the pitcher's mound. As I moved closer, I saw that it was Mo Rivera. He was sobbing. Great racking chest heaves and tears made it almost impossible for him to stand on his own. Lee was trying to pick him up, but it was like trying to lift up an armful of water. Eventually, the two of us did get Mo on his feet. I'd never seen Mo that emotional before; I'd never seen anyone lose it like that before. Of course, back then I couldn't have known what was going to happen ten years later on that same mound, and how a whole bunch of us would be in tears seeing Mo on that familiar rise of dirt.

I said before that I'm a competitive person, and as a result I sometimes tend not to remember the good stuff as well as the bad stuff—such as the 2004 American League Championship Series. Using the word "collapse" may seem a bit insensitive in this context, but when we lost the ALCS to the Red Sox in 2004 and my Mets failed to make the playoffs in 2007, that was the kind of language used.

In my mind, each of these events was a kind of perfect storm—all kinds of influences and circumstances coming together to produce a very, very undesirable result. What made that loss to the Red Sox so tough and yet so believable, despite how much of a horror show it seemed to be, was this. We won 101 regular-season games. The Red Sox won 98. We finished second in the league in hits, first in homers, and first in walks, but eighth in batting average. Walk and home run numbers like that mean that we were a pretty patient bunch and jumped all over mistakes. Pitching-wise, this was a team still in transition. We no longer had Roger Clemens. We no longer had Andy Pettitte. Our starting pitchers with the most wins were Javier Vázquez and Jon Lieber, with fourteen each. No disrespect, but I don't think that Vázquez and Lieber are going to come up in Hall of Fame discussions. They were solid major league pitchers, but certainly not dominant. Mike Mussina didn't have as strong a year as he would have liked, going 12-9, while our big free agent acquisition, Kevin Brown, also underperformed at

10-6. We also gave up eighty-nine more hits than innings pitched, and that's never a good thing. Mo was terrific, however, saving fifty-three and allowing thirteen fewer hits than innings pitched.

When we lost to the Diamondbacks in 2001, they'd had their dynamic tandem of Randy Johnson and Curt Schilling. Those two showed how important it was to have that really strong front end of the rotation to do well in the postseason. We'd had that in years past, but not in 2004.

None of that seemed to matter when we won the first three games of the ALCS and were on the verge, with a one-run lead in the ninth and Mariano on the hill to close out game 4, of sweeping the Red Sox. You don't expect the greatest closer in the game to walk the leadoff hitter. You hate to see that happen anytime, but with Mariano out there, we all then expected him to saw someone off, get a ground-ball double play, and make that walk irrelevant. Instead, the Sox stole a base, eliminating the double play, and now a single would tie it up. At that stage the game turned into an extra-inning bullpen battle, and we all know that those can go either way.

Still, even after losing game 4, we were sitting pretty. Up three games to one, with history on our side and a loose and confident bunch of guys, many of whom had been there and done that before in other postseason series.

So what happened?

The deeper we went into the series, the more our flaws were exposed. Our starters, with the exception of Kevin Brown in game 7, were effective if not great. We got beat by guys on the other side coming up huge in clutch situations. David Ortiz hits a big home run. How many times have you heard that? David Ortiz drives in the winning run with a single in the fourteenth after two walks preceding that hit. How many times have you heard that? Esteban Loaiza had pitched out of the bullpen a gutty three and a third innings, but those walks ultimately spelled our doom in a classic game 5.

Game 6 was a classic example of how things can turn around so quickly in a baseball game. Jon Lieber retired the first two batters on ground balls. He seemed to be cruising along. Five batters later, four runs were in and a lesser-known guy, Mark Bellhorn, had become a hero by hitting a three-run homer. How many times did we do something like that to our opposition? The tables had just been turned. I don't think anybody expected us to sweep the Red Sox, and we were on the verge of it. Nobody expected the Red Sox to come back and win four in a row, and yet they did.

And yes, we did get tight as the series went on. Some of that patience at the plate we'd exhibited all year long went away. Up until that final out was made, though, I still believed that we had it in us to win that last game. We were that good, but we didn't do the things we'd normally done all year to be successful. And it wasn't like I felt helpless at times, like I was in a dream and falling and clutching at anything I could find to stop the descent. The games were close. We were within a pitch or a hit or two of ending the series several times, so the word "collapse" never really entered my mind. That implies something sudden and catastrophic. I suppose you could use that word to talk about the entire series, but as players and coaches and staff, we look at games a bit differently. You're so focused on each pitch of each at-bat in each particular game that it's always a series of very small instances that add up to an out, a loss, a season ending.

Only after it's over do you go back and look for patterns and explanations. You look at your body of work in the regular season, the performance in the majority of the games in the series, and there's nothing that really jumps out at you as a single major fault or cause. Was the 19–8 blowout win in game 3 ultimately a bad thing for us? No. Looked at logically, one thing doesn't have anything to do with another. Completely different ball games. Just because one thing occurred before another doesn't mean that A caused B or that it even contributed in any way. That's the logical response, but most people don't want to hear that. And truth be told, most players don't respond logically. You don't go up there thinking that just because a pitcher has gotten you out twenty-one out of the twenty-three times you've faced him, which means you're hitting .109 against him, but you're a .280

career hitter overall so your chance of getting a hit in this particular at-bat is almost three out of ten. No. You go up there with belief and guts, and those are emotional responses.

And I think we just saw the same thing in 2013 with the Red Sox victory. Big Papi came up huge. Think of a team as a pack of wolves. You have your leader of the pack, the alpha male, and he runs the show and provides safety and security for the rest of the guys. Truth is, as much as many players dream of being the hero, it's a rare few who are comfortable taking command. Most of us want to have someone on our team—in our pack—who can lead by actions if not by words. I really believe that in 2004, if it hadn't been Big Papi getting those big hits, we would have won. Why? Because when your alpha guy is going well, that takes pressure off the rest of the team. It just does. As a manager or a coach, you want to create an environment conducive to success. Nothing is more conducive to success than your big guys coming through. Why do some guys who aren't the big names sometimes become heroes? A lot of the time it happens because they are relaxed. Expectations are lower, and pressure doesn't get to them as much.

We're irrational beings playing an irrational game. Of course, we were thinking at some point that if Johnny Damon had hit that fly ball in any other park but ours, it would have been a routine out. But we quickly had to tell ourselves not to think that way, because he was in our park and that's just the way it goes. You're constantly veering back and forth between logic and emotion, and I sometimes think that's what momentum really is—a shift in one direction or the other between those two poles. The thing is, you can't say that one is better than the other. Sometimes logic is good, sometimes it's bad. Logic told us that our chances of beating the Red Sox one out of the next four games were excellent. Emotion told the Red Sox that they could come back. Logic told us that our track record of success combined with the fact that *no* team had ever lost four straight after winning the first three made our likelihood of winning very, very high. We weren't kidding ourselves in thinking that we would win. Logic told us it was true!

Many of the same things can be said about what happened in 2007 with the Mets. Talk about walking the fine line between the rational and the emotional. Some in the organization questioned why I wasn't as fiery and passionate as a manager as I'd been as a player. I'll admit that there's truth to that observation. I wasn't as fired up every day as a manager as I was on the field. With rare exceptions—Billy Martin being about the only person who came close to being as fiery in the dugout and clubhouse as a manager as he was as a player—I don't think you can succeed by wearing your heart on your managerial sleeve. Again, it comes down to emotions and logic. Getting fired up can mean a lot of things, and getting on players or umpires is one way to express that. Some players don't respond well to that kind of leadership. Some do. You try to individualize your approach in dealing with guys, but then you run the risk of being accused of playing favorites or being inconsistent or a number of other criticisms.

I felt like while I was managing the Mets I was being myself. I wasn't trying to be like Joe, and I didn't have a WHAT WOULD JOE DO bracelet on my wrist. Joe Torre was a great person to learn from, but I couldn't copy him any more than Joe himself tried to copy anybody else. You have to be genuine because players, most of them at least, have very good BS detection systems. I wasn't dispassionate about the game as a manager, far from it, and I had my players' backs in ways that may not have been obvious, but I wasn't one of those guys who saw the value in getting kicked out of a game or mixing it up with umpires just to make it obvious to the folks in the upper bleachers that my players could count on me.

That was a strategic move on my part. As a young manager, I had to earn the respect of the umpires as well as my players. I saw how veteran managers "worked" umpires and got away with things that might have crossed some lines. They had earned the right to do that by establishing goodwill early on. Umpires are human beings. They do remember how you've treated them and it can't help but influence how they make calls. You hear about that all the time in the NBA, how veterans and superstars get the benefit of the doubt. I was looking long-term and wanted to set a tone: I wanted the umpires to know that the Mets and their manager weren't whiners. I believed that in the long run—over a season and over a managerial career—we'd get more calls if we didn't chirp on the umpires too much, and then only when it was absolutely necessary.

I also didn't want to be too demonstrative and have overly negative reactions when things went bad on the field. Remember that idea of a team as a pack and an alpha male as a leader? Well, that pack leader, that alpha male, has to exude calm authority. Leadership is best when it is calm and exudes control. That makes the rest of the pack feel secure. I was also very aware that my team literally had their eye on me. That was true of the guys in the dugout who could see me right there, and also the guys in the bullpen watching on TV monitors that frequently showed shots of me and the rest of the staff. I never wanted to do anything that could be construed as showing up a guy who messed up. I did a lot of cheerleading as well. Was I as passionate, fiery, and effusive as I was as a player? No. But that was by choice. I wanted to produce the best environment that would allow our guys to succeed. I still believe that's what we did most of the time. Could I have been better at reading the ball club and understanding the team's needs? Absolutely.

Here's where coming from the Yankees proved to be a bit of a disadvantage. I was used to being around veteran leadership with a proven track record of success. Those guys on Yankee teams were low maintenance. As a result, when I came to the Mets, I respected the veteran presence we had on the club. I took for granted that the core leadership there had the same kind of winning knowledge that the Yankee clubs had had. I checked in with the Mets' core group, and I heard a lot of "We got this" from them. They didn't want to have a lot of meetings and things, and I tried to respect that. The truth is, I should have done a better job of reading between the lines and recognizing that the "We got this" message wasn't an accurate reflection of the reality in the clubhouse or, to a lesser extent, on the field. I take full responsibility for that and consider it a very valuable lesson learned.

As a former infielder, I found making the transition to managing a pitching staff to be difficult. If I hadn't been committed to having my players' backs, I would have gone off more than once about things like bullpen issues. Logically, I couldn't understand at first why some pitchers only wanted to come in the game to start an inning, or why others didn't want to start off an inning. I wasn't a pitcher, and it didn't make sense to me. I heard some grumbles from the bullpen about how I was managing the staff, but I tried to be patient and learn from it. I didn't go off on them, in the same way I didn't go off on umpires. I wanted to have good relationships with people and thought that was a more productive approach.

That 2007 club was talented, no doubt about that, but I don't think they had the chemistry of the championship teams I played on in the late '70s or the chemistry of the Core Four (Jeter-Pettitte-Posada-Rivera) teams. Guys got along and had fun for the most part, but I don't think that they all knew how to win. I know for a fact that as the season played out it became clear that we had some areas of weakness, particularly in the pitching staff, that proved too tough to overcome. Put simply, we had a few guys on the staff who weren't ready for the major leagues at that point. That's no knock on them. It's tough to learn the game when so much is at stake.

We also had some holes to fill with Pedro Martinez out after rotator cuff surgery; he'd come back to make only five starts the entire year. We still had the great Tom Glavine, who was closing in on 300 wins after pitching well over 4,000 innings in his career. But he was forty-one years old—how durable was he going to be? And how many teams want to pin their hopes on the arm of a forty-one-year-old?

Tom was very, very solid for us all year, but in a bit of irony, Tom the Met Killer got a bad break that year. By then, QuesTec and the Umpire Information System were being used more widely around the league. Tom had made a living for years by getting borderline—well, really not so borderline—pitches off the plate. He had such great control and command that umpires rewarded him with the benefit of the doubt. Tom wasn't alone in that, but I'll use him as an example. Once the UIS began to be used as a measurement tool to evaluate umpires' performance, the benefit of the doubt went more or less out the window. Ask any manager or umpire and they will tell you that it changed how the game gets called.

I can't tell you the number of times I argued with an umpire about a call and heard some variation on: "I know it was close, but I can't make that call anymore. If I do, my supervisor is going to be all over me with his QuesTec data. Sorry, but my job's on the line here." I'm not making excuses for Tom—after all, as a Hall of Famer, he doesn't need me to defend his record—but the reality is that he couldn't pitch with the same degree of fineness as before because that technology wouldn't reward him. He wasn't the only pitcher having trouble with the new system, but as one of the few with such mastery of location, it probably hurt him more than most.

As Rick Peterson, the pitching coach, and I calculated it, with Pedro out and El Duque, also forty-one years old, a question mark health-wise, we were going to have to get some strong performances from our other starters and bring in some guys on a spot basis to fill the gaps. Hernández wound up starting twenty-seven, Glavine thirty-four, John Maine thirty-two (double his previous season high), and Óliver Pérez twenty-nine (his most since 2004), and things were going well for us. But we knew two things—fatigue and the law of averages might catch up to us. The previous season we were near the top of the league in an important category—ground-balls-to-fly-balls ratio. We had a solid infield defense, and you always like to see your pitchers have more ground-outs than fly-outs. In 2007 we were a fly-out team, but our outfield defense wasn't as strong as our infield defense. In the end, we had twenty-four fewer double plays in 2007, and that is significant, especially when you realize that we finished sixteenth out of sixteen teams in that category.

Older arms, younger arms, newly stringent strike zones, not nearly enough ground balls and double plays—all that spelled potential trouble. We knew it and were concerned about it, but the financial realities of the game are such that you're sometimes forced to go with who you've got. We had to fill in some holes in the rotation, and at the end of the year we looked at the results. We figured there were twenty-four games started by six different guys. Their collective record was 4-12, with eight no-decisions and a combined ERA of 9.95.

Let's take Mike Pelfrey out of that equation. You have to remember that he was our number-one pick in the 2005 draft and had seen only four games in the major leagues in 2006 before being rushed into the rotation to start thirteen games for us. In those remaining eleven starts, the rest of the spot starters were 1-4. At season's end, everyone was looking for those two magical wins that would have meant the difference between escape and collapse. I could point to those twenty-four games and say that if we had had someone to start those games who was big-league ready, we would have won at least two more than the four we did manage to win.

Some things just defy the numbers. You try to do the best you can with the available data and personnel. In one of the infamous games in mid-September when the Phillies swept us in a three-game series at Shea, I wanted to tell the statistics to shut up. We were up 3–2 going into the top of the eighth. Billy Wagner wasn't going to be available, so it was bullpen by committee to close out the victory. We went with Pedro Feliciano, who'd given up an unearned run in the seventh, to start the inning facing Aaron Rowand. Why? Rowand was 0-for-5 in his career against Feliciano. We had another choice. We could have gone with a righty-versus-righty matchup by bringing in Jorge Sosa. We figured if we did that, they'd go with Greg Dobbs. Dobbs was a great pinch hitter, and we wanted to keep him on the bench. We liked the Feliciano-versus-Rowand matchup better. Of course, Rowand hit one out to tie the game that we eventually lost. Twenty-twenty hindsight will tell you that was not the right move, but the numbers told us something different. Given the exact same set of circumstances, we would have made the same move.

I could go on, but the point is that so many different factors play into a single confrontation between a hitter and a pitcher and influence the outcome. That's true of what transpires both on the field and behind the scenes. There are no excuses for going 5-12 down the stretch and losing a seven-game lead. I can offer only partial explanations, but to the bitter end, I still believed in those guys and thought every day that we were the better club and would win. We chose the wrong time to go into that tailspin, and a very good Phillies club got hot at the right moment. I'm enormously proud of the job we did as a staff and how the players performed. In late August, when we got swept in Philly and saw our lead dwindle from six games to two, we then ran off a streak of nine wins in ten games. That's the kind of heart we had.

I just heard the new Chicago Bears head coach use the term "good amnesia" to describe what his team needed to rebound from an embarrassing loss. I like that. Players and coaches need to have that kind of forgetfulness, the kind that keeps the past from affecting you to the degree that you end up injuring your chances the next time. I believe that there is always going to be a next time. Learn from the bad times, grow from them, and don't repeat the same mistakes, while also understanding that sometimes you will do your best and come up short.

I can honestly say that there was no failure of will or effort down the stretch for the 2007 Mets. That would be unforgivable in my estimation. I've forgiven myself and am at peace with how I chose to handle matters. Sure, like reading a team's needs better, there are a few things I'd have done differently. But I've learned and moved on.

Just to show you how much I've learned, I want to talk about the great experience I had in 2006 with the Mets. The year 2005 saw us taking strides in the right direction, but 2006 was special to me in so many ways: I've related the difference between winning championships and experiencing clubhouse celebrations as a player and as a coach. Doing so as a manager was something new and added immensely to my experiences in the game I love. I often referred to players as my guys, my kids, etc. But when I became a manager and even more directly helped to influence their growth and development in the game, those terms took on a deeper meaning. I experienced a kind of parental satisfaction when I saw them doing well.

One of the guys who I was most pleased to see develop into a real force in the game during my tenure with the Mets was Jose Reyes. I still get chills when I think back to those days and nights at Shea when the fans would do their best soccer-fan imitations and join in that lilting "Jose, Jose, Jose!" chants in serenading their guy. Jose had been plagued by injuries early in his career, and I made it one of my priorities to keep him healthy. I also made it a priority to keep him on track mentally. Like a lot of young guys, Jose could get down on himself when things weren't going his way. That's natural, but it's a tendency that you have to fight if you're going to succeed at a high level over the long haul.

I liked Jose a lot as a person, but I especially liked what he could do for our ball club. He perfectly fit my idea of what a top-of-the-lineup igniter should be like—good speed, lots of contact, high on-base percentage, etc. I knew that as Jose Reyes went, so went the club. As a result, early in 2006 I sat him down and told him that I was going to be on him in way that might seem unfair. And I was. After all, he was only twenty-two years old. I told him that I needed him to be strong for me, and that the things I might end up saying to him were always going to be constructive criticisms. I told him that I loved him and that he was going to be my guy, but he was going to have to get used to the idea that I was going to be harder on him than on anybody else in the club. I was thinking that he was going to be a future leader of the ball club.

I was fortunate to have Jerry Manuel on the staff. He could keep an eye on things and keep his ear to the ground. He seemed to have a special sense of knowing when a guy needed some loving, some nurturing. He'd let me know who was feeling underappreciated or whatever, and I'd make sure that I spent some time with that guy. I didn't rely solely on Jerry for that; I kept track of the guys myself, but having multiple pairs of eyes and ears and maintaining good relationships with players was ultimately more important than how you handled double switches or any other bit of game strategy.

I started out in '05 and made it clear that I wanted to have a real professional attitude. That meant no loud music in the clubhouse and no facial hair. A lot of people thought that I was trying to Yankee-fy the Mets, but the few rules that I laid out for the guys were no different from the policies of a lot of clubs. After experiencing some success in 2005 and seeing that we had some good veteran leadership, I backed off on some of the rules a bit. We put in place a rotating disc jockey system. Generally that meant that whoever the starting pitcher was going to be that day was the one to select the music that played over the loudspeakers. Guys could listen to whatever they wanted to through their earphones, but my only request was that they keep the volume down a bit so that the journalists could get their job done without having to shout. That was the general tone of respect I was trying to create, and along with that, a sense of fun.

It also helped that we had some other veterans join the club in the off-season: Carlos Delgado, Billy Wagner, Paul LoDuca, and Julio Franco among them. With that nice mix of veterans and youngsters it was easier to loosen the reins a bit. There was a real sense of excitement in camp, and the organization's marketing slogan, "The team. The time. The Mets," felt like more than just words.

Once we got off to a really strong start in 2006, things seemed to take on a momentum of their own and the real fun began. Finishing April with a 16-8 record and a six-game lead was just what we wanted. For me, a key point in the season was a 1–0 victory we had over the Diamondbacks to close out May with a 32-20 record. Though neither Pedro Martinez nor Brandon Webb was involved in the decision, they were locked in a tight pitchers' duel deep into the ball game. At the time we had the second best record in the league (behind the Cardinals) and Arizona had the third best. That series with them was a good test, and it showed me that Pedro was still the gutsy competitor I knew him to be.

To be honest, I was worried about how my run-ins with Pedro might affect our ability to sign him as a free agent. After all, you may have to turn the page in this game, but that doesn't mean you also don't put a bookmark there. When Omar told me we were pursuing him, I shared those concerns. When Pedro came to spring training, I had a talk with him about our shared past. Pedro seemed to think it was a nonissue, and to an extent it was. Still, when you feel like you've been burned by a guy in the past, it takes some time to get over that.

His performance against the Diamondbacks helped put a lot of that past negative stuff in better perspective.

Unlike a lot of big stars, Pedro is a fun-loving guy and a great teammate, somebody who loves the camaraderie and wants to help make everybody better. During the final, forgettable homestand of 2007, I heard a commotion in the clubhouse one afternoon and found out later what caused it: Pedro was cavorting around wearing nothing but a necktie. He had the place rollicking with laughter. It was a nice sound to hear at that particular time, perfect for loosening up.

It worked about as well as my pep talks, but at least he was trying.

When other guys are pitching, you'll often see Pedro in the dugout, making suggestions and offering reminders to the guy on the mound. You won't see many pitchers of his caliber who will take that kind of interest in less-talented colleagues. When he's pitching, he's just as quick to back up his fielders and hitters. If you make an error behind him, he's never going to show you up, never going to go into histrionics the way some guys do. And if you drill a Met or two when Pedro is on the mound, you can be pretty sure one of your guys is going to go down the next inning. Not that the manager would know that, or have anything to do with it, or approve it . . . no, sireee. We'll get to more on that in a minute.

While Pedro has his comedic interludes and antics, on the mound he's an assassin, someone who competes with the best of them and will cut your heart out to win. That's how all the best competitors are. I hated it when I saw guys like Chase Utley or Chipper Jones come to the plate in a big spot. They play the game with an angry, edgy intensity—but a controlled intensity. They may not always succeed, but damn, you knew they were going to come after you. You knew they were going to do whatever they had to do to win. It's a characteristic of all winning ballplayers. Long after his days of blowing people away with 95-mile-per-hour heat were behind him, Pedro could still dominate you with deception and location. He has made the transformation from power pitcher to finesse pitcher as well as anybody ever has. The metaphor is probably overused, but he's like a master artist at work when he pitches. He paints corners, dabs a fastball here, applies a cutter there. His pitching intellect is as good as anybody's I've ever seen.

Tom Glavine was our number-one starter and he contributed in a big way during that opening surge. What I liked about Tom was that he was a calm presence on the mound and in the clubhouse. We had guys who liked to be a bit more raucous and flamboyant, so it was good to have some low-key guys to keep that in balance. By the middle of June, Tom was 10-2.

We had some memorable moments during the regular season. Billy Wagner earned his 300th career save. Jose Reyes hit for the cycle. On July 16, against the Cubs, we hit three home runs in the sixth inning. That's great, but nothing remarkable except for the fact that Cliff Floyd and Carlos Delgado both hit grand slams in that inning. I'd been around the game a long time, and I'd never seen that one before. We were in first place everyday except for the second day of the season.

A bit of George Steinbrenner popped out of me as we approached clinching the division to end almost two decades of Eastern Division frustration. The Boss was a bit superstitious and he never liked to get too far ahead of things. So, whenever we were in a position to clinch a playoff berth or win a series, he'd be down in the clubhouse preventing the media from getting into the clubhouse to cover the victory celebration. He didn't want to jinx it, and I felt the same way when I saw the cases of champagne being unloaded, bunting being unboxed, and the rest of that going on. I put an end to the premature preparations. Maybe it was our tempting the baseball gods that had us lose three in a row in Pittsburgh. That prevented our celebration, but the good thing was it put it off long enough for us to return home to face the Marlins. Fittingly, Steve Traschel was on the mound. He was the guy who'd been with the Mets the longest and he was solid all year for us, earning his fifteenth win in that Eastern Division clincher.

Even though Pedro Martinez was injured and wouldn't participate in the playoffs, he was one of the guys on the top step of the dugout, dancing in place with his goggles on as Cliff Floyd settled under a routine fly ball to end the game. We had the best record in the major leagues, and I got my first taste of managerial-success champagne. That we ended the Braves' long run was especially sweet. They were, and are, a great organization and the kind of sustained achievement they had was what we were looking to build in Queens. And yes, it did matter to me that we'd eclipsed some of the Yankee spotlight that year. Yes, we had the same regular-season record as the Yankees, but as I spent time in the city, it felt like the Mets' success had set off a different vibe. Don't get me wrong, I'm proud of my Yankee affiliation, but I pointed out earlier that New York has always been, in my mind, a National League city. I felt like we had won the division for the men and women of New York who had to grind out their daily living, that we were the lunch-bucket warriors, the Mets of the people.

I would have loved to have squared off against the Yankees in the World Series. That would have been great for the city and great for New York. Unfortunately, neither team got far. After we swept the Dodgers in three games, a result that, frankly, surprised me given the state of our starting rotation due to injuries, we took on the Cardinals.

Seventh games are always fraught with tension, and one of the lasting memories I have of that game was seeing Endy Chavez go back on a fly ball off the bat of Scott Rolen. The score was tied 1–1 thanks to Ollie Perez coming up big for us in a huge start. Endy went back and I jumped up onto the top step hoping against hope. He leaped and, with his arm extended over the fence, gloved the ball. A whole lot of white was showing at the tip of that glove, but he had it. When he threw the ball back in to double up Jim Edmonds, I shook my head and, getting ahead of myself in a way I probably shouldn't have, thought, *We're going to the big show.*

Another lasting memory is of Endy turning to watch helplessly as Yadier Molina's tie-breaking home run flew into the stands. We had our chances, but when Carlos Beltran took strike three to end the game, that bittersweet feeling of being gut punched in a big game flooded my body. Carlos had a sensational year for us and for him to stand there and take that pitch was not the way anyone wanted to see the season end. I know that Carlos caught hell for that, and that some people misinterpreted his cool demeanor for a lack of passion. The man did have ice water in his veins, but that was needed to cool his incredible desire to win. Some guys handle pressure differently, and just because you're not a fist-pumping screamer doesn't mean that you don't care. Intensity and passion wear many different uniforms.

Despite what happened in 2007 and with my firing in 2008, I remain very proud of the things we accomplished while I was wearing the Mets uniform. I walked into that last meeting with Omar Maniya thinking that I was going in there to fight a battle to save the jobs of a couple of coaches. In the end, that battle was already over, the decision about my fate as manager already decided. I wasn't happy about the decision and felt then, much as I do today, that if given the opportunity, my staff and I could have contributed to the kind of sustained excellence that the Braves and Yankees had enjoyed.

I know a thing or two about having patience and working hard for getting what you want. Nobody handed me anything and nobody took anything away from me either. I still believe I have what it takes to lead a group of men and still have a passion for competition that led me from the projects to the headlines. Next time, that large type will be announcing a victory and not a loss.

CHAPTER 11

Making Some Tough Calls

A few weeks ago, a bunch of my teammates from the '78 and '79 clubs gathered in New York for a kind of informal class reunion. Steiner Sports, the memorabilia people, had put together a signing and a presentation where a few of us were asked to be up on a dais to answer some questions. That part went about like I expected. We were asked why those two teams were so good, how we were able to overcome that fourteen-game deficit, and so on. When it was my turn to speak, I said that I wasn't going to be as long-winded as Reggie had just been—he laughed, and so did the other guys up there, Lou, Goose, Bucky, and Mike Torrez among them.

We all talked about how much *fun* we'd had playing together. I thought that Goose had some great things to say about coming in, being handed Sparky Lyle's job on a silver platter, as he put it, and screwing things up every which way. He took credit for putting us in that hole so that we could make our historic comeback. Goose also told how Thurman would come out to the mound during that first half of the season when Goose was stinking up the place and ask him, "Hey, Goose, how are you going to lose this one?" He'd trot back to the plate laughing, and Goose would yell at him, "Get your ass back there and we'll find out."

Mike Torrez, who was with the Red Sox and gave up Bucky's legendary home run, talked about the broken bat/corked bat that Mickey Rivers may or may not have slipped him, and we all just laughed and laughed. Later on, after the official event, the guys all got together and it was more of the same. I got in a couple of more lines about Reggie dressing down for the event—he was the only one in a suit and tie—and he shot back a few lines, and we all just enjoyed being together again.

Later on during the presentation, members of the Core Four were there, in particular to pay tribute to Mo. It was great to see them and to be pretty sure that somewhere down the line, maybe thirty-five years from now like it had been for my teammates and me, those guys will get together and do something similar. When they do, I know the memories will flow and the barbs will fly.

Having witnessed up close so many generations of Yankee talent, I'm asked all the time about how my teammates stack up against the "kids" I've helped coach. Let me say this from the outset. Today's players have tremendous skills. They are incredibly well prepared physically to play the game. For example, they eat better than we did. I can remember giving one of the batboys $10 to run to a local Bronx McDonald's and bring me back a pregame meal. So no matter whether I talk about Graig Nettles versus Scott Brosius or Thurman Munson versus Jorge Posada, I'm comparing some really, really fine athletes and baseball players. I don't want to turn this into a "back in the day we were tougher" or whatever kind of exercise.

I know that fans love to have these kinds of debates, so in my role as table setter, here's some food for thought. Before I get to that, though, here're the ground rules. I'm choosing between Yankee players from my playing days with the team (1976 to 1988) and my years coaching the Yankees (1994 to 2004). I won't be going all the way back into the rich tradition of Yankee greats, though I will mention some of them in context. I'll mention some of the guys I managed in my time with the Mets, just to enrich the discussion. The last thing I want to do is offend anyone, but to make this a good exercise to start a discussion, I had to make some tough calls.

Also, to keep things interesting, I'm not going to do this in 1–9 position order. I'm going to start at first base.

I was sad for Don Mattingly when his back began acting up and robbed him of his power, and sadder still that Donnie never got to play in a World Series.

	G	PA	AB	R	H	2B	3B	HR
14 Yrs	1785	7722	7003	1007	2153	442	20	222

RBI	SB	CS	BB	SO	BA	OBP	SLG	OPS
1099	14	9	588	444	.307	.358	.471	.830

Tino Martinez had some big shoes to fill when he took over as first baseman in 1996. It's never easy to replace a fan favorite and a guy who performed as well as Donnie Baseball. Tino had some great years with the Mariners, and when we got him in December 1995, along with Jeff Nelson, we knew we were getting a quality major league hitter and a fine defensive player as well. We were also getting a very intense competitor, a guy who, though he played only seven years with us, contributed every year on the team, becoming a crucial support to the Core Four.

Tino had a bit of perfectionism in him, like most great players do, and I bumped up against that on one occasion. We were playing the White Sox in the "New Comiskey," or what is now US Cellular Field. When a ball was popped up toward first base, some miscommunication went on. After the inning was over, doing what I was being paid to do, I went over to Tino to talk about what happened. Some people believe that you should wait until after the game to go over any lapses or situations that you think might have been handled better. I believe that if you approach the guy the right way between innings after the incident occurs, you can better dissect the situation and come up with a solution. I don't believe in getting in a guy's face, but ultimately that's what happened between Tino and me. A few words were exchanged once he took a tone and an attitude with me that wasn't what I would call respectful.

A few guys had to separate us, but we both settled down, and later Tino apologized. "Will-o," he said, using the nickname a lot of guys used to address me, "I was wrong. I was pissed off about screwing up, and I took it out on you."

I explained to him what I just stated earlier—that I was just trying to do my job, dealing with a problem when it occurred so as to prevent the same thing happening later in the game, and so on. I wasn't happy with myself for not just walking away, but when it comes to matters of respect I have a hard time backing down. The point, though, is that Tino was tougher on himself than anyone else could ever be.

That includes Yankee fans, who got on him pretty good when he got off to a slow start in '96. He eventually turned things around, and I think that a guy with less fight in him than Tino might not have been able to do that. He led the team in RBI and helped the team win its first championship in eighteen years that season. He had an even better '97, finishing second in the American League MVP voting. In '98, when we began our run of three in a row, he hit what some people consider the most important home run of the World Series. We swept the Padres 4–0, so it's easy to sweep that home run under the rug, but at the time it was huge. We were down 5–2 going into the bottom of the seventh, when he belted a grand slam off the left-hander Mark Langston deep into the right-field bleachers to break the tie and put us up 9–5.

The number that always jumps out at me about Tino is his RBI total. To me, that's how you judge middle-of-the-order guys. At the risk of sounding too full of myself, Donnie benefited from having some pretty good table setters in front of him, with Rickey and me doing our thing. Maybe more important, he had protection in the form of Winfield, Baylor, and Griffey hitting behind him. The same is true of Tino—though he hit sixth that Series—but you've still got to take advantage of having those runners on base. Both Tino and Donnie did.

Numbers can be deceiving, particularly in Don's case. In his prime, he was outstanding, but those back issues really hampered his productivity. If you look just at these averages in the triple crown offensive categories over their careers with the Yankees, it's pretty easy to make the case that Tino deserves my nod:

PLAYER	HR	RBI	BA
Don Mattingly	16	79	.307
Tino Martinez	27	105	.276

When you factor in the number of World Championship rings each won—four for Tino and none for Don—the scales tip even more in favor of Tino. That he struggled greatly in 2000 is undeniable (16, 91, .258), but he had a huge postseason and World Series for us when we won our third consecutive title, this time in the super-pressure-cooker Series against the Mets.

All that said, I don't think that the Yankee teams of Don's era, especially during his really productive years, would have been able to win as often as they did without him in the lineup. We were so loaded with talent up and down the lineup during Tino's years that, as important as his contributions were, we still could have won. Maybe we wouldn't have won all four of those World Series, but we'd have been right there each year.

Timing is everything, and one of them really benefited from it, while the other didn't. I'd like to call first base a toss-up, but you know we keep score for a reason, so in a decision that might be a little bit of my heart overruling my head, I've got to go with Donnie Baseball on this one—but only by a hair.

I've also got to give a shout-out to Chris Chambliss. Not only did he provide me with one of my greatest thrills in my earliest days in the big leagues, but he was a tremendous teammate and a guy who has continued to give back to the game for years and years.

	G	PA	AB	R	H	2B	3B	HR
7 Yrs	1,054	4,244	3,770	566	1,039	189	11	192

RBI	SB	CS	BB	SO	BA	OBP	SLG	OPS
739	17	10	405	546	.276	.347	.484	.831

Deciding who was the best second baseman I played with is tough for the obvious reason. I don't want to come across as arrogant, but the thing is, I held down that position for a lot of years with the Yankees. The Yankees have had some great players at the position, but only two Hall of Famers, both of whom were elected by the Veterans Committee—Tony Lazzeri and Joe Gordon.

I may be biased because I played the position and had my own strong sense of what your responsibilities were—help anchor the defense up the middle, turn double plays, steal some bases, and get on base for the big guys in the middle of the lineup—but I think that judging second basemen and their value is harder than it is for any other position. I feel qualified to make that statement because I spent my whole career evaluating the other guys who played the position while I was playing it myself.

In some ways, I took on a mind-set that might sound more appropriate to basketball. Sure, I wanted the team to win, I would do anything I could to help us do that, and I studied the opposition's pitchers and their hitters' tendencies, but I also thought of the matchup between me and the guy playing my position. Obviously, I couldn't tally points scored against each other, like in basketball, but this was one of those game-within-the-game things for me. I wanted to know how I stacked up against those other second basemen with respect to each game, series, season, and career.

When I really was slumping or felt like I needed a little more incentive, instead of feeling sorry for myself because I was 0-for-10 or 0-for-15, I'd try to go into the game and just make it personal with

Frank White, Lou Whitaker, or Bobby Grich. "I'm going to outplay this guy today. I'm going to be better than him today. All-Star Game's coming up. I want to beat him out, so I'm going to play well." Motivation takes a lot of forms. I wasn't the only guy who took that position thing personally. Because he was viewed, I think, as the poor man's catcher, Thurman got off on that too. So when he had a big stage, he had someone to measure up to like Johnny Bench or Carlton Fisk.

Bobby Grich of the Orioles was in our division the first year I was with the Yankees, but left for the Angels after that. He had a lot more pop than I did, and my 54 career home runs pale in comparison to his 224, but as they say, different horses for different courses. I wasn't expected to produce that kind of power, and he fit into his lineup well. We did share one trait—a good eye at the plate. I averaged nearly two walks for every strikeout (91/50) per 162 games. While Bobby averaged nearly as many walks as me (81), he struck out more than twice as often (103) per 162 games.

It's funny that I find myself falling into the same trap here—mostly talking about offensive numbers in evaluating the relative strengths and weaknesses of second basemen. That's how most people do it, and truth be told, as much as the Gold Glove Awards are, by definition, about defensive play, offensive statistics creep into that evaluation and honor as well. I understand that, as with some other awards, the criteria are subjective, but I also know that they don't hand out the Gold Glove Award to the guys with the best fielding percentage, most double plays turned, or what have you. Managers and coaches do the voting, limited only by the rule that they can't vote for one of their own players. They don't all use the same set of criteria, and there's no unanimity, even among these professionals, as to what constitutes "defensive excellence." We might agree on some things, but how we value them and the other variables that go into saying what's best, all that is pretty subjective.

I'll go on record saying this. I think I deserved the Gold Glove a couple of times when I led the league in a couple of defensive categories. I'm no conspiracy theorist, but the award was created by Rawlings, which continues to sponsor it and whose name it bears. Rawlings is a fine company, they make really outstanding equipment. During my career, I just happened to like and mostly use either Wilson or McGregor gloves. Middle infielders today don't do this so much, but guys like me had a habit of using the smallest glove we could find. The Wilson 1168 was one of the smallest gloves available, and I got used to using it and stuck with it.

I remember as a kid going to the sporting goods department to buy a new glove and being in heaven. The smell of all that leather was intoxicating. I had to have a glove with Mickey Mantle's name on it or Frank Robinson's or the name of someone else who was equally prominent. Size didn't matter so much to me then. Later on, I saw the glove as an extension of my hand, which it literally is, and I used to treat it like a body part. I babied that thing, often using baby oil to soothe and soften and break in a new one. Sometimes I'd use shaving cream as well, figuring anything good for the skin was good for my glove. Guys have their own beliefs about how to break in a glove: you have dunkers (guys who submerge it in water) and wrappers (guys who put a softball in the palm with rubber bands around the outside of the glove to form it), but I was a tried-and-true pounder. I'd just take a ball or my fist and pound that leather until it softened. My mother used to have to stop me when I was walking all around the house with my new glove, creating a ruckus with all the noise.

I think I knew that other methods would have gotten the job done, but I wasn't going to take any shortcuts. Job worth doing, job worth doing well. I tried my mother's patience when I would lay my glove on the ground, take the barrel end of a bat, and pound it into the leather like I was churning butter or stomping grapes or some such thing.

My point about the gloves is that, though I used Rawlings gloves early on in my pro career—an XPGS model—I mostly used Wilson. I can't say for sure that some consideration was given to Rawlings guys over any others in Gold Glove voting, but I can say this for sure. Where you played the majority of your game—in other words, your home field—could make a big difference in how you performed defensively. Two guys I competed against and considered my top competition at the position were Frank White and Lou Whitaker. Frank played for the

Royals, and Kansas City had a turf infield with just the dirt cutouts around the bases. Come on! Are you trying to tell me that a guy playing on a carpet, where the hops are true and predictable as can be, is a better defensive performer than someone who spent most of his career in old Yankee Stadium?

Old Yankee Stadium had a drainage system that was, well, old. "Antiquated" might be a better term. Back then, the only drainage areas were in right-center field. As a result, the field had to be sloped toward those drains. That was true mostly of the back part of the infield, where you normally positioned yourself as a second baseman or shortstop, so some ground balls were coming at you downhill. That imparted a bit of top spin, and balls would come up on me a lot. I had to adapt to that, of course, and took to fielding grounders like everything was going to short-hop me. Sometimes balls stayed down, though, and that style wasn't conducive to fielding these flat grounders. All you can hope for is consistent hops, and turf gives you that more than a grass infield does.

I got to be friends with Frank White over the years, despite our kicking the Royals' butts so often in the playoffs. We'd tease the hell out of each other. He won the Gold Glove eight times, including six in a row from 1977 to 1982, some of my prime years. Frank had some tough shoes to fill, replacing the Royals' beloved Cookie Rojas. It's tough to replace a Cookie in the fans' hearts, I always say. But Frank gradually won them over, as he did the voters.

Let's look at 1978's statistics, and I'll let you be the judge:

DEFENSE	INNINGS	CHANCES	PUTOUTS	ASSISTS	ERRORS	DOUBLE PLAYS	FIELDING %
Frank White	1194.1	726	325	385	16	96	.978
Willie Randolph	1144.2	712	296	400	16	80	.978

OFFENSE	AB	HITS	RUNS	2B	3B	RBI	OBP
Frank White	461	127	66	24	6	50	.317
Willie Randolph	499	139	87	18	6	42	.381

I could go on, but I think you get my point—there was a slim margin of difference between the two of us. What effect did playing for the Yankees have on my performance? Who knows? And if offensive capability played a part in it, I was right there with White and exceeded him in the statistic that metrics fans love—on-base percentage (OBP).

Please understand that I mean no disrespect to Frank. We're good friends, and he and I have hashed this out over the years. Even during our playing days, the conversations went something like this:

"Hey, man, Frank, why don't you let me have one of those Gold Gloves? You can only wear one at a time."

"No, Willie. Can't do that. Man, I got all the gold."

"You know what?"

"What's that?"

"I'll tell you what. You can have all the gold. I got all the diamonds." I'd wiggle my ring finger letting him know what was most important.

"SOB," he'd mutter.

"But hey, anytime you want to swap out one of those gloves, I've got a ring I could let you have."

Truth is, I wouldn't have swapped one of those rings for any personal award. I will say this, though: in 1980—another of Frank's "catch 'em on the carpet" Gold Glove seasons—I did win the Silver Slugger Award, which is for the best offensive and defensive combination at each position.

I'd have to say some of the same things about Lou Whitaker of the Tigers. He had an advantage playing at the old Tiger Stadium for half the season. I think they mowed that infield only on full moon Tuesdays or something. You needed a machete to go into that thick stuff to try to bare-hand a ball. You could stick your hand in that deep grass and come up with a starter off a Chevy instead of the Rawlings baseball you were fishing for.

Lou won a Gold Glove from 1983 to 1985, assuming control of the award from Frank. Let's see how I stacked up against Lou in '84.

DEFENSE	INNINGS	CHANCES	PUTOUTS	ASSISTS	ERRORS	DOUBLE PLAYS	FIELDING %
Lou Whitaker	1,195	710	290	405	15	83	.979
Willie Randolph	1,248	766	334	419	13	112	.983

OFFENSE	AB	HITS	RUNS	2B	3B	RBI	OBP
Lou Whitaker	564	127	66	24	6	50	.377
Willie Randolph	558	161	90	25	1	56	.357

I'll admit that Lou had a more productive year at the plate, with more hits, RBI, and home runs (thirteen to my two), but again, my defensive numbers are better than his across the board, and this is for a defensive award. As I stated earlier, offensive stats sometimes come into play, and the only thing that I can figure is that in '84 that factor influenced the Gold Glove voters.

Believe me, I'm not bitter, but I'm like most anybody. Getting a bit of validation from my peers would have meant a lot to me. I knew I was a good fielder, and I think others in the game did as well, but I just didn't get the gold; instead, I came up with the silver.

As I mentioned previously, I took pride in working with Yankee second basemen, especially Chuck Knoblauch and Alfonso Soriano, to help them maximize their abilities at the position. Even though he seems to have played his last game in pinstripes, today Robinson Cano is considered by many to be the equal of any second baseman in Yankee history and perhaps one of the all-time greats at the position. Robby just finished up his ninth year with the Yankees, so he's had a fairly extensive body of work there that makes the 162-game average somewhat fair in assessing how he compares to my group. (One of the things that Frank, Lou, and I had in common was longevity: Lou played nineteen years, and Frank and I enjoyed eighteen-year careers.)

With a .309 batting average, 24 home runs, and 97 knocked in, his 162-game average shows him to be an offensive force. Add in his .355 on-base percentage and you've got a guy with a good combination of power and plate command. After my coaching tenure with the Yankees was over, Cano won a Gold Glove in 2010, and he's acknowledged as having one of the stronger arms at that position.

The role of the second baseman has evolved, just as the game has, and I understand the pressures that guys are under these days to produce the big numbers. Agents, peers, and to some extent management focus on those offensive numbers, and it's hard to argue against Robby Cano being superior to the guys in my day, including me. He's the kind of guy you can build a ball club around, and he's only thirty years old, having made his debut at the age of twenty-two. The only thing working against him is his performance in the postseason. He's hit only .222 in eleven postseason series. That's a big drop-off from his regular-season stats. By comparison, Frank White hit .213 in nine postseason series, Lou Whitaker hit .203 in three, and I hit .222 in eleven. Those numbers reflect the smaller sample size in the postseason and also the fact that in the postseason you're facing other teams' top starters.

Here's another way to compare players and their relative values. The sabermetrics people devised something called wins above replacement (WAR). Here's how Fangraphs.com explains this statistic:

> WAR basically looks at a player and asks the question, "If this player got injured and their team had to replace them with a minor leaguer or someone from their bench, how much value would the team be losing?" This value is expressed in a wins format, so we could say that Player X is worth +6.3 wins to their team while Player Y is only worth +3.5 wins.

I'm not a statistician, but I've been told that WAR is an approximation of value and that any differences less than one or two wins is not significant. Here's how the four second basemen stack up:

PLAYER	OFFENSIVE WAR	DEFENSIVE WAR
Frank White	22.1	21.4
Joe Morgan	103.8	3.3
Bobby Grich	62.2	16.2
Lou Whitaker	67.0	15.4
Willie Randolph	52.7	19.4
Robinson Cano	42.5	6.3

I'll leave it up to you to draw your own conclusions on this one, but the thing that really stands out for me is how much of an offensive force Joe Morgan was. I can't say that he was a defensive liability, but that low defensive WAR number tells you something as well. The same is true of Robby Cano, even though he was a Gold Glove winner. Regardless of whether you favor offense or defense, the great thing about baseball is that you have to play both sides of the ball, so to speak. That's what makes these kinds of debates so fun and so exasperating.

CHAPTER 12

The Left Side

Now that I've covered the right side of the infield, it's time to cover the left side. I'm going to make this really easy. Derek Jeter. The Captain. DJ. Jete. Whatever name you want to use, the answer to the question about who was the best will always come up number 2. Jeter has been a Yankee since he started shaving. He won four titles in his first five years, and five overall. He may have grown up in Kalamazoo, but he has long since been adopted as New York's own, a player with a dignity that matches his talent. That's tough to compete with.

I mentioned before that thirty-three different men played shortstop alongside me, and no disrespect to anyone who ever put on a major league uniform, and in particular the Yankee pinstripes, but Derek Jeter is a better shortstop than any of them. The man can play the game. Offensively and defensively, he's been a standout for a lot of years, and I have enormous respect for him as a person and as a player. The year 2013 marked Mariano Rivera's departure from the game, and he was universally respected in a way that I found unprecedented. I can't say that Derek has as many admirers as Mo did, because the Yankee closer was a once-in-a-lifetime kind of guy. In my mind, Derek is a once-in-a-generation type of player and person. There's a chance we could see his likes again, but I have my doubts that anyone could top him.

To me, one of the most remarkable things about Derek Jeter is that you can't tell if he's 0-for-50 or 50-for-50. You can't tell now, and you couldn't tell when he was twenty-one either. His approach, his effort level, his belief in himself and his team's ability to beat you, never waver. Remember in 2004 when Jeter was in an 0-for-32 slump in April? You know it had to be working on his head. He was actually getting booed in Yankee Stadium! Imagine that. He had to have been ticked off. But he never showed you any of that. Not a speck of it. And then he hit a ball into the monuments off Barry Zito and was on his way and took his team with him. That's grace under pressure, even when the pressure was undeserved.

Derek's cool extends beyond the field of play as well. I said that, back in my playing days, being with the Yankees was like being a rock star. Well, for Derek, playing shortstop for the Yankees and winning all those championships was like being a rock star, an Internet start-up billionaire, and an Academy Award–winning actor all at the same time. Except, instead of clamoring to get into the spotlight, Derek has fought like hell to keep his private life private. That's hard to do, but he's always managed to fight off the media hordes.

Derek's a good-looking guy, and he's dated some very attractive women over the years. It shouldn't come as a surprise that a ball club is a lot like a bunch of high school–age guys hanging out with one another. There's very little that's off-limits, and guys will frequently ask Derek about his dating life. As far as I know, about the only response he's given to those kinds of questions is that grin of his. I don't know if he understands that only inflames guys' desire to find out what's really up, but he has never dished any dirt, at least that I've heard. All I can say is that it is very good to be Derek Jeter.

I've been in baseball all my adult life, and as much as I love the game, I don't like going to watch games that I'm not a part of. Let me clarify that. I like going to the games if I can sit in the stands, have a beer, enjoy a good hot dog, and just be a fan. That's not always possible. Most of the time when I do go to a game now, I'm up in one of the boxes or suites, and I'm uncomfortable up there. I feel too disconnected from the action.

In 2011 I told my son, "Do what you have to do at work to get the day off, but we're going to opening day at the Stadium."

My good friend Mitch Modell of Modell Sports let us use his tickets. We were about four rows back of the Yankee dugout, enjoying these great seats. Something came over me, and I decided I was going to do something I could never do as a coach or a manager.

Derek Jeter strolled out of the dugout and sashayed into the on-deck circle. Now, I know that Derek knows that all eyes are on him, but he likes to pretend like he's completely unaware of his surroundings. I know better. Part of Derek's cool is how he can carry on a conversation with the fans in the stands while getting loose in the on-deck circle, stroll to the plate, and be completely locked in. I couldn't do that. I had to be completely focused and block everything out of my mind.

Knowing what I know, I shouted, trying to keep my voice disguised, using a gruff kind of bellow, "Jeter, you suck!"

I checked my peripheral vision, and I could see a few surprised faces around me.

"Jeter, you suck!" I yelled again, knowing full well that I was going to get a lot more puzzled and probably angry looks. They were like, *Who's that guy giving Derek a hard time? Where the hell does this guy think he is?*

I let that sit until the next time he came up, and I repeated the routine, "Jeter, you're terrible!"

This time I noticed that a few fans had recognized me and were pointing and talking to the people next to them.

"Jeter, give it up. You suck."

I knew that in his first at-bat Derek had heard the heckling. I could just tell by how he cocked his head to one side a bit. He refused to look anywhere but at home plate and the pitcher's mound.

That second at-bat, after I'd gotten on him twice, he took a practice stroke and let his shoulders turn fully. That made his head pivot around so he could scout who was getting on him. When he saw me, he started cracking up. He shook his head and said, "You son of a bitch, Will-o."

I looked at my son and said, "I can die and go to heaven now. I heckled Derek Jeter at Yankee Stadium."

And then, in typical Derek Jeter fashion, he stepped up to the plate and doubled down the right-field line, going with the pitch.

If there's a baseball team in heaven, I'm pretty sure that Derek Jeter will be roaming around the middle of that diamond.

There's no point, really, in recounting all the rest of Derek's numbers and accomplishments. Everyone who has followed the Yankees closely has their own private list of Derek's top ten greatest feats. I mean, how many guys are going to have the time they backed up a play go down in history as such a great accomplishment? I'm not trying to diminish the importance of that effort, but it just goes to show how complete a ballplayer Derek is, how he always looked for ways to gain an edge in a competition (without ever crossing the line into doing something illegal or unfair), and how he seemed to always show up at the right place at the right time to do the right thing.

Now, I've done some acting—if that's what you can call playing yourself—but Derek took on a real challenge and showed his cool factor by hosting *Saturday Night Live* in December 2001. I mean, c'mon. That show is *live,* it's a cultural institution, millions of people were watching, and the man stepped in there and just did his thing. And who can forget the circumstances surrounding that appearance. This was just months after the attacks of 9/11. The city was still grieving, still looking for a way forward, trying to figure out how to get back to normal, and Derek was asked to host the show. Talk about pressure.

Back in September 2008, Derek demonstrated that he really has a sense of history and tradition. A few days before, he'd just broken Lou Gehrig's record for most hits in Yankee Stadium history. When he was presented with a crystal bat on that occasion, he said that playing in Yankee Stadium was like performing on Broadway. Well, he definitely has a flair for the dramatic, getting that hit just days before the old Stadium was to host its last game. On that final Sunday night of the season, 54,610 people jammed into the ballpark to bid it farewell. A bunch of us were there—Yogi, Whitey, Goose, and Ron Guidry, among them. Even Bernie Williams made it back for the first time in two years.

I remember being struck by the fact that there were so many widows and surviving family members of the Yankees I knew and some I'd played with. David Mantle and Randy Maris, Billy Martin Jr., Michael Munson—all sons of Yankee greats—plus Cheryl Howard, Kate Murcer and her kids Todd and Tori, Helen Hunter, Cora Rizzuto, all either wives or children of former players. I'd just been fired by the Mets that June, and it was really heartwarming to receive the kind of ovation I did from the Yankee faithful. I can't thank them enough for that. I'm not sure what possessed me to slide into second base, nearly taking out a cameraman, but you get out on that field and you just want to do what you did for so many years.

After the game, Derek stepped up to a microphone in front of all those fans and dignitaries to address the crowd. More than one journalist commented later on the other great speeches that had been delivered on that spot. I can't say that Derek's was as eloquent or as memorable as Lou Gehrig's, but it was from the heart. Derek later said that he hadn't scripted anything. He wasn't sure until before the game that he was going to speak, but his words spoke volumes about him and how players felt about the organization and the city.

"For all of us here, it's a huge honor for us to put this uniform on and come out here and play every day. There's a lot of tradition, a lot of history, and a lot of memories. The great thing about those memories, you're able to pass them along from generation to generation. And while a lot of things are going to change—we're moving across the street—there are a few things that aren't going to change. That's pride, tradition, and most of all, we know we have the greatest fans in the world."

Later Derek spoke about how nervous he was to do that speech, but it never showed. He also said, "When I was younger, I used to get really, really nervous when you have to do an oral report in front of twenty-five people. I guess I've come a long way."

I have to agree: he has come a long way, and it has been a privilege to witness so much of that progress firsthand.

Whenever I've been asked about Derek, I always say that what makes him so special is that he always answers the bell. You don't get to 3,000 hits except by playing all the time, through injuries and everything else. Unless you've been deeply involved in the game, you can't really appreciate what it is like to be able to have someone you can count on the way the Yankees have counted on Derek. Penciling that name into the lineup, game after game, year after year, knowing that you are going to get a high standard of effort and performance, is invaluable in this game. I know there's no official award for most invaluable player, but Derek Jeter would have been up for it every year I was with the Yankees as a coach.

IF I WERE TO mention the names Staiger, Ashford, Moronko, Kiefer, and Silvestri, you might think I was talking about a high-powered Wall Street legal firm. If you're a Yankee fan, you'd recognize them as just a few of the men who played third base during my tenure with the club. More familiar names would be Nettles, Rodríguez (Aurelio and Alex), Hobson, Brosius, Boone, Ventura, and Zeile. One thing most of these guys have in common, along with more than a dozen others, is that their tenure at the position didn't last very long. Graig Nettles was with the club from 1973 to 1983, and Alex Rodriguez began his Yankee career in 2004. As much as Scott Brosius and Aaron Boone have contributed to Yankee history and fond memories for Yankee fans, the two of them combined played four seasons in pinstripes.

For as much as the Yankees have enjoyed a long and rich tradition of greatness, only one Yankee, Wade Boggs, has made it into the Hall of Fame. And Wade played with the team for only four years—most people think of him in connection with his years with the Red Sox. Besides Wade, only ten other third basemen have made it into the Hall, so maybe it's not so unusual that the Yankees, like a lot of other clubs, don't have a Brooks Robinson, George Brett, or Mike Schmidt on their roster of greats.

For me, it comes down to Nettles versus Boggs versus Rodriguez for the all-Willie honors. Until Graig left the Yankees to return to his hometown of San Diego, he anchored that position. Turning the 5-4-3 double play, going around the horn, as the expression goes, is one of the great joys of playing the game. I don't know the exact number of double plays that Graig and I turned, but when you've done something with another player hundreds of times, you grow comfortable with him and know his tendencies. Sure, a 6-4-3 is sweet, but there's something about getting that feed from the third baseman that makes the play special—mostly because the throw comes from a greater distance and consequently the ball travels all around the infield. On one particular double-play ball hit to Graig at third, though, I wasn't so in love with the transcendent beauty of the play.

I was the guy, after all, who got knocked halfway into Death Valley by Hal McRae, the Royals' DH. A former football player, McRae broadsided me with a rolling body block that the Royals tried to pretend was a good, clean takeout slide.

Yeah, sure. If McRae wants to call that clean, then he's not just an overly aggressive player.

He's a liar.

The *Washington Post* called it "the slide heard 'round the world." I don't know about that. I just know it was a cheap stunt, and I was pissed.

The play came with one out in the sixth inning of game 2 of the 1977 ALCS. We were up, 2–1, at the Stadium. Fred Patek doubled, and then McRae walked. Ron Guidry, our starter, got George Brett to ground to third, one of the few times we were able to get George out. It looked to be a perfect double-play ball. Graig fielded it cleanly and threw to me. I knew McRae, a thickly built man who came up with the Reds and was known for being a hard-ass, would be coming hard.

I didn't know he'd barrel right past second and lay me out a good five to seven feet behind the bag.

"I told Fred [Patek] that they weren't holding me on so he should go all the way because I was going to get the pivot man no matter who he was," McRae said later.

It was as hard as I've ever been hit on a ball field, and the impact sent me flying. And if that wasn't enough, McRae clutched onto me so I couldn't go get the ball, which had rolled away, allowing Patek to race home from third to tie the game.

When McRae finally let me up, I was so furious I picked up the ball and fired it into the Royals' dugout. Billy Martin came out and railed to the umpires that McRae should be called for interference and Patek should return to third. The fans were booing McRae hard. Billy was asked later if there would be payback.

"If it takes 1,500 years," he said.

The next day we were doing our pregame stretching when I noticed Cliff Johnson, our six-four, 225-pound DH/catcher, walking over to the Royals' side of the field. Cliff was an amusing guy in a goofy way, though often he took things too far. He used to tease Thurman all the time about being captain, addressing him with mock servitude: "Hello, Captain." Thurman told him to cut it out. Cliff kept it up until one day he pulled his "Captain" routine for the umpteenth time and Thurman picked him up and tossed him on top of a garbage can. It was the same sort of behavior that resulted in Cliff and Goose Gossage fighting in the shower at the start of the 1979 season, an altercation that left Goose with a broken thumb and the team without a closer for six weeks. I was ready to let Cliff have it myself once. I used to keep a little boom box in my locker. I liked listening to jazz before games. Now, I've always been very particular about my stuff. I don't like people touching it or messing with it. I was like that as a little kid—remember Galileo Gonzalez and the sandwich?—and never outgrew it. Cliff used to mess with the boom box all the time, mostly because he wanted to mess with me. After a tough loss to the Rangers, Cliff did his thing, turning up the volume. We came into the clubhouse, and my music was blasting. I didn't need the FBI to find out who did it.

Billy was not pleased.

"Who the hell has the [bleeping] music on?" Billy hollered. I went to my locker and turned it down. I was embarrassed and ticked off that Cliff would do that. As he lumbered toward me I snapped. "You ever touch my music again, I'll . . . I'll . . ." I was up near his chest now. Cliff smiled, as if to say, *Look here, little fella, you really want to have a piece of me?*

I came to my senses quickly and backed down.

Cliff wasn't so amused the day he went to visit the Royals. He found McRae and wasted no time opening up the dialogue.

"I don't appreciate what you did to my boy at second base yesterday," Cliff said. "Why don't you pick on someone your own size? If you want to take it up right now, you and me, we can do that."

McRae was not interested in discussing it with Cliff. I appreciated Cliff watching my back very much.

Graig was an innocent bystander pretty much, so I couldn't blame him for everything that went on. Later, after cooler heads prevailed and we'd won the series, Graig said that my throw into the Royals' dugout would one day be remembered in the history books as another shot heard 'round the world, joining the assassination of Archduke Ferdinand and the Battle of Lexington and Concord. He was proud to be a part of it.

Graig won a couple of Gold Gloves in '77 and '78. He made a total of twenty-one errors in those two seasons combined.

More than that, as I've talked about before, he was a great teammate, a guy with a remarkable wit. I don't know how much of that came from being from laid-back California, having attended college (San Diego State University), or what, but he could crack me up and help diffuse tensions with just a few well-chosen words.

From 1976 to 1978, when we revived ourselves and went to the World Series three straight times and won two titles, Graig had his finest seasons, and that means a lot in my mind. Sure, we had Thurman as one of our leaders, and he did win the MVP Award in '76, but where Thurman was fiery and sometimes ornery, Graig's cool demeanor helped to balance Thurman's intensity. Not everyone can go with their foot mashed down on the accelerator all the time. Watching how Graig handled the ups and downs and the ebbs and flows of a season helped me enormously. And his 37 homers and 107 runs driven in in '77 helped the team enormously. Seemed like every time we needed a big hit, Graig stepped up and delivered.

I joined the Yankees' coaching staff in 1994, the strike-shortened season, and the year after Wade Boggs signed with the club. For those ninety-two games, I marveled at the man's ability to handle the bat. He hit .342 and had 61 walks and 29 strikeouts before the season was halted. No surprise there, really: from 1982 to 1996, he never hit below .300. That's just a crazy kind of consistency, as consistent as him eating chicken every day. In his five years with the Yankees, he averaged .313. He wasn't much of a power guy for a third baseman, and he didn't take advantage of our short porch in right field, but the man was an offensive machine, with a career .415 OBP.

He could throw some leather as well, winning Gold Gloves with us in '94 and '95 and multiple Silver Slugger Awards throughout his career. He even climbed the hill for us once, in 1997, at the age of thirty-nine, facing four hitters, walking one and retiring the rest in the eighth inning of a 12–4 loss in Anaheim. He had a dandy knuckleball, and fans at the Big A gave him a standing O. I don't know if he could have extended his career tossing that thing, but before he retired in '99 he pitched again—for the Devil Rays, as they were then known—this time surrendering a run in one and a third innings of a blowout loss.

It's almost impossible to talk about Alex Rodriguez and his role in Yankee history without some discussion of the controversies surrounding him. Believe me, I wish we could just talk about baseball and the things that take place on the field, but that's a naive take on what is an industry, not just a sport. And I don't want to heap all of this on Alex, because it's obvious by now that a lot of guys are involved in the performance-enhancing drugs (PED) controversy. But there's a reason why I bring it up now when I'm talking about all of these comparisons among players. What troubles me is this: I love the game. I love talking with my son, going to the barbershop and hearing the debates about who's better than whom. That's been a great part of the game for so long, and I still get caught up in it, but now there always comes a point in these discussions when I'm like, "Whoa! Let's hold on here. I don't know if I want to keep doing this, because there's an elephant in the room."

I'll admit that baseball has a problem, and one that's been going on for a while. We didn't want to deal with something that we all knew was going on. To what degree—or depth, I guess—we put our collective heads in the sand isn't for me to debate, but I know that it *hurts* me on a deep and personal level to know there's always going to be a shadow lurking around the edges of any talk about players of this era, or comparisons of players of different eras. Simply put, the playing field wasn't level during my time in the game, and that makes some of these comparisons I'm doing feel false somehow.

I never saw anyone do it, and that's what I told George Mitchell's investigators when they came and talked to me in the spring of 2007. I was in Port St. Lucie, preparing for my third year of managing the Mets. I met with them in a room adjacent to general manager Omar Minaya's office. It was just two investigators and me. They asked me mostly about Jason Giambi, Roger Clemens, Knobby, and Brian McNamee and about what I observed in my time with the Yankees. I wasn't about to deal in guesswork and hunches or talk about who I thought might have done what, because that wouldn't have been fair to anybody. But I didn't gloss over anything either.

I first became suspicious about guys juicing when I'd see little middle infielders hitting home runs to the opposite field, or going oppo, as we say. I had my head in the sand for a while; I think most baseball people did. But when all of a sudden the ball starts flying off bats as if guys are hitting a three-iron, well, you can't help but notice the difference. You'd see guys go home for the off-season with one body and come back February 15 with a whole different body. It was like, "Whoa, what happened to you? What vitamins are you taking?"

To me, the before-and-after pictures of these athletes told the tale. Mark McGwire, Barry Bonds, Roger Clemens, Jose Canseco, and

Sammy Sosa were lithe guys with a kind of coiled, sinewy power when they came up to the big leagues. But late in their careers—at ages when previous generations had long since retired to coach or tend bar—these guys were Macy's Thanksgiving Day Parade floats.

I have a theory about what happened. Ballplayers are competitive. They have an extraordinary chance to make millions of dollars. They see rival players bulking up and feel like suckers for maintaining their natural builds. Some know that bulking up gives them the edge they need to make it to the big leagues. Others know that it can make the difference between so-so or good careers and superstar careers. And so they start talking behind the scenes with doctors and teammates about how to bulk up. And here's the kicker—baseball, until 2002, didn't have any power to test players. Not until 2005 did players suffer serious penalties for testing positive for using PEDs.

It goes without saying that baseball is not the only sport to have faced problems with PEDs. Athletes like Lance Armstrong (bicycling), Marion Jones and Ben Johnson (track and field), and Bill Romanowski and Lyle Alzado (football) are just a few famous cases in other sports. Supercompetitive athletes always look for an edge. It could be statistics, videos, or new training techniques. Or it could be drugs.

After a while, you simply couldn't ignore it anymore. We couldn't say we didn't know. Because we did know. It's true I never saw anyone take anything, but did I see guys' muscles getting bigger, and the ball going farther? No doubt about it. We talked in the coaches' room about it all the time. We all participated in the charade by looking the other way, the same way the owners and GMs and managers and virtually all of the media did.

I wish I could say I am surprised that performance-enhancing drugs became so popular, but I'm not. For generations, major leaguers popped "greenies"—amphetamines, or "uppers"—to keep up their energy through the long, grueling season. Some teams had two coffee pots—one filled with standard-issue java, the other with spiked java. I sipped the spiked java a few times in my career, but I never liked the way it made me feel. It would make me jumpy. It didn't feel right, didn't feel natural. Caffeine was enough for me. I felt no need to go for anything stronger.

I have very mixed feelings about the parade of names coming out from the supposedly anonymous list of players who tested positive for banned substances from 2003. On the one hand, I'm glad that guys who cheated are having to face the music and we can begin to maybe put this steroid era behind us. But where is the fairness for the other guys who cheated whose names have not been made public? How does that work exactly? If some of the 103 names on the list are getting out, they all should be released, if for no other reason than to protect the innocent—to prevent the guys who competed clean from getting unfairly lumped with the cheaters. Either way, you hate to see the sport you love get dragged through so much dirt. Then again, we collectively piled that dirt there, every shovelful. Now it's become our very own Superfund site—it's up to us to clean it up.

What bothers me most about the steroids issue is the way it taints the historical part of the game. I love baseball history. So much of that history is tied up in numbers and statistical achievement. Before steroids surfaced, you could have a legitimate debate about who was the better player, Barry Bonds or Willie Mays, Barry Bonds or Hank Aaron. Now how do you compare players? How do somebody's achievements stack up if they've been chemically enhanced? Barry Bonds was a sensational hitter long before anybody ever heard of BALCO, but can we say for sure that we know how many of his home runs would've gone out without the added strength he developed well after his thirty-fifth birthday? No, we can't.

What I do know is this: when it comes to steroids in baseball, everybody and everything loses. The game itself loses credibility. Fans lose because they don't know what they can believe and what they can't believe. And the players themselves lose, for even if you wind up winning a few home-run titles and signing a big fat contract or two, you still have to live in some amount of fear, wondering if you are going to have your own A-Rod or Manny Ramirez moment. You still have to wonder how getting caught would affect how you are remembered long after you are through playing. You may never get caught—lots of dirty athletes have sailed through drug testing over the years, whether because they are using a designer steroid that isn't covered in the testing or because they use an effective masking agent—but you have to know the mood will turn ugly fast if you do get caught. Just look at how fast things went south for Mark McGwire. Not only has his alleged performance-enhancing drug use kept him out of the Hall of Fame, but his evasive congressional testimony—his statement that he wasn't there to talk about the past—made him an object of ridicule.

I played with Mark McGwire, and I like Mark McGwire. That doesn't earn him a lifetime pass. Not at all. I just find it sad that his reputation is pretty much in tatters and that instead of being remembered for hitting 583 home runs and being a twelve-time All-Star, he's remembered as the guy who refused to come clean before Congress. Maybe returning to the game as a hitting coach will help repair the damage to his reputation, but that remains to be seen.

I'm not saying that everybody was using PEDs, far from it. But another thing that troubles me is the way the actions of some players cast suspicion on the rest of the guys. That's putting it politely, so let me say what I really mean. It pisses me off.

I don't like talking about guys I competed against at second base, like Frank White and Lou Whitaker and the rest, while ignoring Robbie Alomar and what he did in the game. He came along and kind of obliterated some of our accomplishments. He was a tremendous ballplayer who made it into the Hall of Fame, but when you look at his numbers and see when he had his most accomplished seasons offensively, is he then guilty by association? Does everybody from that era have their accomplishments diminished as a result of those unfortunate circumstances? The truth is, that's the way some fans see it—everyone guilty till proven innocent. That view is understandable, but still terrible.

I know how I would feel if I was playing in such an era of suspicion. I'd be frustrated that my accomplishments were being tarnished because of what other guys were doing. I don't know if I would have had the balls to be a whistle-blower myself, so I can't really point a finger at any of the players who didn't raise hell about what they knew or at least suspected was going on. A few guys spoke out—Frank Thomas of the Chicago White Sox is one who comes to mind, but he was a lone voice in the wilderness. Now he's recognized as someone who was ahead of the curve, but back then nobody really paid that much attention to what he was saying.

Like a lot of former players, I'm saddened by the whole thing, as are a lot of fans and even others who don't really care all that passionately about the game. As I was working on this book, the Ryan Braun suspension was handed down. I knew and worked with Ryan while I spent time on the Brewers' coaching staff. Here's where this gets even more tangled in my mind. I heard Ryan issuing denials. He's a very bright, articulate young man, he was so adamant and so well-spoken, and I had no firsthand evidence that would make me doubt his statements, so I believed him. Was I turning a blind eye? I don't think so. It wasn't even a case of me wanting to believe that he was clean. It wasn't like I had a long-term, heavily invested relationship with him or the Brewers. I do have that kind of relationship with the game, though, and I would do anything to protect its integrity. So if I state that I didn't know what was going on or that I believe somebody who denies using, does that make me a co-conspirator, a cover-up artist?

The issue is so complicated that I find myself getting turned inside out and into knots when I try to make sense of it all. That's how I feel about Alex and his contributions over the years to the Yankees and where he fits in historically. I'd like to just look at his numbers and say, "Hey, the man can play the game and for a time was as good as, if not better than, anybody else out on the field."

Is Alex the Yankee goat at his position? I don't think so, because I wasn't there to personally witness what he did in 2005 and 2007, his two MVP years when he just electrified the league and the game with his brilliance. PEDs and other issues aside, for me to give the guy my nod for my own personal award, I'd need more personal evidence to support his case. Alex's numbers are impressive—beyond impressive, really. He's closing in on 3,000 hits and 2,000 RBI, and he's hit 654 home runs. These are numbers that stack up against those of anybody who's played the game.

I have no problem with Alex as a person. I'm not about to judge him. As is true in any walk of life, baseball is filled with personalities that run the gamut. I got along very well with Reggie Jackson. He wanted the spotlight and did a lot of things to deserve it. I had no complaints about that since I wasn't seeking the spotlight. Same is true with Alex. I understood my role with the Yankees as a coach and knew that none of what was going on was about me.

Because of when I came up and who I played with and what they contributed to the early success I enjoyed in those first few years in the big leagues, Graig Nettles left an indelible impression on me. I can't say the same of any other Yankee third basemen. Some showed flashes of brilliance, no doubt about it, but sometimes the glare from all the off-field stuff was so blinding that those white-hot blind spots lasted all the way through game time and beyond. Being dazzled and being convinced are two different things in my mind. I just wish I wasn't blinded by the lights and could simply enjoy those on-field images of a very, very talented Alex Rodriguez.

CHAPTER 13

The Battery

N obody I ever played with competed harder, or wanted to win more, than Thurman Munson. In thirty postseason games, his lifetime average was .357, a number that doesn't begin to convey both his greatness and his pain tolerance. Thurman was almost always beat up. Good luck trying to get him out of the lineup. He never came up bigger than in game 3 of our annual ALCS meeting with the Royals in 1978, when he belted a two-run homer off of Doug Bird in the bottom of the eighth to give us a 6–5 triumph in the biggest game of the series. He hit that homer with an acutely painful shoulder injury. He never made a big deal out of injuries. He was like Jeter in that regard. He hated talking about them and wouldn't even acknowledge having an injury if someone brought it up. But we knew he was hurting.

Thurman led us to three straight AL pennants and two straight World Series titles. The 1976 Series was over before you could say César Gerónimo, but if a whole bunch of us never showed up, Thurman sure did, hitting .529 (9-for-17) and playing his butt off. I always thought it was a cheap shot by Sparky Anderson, the Reds manager, after he was asked to compare Munson and the great Johnny Bench, who was the Series MVP and hit .533 in the sweep. "Don't embarrass anyone by comparing them to Johnny Bench," Anderson said. I'm not saying Thurman was Johnny's equal, but you're darn right I am saying he is in the same sentence. He was a total winner in every way, and there's a long line of guys on those Yankee teams who would offer the same opinion. Reggie and other guys got more publicity, but to a man, the guys on that club knew who the biggest gamer on the team was.

"If there were two outs and a runner on second and we needed to get the run in, Thurman was the guy we wanted at the plate," said Paul Blair, one of the best defensive outfielders ever to play the game.

It's impossible to project into the future how his eleven-year career statistics would have compared with some of the other all-time great catchers. Who knows what kind of toll playing behind the plate would have exacted from him, but in seven of his nine full seasons in the big leagues, from 1970 to 1978, Thurman received Most Valuable Player votes, and he won the award in 1976. Whenever I talk about Thurman, I describe his as the total package—he could run, hit, call a great game, throw, and pounce on balls in the dirt and bunts laid down in front of him. It was his leadership that set him apart, though.

My former teammate Elliott Maddox said it best. Thurman could get on you about applying yourself better. That was how you knew he liked you; otherwise, he would have just ignored you. Elliott joked about Thurman loving him because he got a lot of attention from the man. Well, a lot of Yankee players and fans loved Thurman Munson in return.

From 1997 to 1999, we saw a gradual shift as Joe Girardi eventually gave way to Jorge Posada manning the position full-time. By 2000, with Girardi gone, Jorge was fully in control of the position, and except for 2008, when Jorge went down with a shoulder injury, it would stay that way until 2011. Jorge played in nearly 1,600 games, the vast majority of them behind the plate. Joe Torre would try to give him some rest by having him DH and play first base, but that doesn't diminish how much of a workhorse he was for all those years. As it was with Derek, being able to put that same name on the lineup card time and time again was a nice bit of security to have.

It's also nice to have a productive left-handed hitter in the lineup, particularly at the catcher's position. The following numbers don't tell the whole story, of course, but they give you a pretty good summation of Posada's career:

	G	AB	R	H	2B	3B	HR	RBI	BB	SO	SB	CS	AVG	OBP	SLG	OPS
Total	1,829	6,092	900	1,664	379	10	275	1,065	936	1,453	20	21	.273	.374	.474	.848
Season Averages	107.0	358.4	52.9	97.9	22.3	.6	16.2	62.6	55.1	85.5	1.2	1.2	.273	.374	.474	.848
Post-season Total	125	416	53	103	23	1	11	42	70	109	3	3	.248	.358	.387	.745

Of course, catchers help anchor the team's defense and can offset another team's running game. Jorge had a fine arm and a good release, but I think even he'd admit that he wasn't as strong defensively as some of his contemporaries at the position. One number that stands out is passed balls. Anytime you allow a runner to advance without putting the ball in play, you're hurting your club. Just as with pitchers' walk totals can be somewhat misleading—the number of times you unintentionally *or* intentionally walk a hitter—the same can be true to an extent with passed balls. The makeup of the staff can affect the number of passed balls, for instance. When guys have good heavy sinkers, split-finger pitches, or nasty curveballs, a certain number will get away from the catcher. However, the official scorer will rule them passed balls when he sees them as pitches that shouldn't have gotten past the catcher.

GP	GS	FULL	TC	PO	A	E	DP	FPCT
1,574	1,450	8,400.0	10,802	10,016	696	90	81.	992

RF	ZR	PB	SB	CS	CS%	CERA	DWAR
11.48	.386	142	657	245	.272	4.42	—

The gold standard for catchers in Jorge's era was Iván Rodríguez. Pudge played four more years in the major leagues (twenty-one to Jorge's seventeen) and only had 109 passed balls in that time. He also had an amazing gun for an arm, throwing out an incredible 37.8 percent of potential base stealers to Jorge's 27.2 percent. That I even compare Jorge to Pudge says how much I respect him and what he did for the Yankees. Just to complete the comparison, Pudge was also a real force offensively, hitting .296 for his career, knocking out 311 home runs, while driving in 1,332 runs with an on-base percentage of .334. Hall of Fame numbers in my mind, and I'm sure in the minds of many other baseball people.

From 1998 to 2005, New York baseball fans were privileged to have two excellent catchers taking their position behind the plate. Mike Piazza was there the first season I took over as Mets manager, but for years I'd been keenly aware of what he was doing up there in Queens. In this case, the numbers reveal that Mike, a guy with real power, was a superior offensive player:

GAMES	AB	R	H	2B	3B	HR	RBI	SB
1,912	6,911	1,048	2,127	344	8	427	1,335	17

CS	BB	SO	BA	OBP	SLG	OPS	OPS+
20	759	1,113	.308	.377	.545	.922	143

Those 472 home runs, nearly 200 more than Jorge, are huge. His 396 home runs while playing that position easily outpace Carlton Fisk's 351, Johnny Bench's 327, and Yogi Berra's 305. Those are the only guys who have hit more than 300 home runs while catching. When you figure in their total home runs hit while playing any position (including designated hitter), Mike is still on top, followed by Bench, Fisk, Berra, and the late Gary Carter.

Defensively, Mike was solid, allowing 109 passed balls, but he threw out only 23 percent of base runners attempting to steal. Any defensive liabilities he may have presented were offset by those fantastic offensive contributions.

An interesting new defensive statistic is catcher's earned run average (CERA). How much of an influence a catcher has on a pitcher's performance has always been a subject of debate, and CERA analyzes how an individual pitcher performs throwing to different catchers. There's not a whole lot of agreement on how effective a metric this one is, but it does offer some food for thought:

JORGE POSADA	4.22
MIKE PIAZZA	3.79
IVAN RODRIGUEZ	4.72
THURMAN MUNSON	3.22

How effective is CERA as a measurement? And what does this number say about a catcher's value? As a table setter, I'll just throw these juicy questions out for all of you to chew on, but I'll add a little more seasoning to the debate by stating this. Thurman Munson threw out 44 percent of base runners attempting to steal when the league average was 38 percent.

One thing that Thurman and Jorge shared was a bit—well, more than a bit—of stubbornness. Just like I got into it with Tino that time, Jorge and I had a brief run-in when I tried to make certain that a mix-up on a cutoff play didn't happen again. Jorge also bumped heads sometimes with a few of the pitchers on the staff. His primary sparring partner was El Duque, Orlando Hernández. Duque turns into a crazy man when he gets angry. He had almost as many tirades when he was a Yankee as he did big victories, and that's a lot. One time he chased Jorge around the trainer's room, looking as mad as I've ever seen him. I don't remember what set Duque off that time; he and Jorge would argue all the time. I guess that when you're battery mates, sparks are supposed to fly.

I'm probably going to catch hell for saying this, but if I was putting a team together—which I guess I am in writing this—Thurman would have to be my guy over Jorge. The combination of his skills and his leadership ability carry the day in this case. Thurman was the kind of guy you'd want to go to war with, the guy in the foxhole with you who could be counted on to stay in control. You'd sleep well knowing he was on your side and spend sleepless nights worrying about all the different ways he might beat you if he wasn't.

FOR MY ALL-WILLIE TEAM, I'm going to select one right-handed starting pitcher, one left-hander, and a closer.

Speaking of guys you'd love to have on your team and would hate as an opposing player, Roger Clemens immediately springs to mind. As I've said before, I'm sorry that there's so much controversy surrounding Roger, but for now I'm just going to focus on him as a competitor. It helped that in his six years with the team he won two-thirds of his games, going 83-42 in that span. Production doesn't always equal acceptance, but it sure as hell helps.

The right-handed starter I played with who I'd toss in the mix is Catfish Hunter. Like Roger, Catfish enjoyed some of his best seasons with another ball club before coming over to the Yankees. His years with Oakland and Kansas City showed him to be about as dominant as Clemens was with the Red Sox. Roger won 192 games and lost 111 with a 3.06 ERA in thirteen seasons with the Sox. Catfish was 161-113 with a 3.26 ERA in ten years with the As. If you figure that Catfish won 16 games per year for ten years and then add on an additional 48 to bring his average wins per year up even with Roger's, that would put him at 209 wins. That's a lot of assuming, of course, but at least it gives you a better idea of what the two pitchers were like in their prime.

What also clouds the picture when it comes to comparing starters, particularly from my era to the present, is the changing use of bullpens and how that has transformed the game. My first year with the Yankees, 1976, Catfish Hunter had 21 complete games. By today's standards, that's an astounding number. Since 2000, only one pitcher, James Shields of Tampa Bay, has led the league with double-digit complete games, and he had 11. In 2013 the leader in the National League was Adam Wainwright with five, while Chris Sale of Chicago and David Price of Tampa Bay had four each. Cat's 21 complete games in '76 didn't even lead the league—Mark Fidrych had 24. What's even more amazing is that Catfish Hunter had 30 complete games the year before and 181 for his career, for an average of 13 per year.

Straddling the two eras, Roger had a high of 18 complete games in 1987 and 118 for his career, averaging six per season, or less than half of what Catfish did. Guys were expected to chew up innings, and that's what they went out there and did: both Clemens and Hunter averaged around 240 innings per year. (Justin Verlander, one of the more durable pitchers today, averages 226.) What differentiated the two guys is that Catfish relied on guile and deception in his last few seasons, while Roger was able to maintain his status as a power pitcher.

When you look through the list of all-time leaders in Yankee history, two other names pop up—Mike Mussina and David Cone. Mike was a real craftsman, a guy with tremendous command of his pitches. As a former infielder, I like guys who throw strikes, and Mike owns five of the top ten spots in Yankee history for best strikeouts-to-walks ratio. Except for some more obscure metrics like situational wins saved and base-out wins saved, he doesn't appear anywhere else in the top-ten record book for a single season, yet he's tenth all-time in career strikeouts.

David Cone was another New York–New York guy who played for both the Mets and the Yankees. I was surprised by a couple of his numbers. In 1997 he averaged 10.17 strikeouts per nine innings. That's third on the single-season list and just ahead of Roger Clemens's best season in that category. David is also the all-time career leader for the Yankees in that statistic. In 1998 David had about as good a year as any starter I'd ever seen. He went 20-7 with a 3.55 ERA, averaged only 8.1 hits per nine innings, and had a walks plus hits per innings pitched (WHIP) figure of 1.180. WHIP is the go-to stat these days, and here's how these right-handed starters stack up in terms of their WHIP over their careers with the Yankees:

CLEMENS	1.307
HUNTER	1.154
CONE	1.331
MUSSINA	1.212

To put this in better perspective, guys with names like Mathewson, Walsh, Young, Marichal, Koufax, and Seaver have lower career WHIPs—in the 1.04 to 1.12 range—than the ones on my list, and only two pitchers in baseball history who pitched more than 1,000 innings have a WHIP below 1. The great Mariano Rivera just misses that company with a WHIP of 1.0003. With such fine distinctions among WHIPs, you can see that Catfish, at 1.134 for his entire career, not just with the Yankees, is well ahead of Roger Clemens and his 1.173 overall. Those figures put Catfish 45th all-time and Clemens 91st all-time, ahead of both Mussina (127th) and Cone (300th).

The important distinction among these pitchers is how they performed when the stakes were highest. A "big game" pitcher is hard to define, as well as what exactly makes a game "big," but we most often look at postseason performance as an indicator of how a guy rises to the occasion (or doesn't).

PITCHER	POSTSEASON GAMES	W-L	ERA	WHIP	HITS PER 9 INNINGS
Clemens	35	12-8	3.75	1.221	7.8
Cone	21	8-3	3.80	1.356	7.5
Hunter	22	9-6	3.26	1.126	7.8
Mussina	23	7-8	3.42	1.103	7.8

Even a betting man like Mickey Rivers would have a hard time choosing where to place his money, based on these numbers, which include all postseason games these pitchers played throughout their careers. What about on the biggest stages of all—the World Series?

PITCHER	GAMES	W-L	ERA	WHIP	HITS PER 9 INNINGS
Clemens	8	3-0	2.37	.993	6.8
Cone	6	2-0	2.12	1.213	4.9
Hunter	12	5-3	3.29	1.175	8.1
Mussina	3	1-1	3.00	1.278	9.0

I've got to be honest, David Cone's numbers surprised me a little bit, especially the fact that he gave up only 4.9 hits per nine innings in World Series competition. That's impressive. In 29.2 innings, he gave up only 16 hits and 7 earned runs. The man was gutsy, I have to give him that, especially when you consider that he walked 20 men in those 29 innings. That's a lot of base runners, and a lot of jams worked out of. Clemens's WHIP of .993 is also impressive, but in the end, because he was a New York–New York guy, I have to go with David Cone. He pitched in seventeen seasons versus Clemens's twenty-four, so his career totals are behind Roger's by a considerable margin, but I think that David had more of a New York vibe to him as well. To me, Roger Clemens will always be a Boston Red Sox. Some Yankee fans may disagree with that, but I stand by it—unless, of course, Roger fires one underneath my chin. In that case, I'm ducking and diving.

I know that a lot of Yankee fans can't forget David's 2000 season, his last with the team, when he went 4-14. I know that David would like to forget that year. He was out of the rotation by the time the playoffs rolled around, and he only appeared in one game against the Mets. He came on in relief of Denny Neagle in Game 4. We were up 3–2 at that point in the fifth inning. Normally, you let your starter go the full five to qualify for a win, but this being the World Series, and with us having only a one-run lead, and with Mike Piazza coming to the plate, Joe made a gutsy call to bring in David.

Piazza had already homered, and with the bases empty and two out, you knew he was looking to duplicate the feat. David got ahead 1-2 on him, and then retired him on a pop fly to right. He was given an assignment, and he came through, doing what it is that professionals do when called upon. I'll talk more about that Series and the incredible job another real pro, Mike Stanton, did for us down the line. But for now, I just want to remember the look of deep satisfaction on David Cone's face as he came back into the dugout.

I mentioned the Yankee record book earlier, and when it comes to pitching generally and to left-handed pitching specifically for the eras I'm talking about, a couple of names appear more than any others: Ron Guidry and Andy Pettitte. Whether you're talking WAR, ERA, WHIP, wins, winning percentage, or whatever, Gator and Andy are all over the top ten for single-season and career achievements. I've mentioned that guys have really dominant years, but the most impressive single-season performance I witnessed firsthand was Ron Guidry in 1978. He was darn near unhittable, and to this day I've never seen anyone excel like that.

What made that performance even more amazing to me was that, with Ron, you knew what you were going to see—that devastating slider and the fastball. Not too much difference in speed, but good hard stuff down in the zone. He was almost like Mariano Rivera in that way. Hitters knew stepping into the box what they were going to see, but they couldn't do much with it. I was a young guy in '78, and I didn't spend a lot of time with the pitchers, but Guidry was one cool customer, what I call a quiet assassin type. He wasn't going to show anybody up, he was just going to get after them with that filthy stuff of his. Guidry and Mo both had a fluid delivery that made throwing hard seem effortless.

The thing that surprised me about Ron was that he's not a big guy at all. He's an inch short of six feet tall and was listed at 165 pounds, and I'd say that those numbers were both generous "roster" figures. He was one of the best athletes around, though, and he took a lot of pride in his abilities. He played center field and pitched in high school and college, and like Mo, he loved to shag fly balls in the outfield during batting practice. He was a very valuable commodity, and Mr. Steinbrenner was worried that his prize lefty might hurt himself. Who knows how the Boss would have responded if he'd been around to see Mariano go down with his knee injury.

I remember seeing Guidry going after those fly balls—he could cover a lot of ground. He once told a reporter that he didn't like doing wind sprints alone because it was boring, and that he thought that running in the outfield after fly balls for an hour improved his endurance and leg strength. He also added that Mr. Steinbrenner called him on the carpet about his "hobby," but he told the Boss that if he forbade him from doing it, he would just keep doing it.

The funny thing is, Guidry got to do something that Mo wished he could have—he got to play center field, covering hallowed ground in Yankee Stadium. On September 29, 1979, Billy Martin sent Ron out to center field to finish up the ninth inning of a 9–4 win over Toronto.

Ron's second and final appearance in center field got lost in the shuffle because of what else happened that day, August 18, 1983. That was the game we played under protest because George Brett had enough pine tar on his bat to make Noah's Ark watertight. Billy was so pissed off that Brett's home run was allowed to stand that he sent Ron to center field and Don Mattingly to second base for the final out to let the bigwigs of baseball know how he felt. It didn't matter to Ron how he got into the game, he was just glad to have a chance. He never recorded a putout, and that's about the only regret he had.

Baseball diehards have argued the pros and cons of Ron's Hall of Fame credentials. Yogi Berra, who was really tight with Ron, said what a lot of others have stated. Ron's career was short in comparison to most Hall of Famers. He did play for fourteen seasons, and in them he pitched 2,392 innings. That is 263rd all-time. I'm not sure how much that matters with Hall of Fame voters, but I do know that he was a great athlete, winning five Gold Gloves, and a great man, winning the Roberto Clemente Award in 1984.

That remarkable 1978 season was something to behold, and if you're not going to be remembered as a Hall of Famer, then this was one to celebrate in its own right. Ron won 25 and lost 3. He had an ERA of 1.72, with 9 shutouts and a WHIP of .946. He won the Cy Young Award and finished second in the MVP balloting. Most memorable for me was when he took the hill in game 163, that playoff game against Boston. He'd had only two days of rest, but there was no one else we would have felt as comfortable with for that one-game playoff. He pitched into the seventh inning and gave up two runs.

Despite how impressive a person and a pitcher Ron is, I have to give the nod to Andy Pettitte. His 219 wins in a Yankee uniform put him in third place all-time, two places ahead of Ron, who finished with 170. Andy's WAR of 51.5 puts him third all-time, just ahead of Ron in fourth place with 47.9.

I could go on with the numbers game, but I can't really quantify what Andy meant to the Yankee teams he played on. Ron was an important person and teammate too—they don't hand out the Roberto Clemente Award to just anyone—but maybe because I was at the beginning of my career and so wrapped up in my own job, I didn't really see and appreciate at the time what Ron did. I don't mean to diminish his accomplishments at all. As a coach, I got to observe the guys and the game through a different lens, and I saw what that Core Four meant to the organization. My Yankee teammates and I had helped put the club back on its feet, back in my playing days, but those guys took off running. Andy played in eight World Series, seven of them with the Yankees. His World Series stats aren't amazing, but when you include all of his postseason appearances, his line reads like some other guy's full regular season: 19-11, a 3.81 ERA, 44(!) games started, 276.2 innings pitched, 183 strikeouts, 76 walks, and a WHIP of 1.305—all against the top teams in each league. He was especially good at getting his Yankee team into the World Series. He went 7-2 in 13 ALCS starts.

For me, the defining game of his career was in the 1996 World Series against the Braves. We'd dug ourselves out of an 0–2 hole to get to Game 5 evened up. He was facing John Smoltz in a rematch of Game 1, in which Smoltz had owned us, going six innings while allowing only two hits and one run in a 12–1 blowout. Andy, on the other hand, had lasted only two and a third innings and given up seven runs. Andy is as good-hearted a man as any I've come across in baseball, and his faith in God, his admission that he missed his wife and kids, and just his general Mr. Nice Guy image made some people think (though not any of his Yankee teammates or anyone else in the organization) that he wasn't up to the challenge.

Game 5 destroyed every bit of that false impression. He matched Smoltz, another great guy and terrific competitor, pitch for pitch that night in front of a very, very vocal tomahawk-chopping Atlanta crowd. In the fourth inning, we benefited from an Atlanta error and scored a run on Cecil Fielder's double to take a 1–0 lead. In the sixth, Smoltz and Marquis Grissom singled back to back to start off the inning. Mark Lemke, a guy who could handle the bat pretty well, bunted, and Andy pounced on it and threw to third to get the lead runner. That was crucial because he kept the double play in order, and wouldn't you know it, Chipper Jones hit a ball to Andy's left. He fielded it, delivered a strike to second base, and we were out of the inning on that double play. I've seen a lot of pitchers not be able to execute that play—both of those plays actually—and in my mind that was even more of a clutch performance than if Andy had struck out the side after surrendering those two hits.

We held on to win that game and then wrapped it up in Game 6. That was vintage Andy Pettitte. He got knocked around, but he bounced back.

Andy is a stand-up guy, and his admission of guilt regarding PED use shocked a lot of people. How he put up with the "Not Andy!

Surely not him!" reaction I'll never really know. I know it's surprising to say that he showed tremendous character given the situation, but he did. He also showed his humanity, and I think a lot of people identified with him and came to respect him even more. The saying about the truth setting you free really does apply. People are willing to forgive and give second chances. I think that Andy earned that second chance as much as it was given to him. Just like he did in '96, he didn't let people down and made the most of that second opportunity.

CHAPTER 14

In Conclusion

C ue the music. It's closing time. To be honest, if I was going to pick a song to fit Mariano Rivera's entrance into a ball game, one that really matched his personality and not what he was about to do, "Enter Sandman" wouldn't be at the top of my list by a long shot. Being a jazz guy, I might opt for Sonny Rollins's "The Stopper" or, going back to my R&B roots, Miss Roberta Flack's "Killing Me Softly" or Mr. Al Green's "Call Me."

It didn't really matter what song you played, though, because the results remained the same: more consistently and with greater surgical precision than anyone else who ever took on the role of a closer, Mo was going to get it done. I've talked about how comforting it was to pencil in the names of the Core Four, or any other guy who went out there time and time again without much muss or fuss, but Mo made the job of managing a bit easier.

I know that I make this selection at the risk of offending my good friend Goose Gossage. Goose and I have talked about this subject many, many times, and while I see his point, I have to put Mariano ahead of him in my all-Willie selections. Let me clarify that a bit. Mariano earns that top spot for how the game is played today. As Goose often reminds me, he didn't benefit from playing in the era of specialization. The same is true of Sparky Lyle, who also deserves mention in this talk of all-time greats. In 1977, Sparky won the Cy Young Award, the first relief pitcher to ever do that. Why did he win? Well, he had a record of 13-5, he appeared in 72 games, finishing 60 of them, and he pitched a total of 137 innings, with an ERA of 2.17 and a WHIP of 1.197. He had "only" 26 saves, but the rules for what constituted a save were more liberal in Mo's era, when he averaged 39 per year. And I already mentioned Sparky's amazing performance in the playoffs against the Royals that year when he went five and a third innings, one of the greatest relief appearances I've ever seen.

Goose began his career as a reliever, was converted to the White Sox closer role for one season, started for another, and then, from 1977 to 1994, never started another ball game. Taking out that 1976 season when he started, he averaged a little more than 75 innings a year. Take out Mo's 1995 season, when he started ten games and appeared in nine others, and he averaged 67 innings per year. Sparky never started a game in the big leagues, and he averaged 105 innings per year. Crazy. Goose, in his first few years as a full-time reliever sandwiched around that one full season of starting in '76, pitched 141⅔, 133, and 134 innings. If you take away his first season of full-time relief pitching for the Yankees, 1996, when he topped out at 107.2 innings, Mo never pitched more than 80 innings a year, and his total was frequently in the mid-60s. Granted, some of that had to do with how efficient he was, but that's also a result of how relief pitchers generally, and closers in particular, were being used.

So much has been cataloged about Mo's achievements that I don't feel it necessary to go on with statistical analysis. Everyone agrees that he will be in the Hall of Fame one day, and he'll probably be a first-ballot guy. If he isn't, there's something seriously wrong with the voters. People also agree that Mo is a first-ballot, unanimous selection for all-time, all-universe, Hall of Fame human being. He's also one of the guys I love to imitate.

I'm not saying that I'm like the comic Frank Caliendo, who does that great John Madden voice and look. I'm not so great with the voices, but I can do a fair copy of guys' mannerisms on the field and off the field. Mariano is a very humble guy, but let's face it, when you're used to mowing people down with Mo's regularity—I think I'm going to start a petition that all baseball writers from here on out change the spelling of that phrase to "Mo'ing people down"—you get used to a certain level of success. I *love* to do my "I just gave up a hit can you believe it?" look. You know the one. The guy is so fluid with his delivery and so cat-quick that after he releases the ball and it's hit, he turns around with his back to the plate. Sometimes the camera catches his expression—that bug-eyed look of puzzlement, like he's thinking, *Did that just happen? What are these base hits you speak of?*

Most of that look comes from his embarrassment. He believes that he's let the team down when he gives up a hit or a run or blows a save. I make it sound like there's some ego involved there, but mostly that "deer in the headlights" look comes from his feeling that he's disappointed fans and his teammates.

Whatever the source of the look, I used to get a kick out of getting on him for staring in disbelief and dismay for so long after giving up a hit. I'd tell him that he had to get his butt behind third base or home to back up the play.

"C'mon now, your job ain't done when the ball's rolling around in the outfield somewhere."

"I was there. I got there."

"Late. You got there late."

I was mostly kidding, and I wouldn't get on him about those things right away. And if that was as demonstrative as he got—getting bug-eyed—then that was cool with me. You see, some relief pitchers, going back to Dennis Eckersley and his six-shooters and on down the line to guys yapping and making a spectacle of themselves because they got a guy out, Mo never did any of that. He never bitched at umpires. He just put the glove up, saying in effect, *Give me the ball. It's okay. I'm going to get this thing done.*

I loved that about him. I recently had a chat with Jorge Posada and Mike Borzello, who was a bullpen guy with the Yankees for a lot of years, and they both talked about how Mo had command not just of his emotions but of the baseball as well. They both said that they really had a hard time recalling times when Mo threw a ball in the dirt when warming up or even in a game. He was that precise. And from the time he first began to dominate hitters, his delivery never changed at all. He was so refined with his motion, and it was so repeatable, that he never seemed to go through spells of wildness. For his entire career, he averaged 4.10 strikeouts to walks and 2.0 walks per nine innings.

Mentally, Mo is as tough as anybody I've seen. During his farewell tour, he was paid a really nice tribute by the Red Sox organization. So, okay, I admit that I'm a hard-assed, old-school kind of guy: watching him on television as he signed autographs in the bullpen for fans and players troubled me a bit. This was, after all, the *hated* Boston Red Sox, but I knew that if anybody could handle the fraternization thing, it was Mo. Still, when I saw him at the Stadium after that, I gave him a bit of grief about losing his edge. He just smiled, and I could see that sparkle in his eyes letting me know that I was barking up the wrong tree.

I know that the cutter wasn't named because of this, but Mo was like a surgeon out there. To his credit, he established such a reputation with that pitch that I think a lot of guys went out there to face him already having retired themselves. They knew what was coming, and I think some guys had a mental image of the stacks of broken bats that had piled up over the years. Take it from me, there's nothing more disheartening than going up there knowing how a guy is going to get you out and then having him do exactly that. That wears on your mind after a few at-bats.

Pitchers have thrown the cutter since the 1950s, but it didn't become popular until the '90s, when Mo started throwing it. Since on the spectrum it's the closest breaking ball to the fastball—the reason why it's called a cut fastball—it has the greatest velocity. In the hand of some of the best practitioners of the pitch, it's generally four to six miles an hour slower than their four-seam fastball. A hard late-breaking pitch is the toughest to hit because you think you're tracking it and then it breaks just enough to make it hard to really square it up, which is why cutters break so many bats. Some starters, like Roy Hallaady, Dan Haren, Jon Lester, James Shields, and a few others, throw it with great frequency, but not nearly approaching the rate at which Mo used it. In fact, Mariano helped teach the cutter to Roy Halladay. Roy was always a good pitcher, but with that cutter he became great, and I think it says a lot about Mariano that he helped Roy out that way.

Like I said, Mo keeps it cool, and I think this story typifies his approach to life.

One of the great things about playing in Kansas City is the food. The ribs that get served up in the clubhouse, the other barbecue you can get around the city, it's the best food in the country. I've still got in my pantry bottles of the Arthur Bryant's sauce I'd buy when on a road trip there. The day in 2012 when Mo tore up his knee in Kansas City, he was taken to the hospital for evaluation. After that, he took a cab, along with a team doctor, back to the ballpark. He talked them into stopping by an Arthur Bryant's shop so that he could pick up a few racks of ribs to bring back to the clubhouse to share with everybody.

The man had to be in a lot of pain, he had to be down about what effect his injury was going to have on the club's chances, and a whole lot of other negatives had to be floating around in his head. Maybe this story says more about Arthur Bryant's than it does Mo, but I don't think so.

We all talk about giving back to the game and to life, and a lot of players have foundations and those kinds of things, but Mariano is special. He frequently meets with people in the community who are dealing with tough times, and he treats every one of the Stadium employees and the team's staff with so much kindness and respect. The plans he worked out with Jason Zillo in the Yankees' communications department to meet with people all over the country during this past season was the kind of thing you expected from Mo but never thought you'd see from a ballplayer. That's a contradiction, I know, but it shows what Mo is really like as a person. He's so unassuming that it wasn't until this last year that people came forward and talked about all the quiet ways that Mariano had been out there doing good things for people.

The thing is, he was like that as a pitcher as well—quiet and unassuming. I have vague recollections of him being around spring trainings in the early '90s. What I remember was this string bean of a kid with a nice fluid delivery. That's about it—nothing special, nobody who was going to set the world on fire. I spoke with John Wetteland during one of Mo's final games at the Stadium. John said that he knew at the time. He could see that Mariano had it. I was an infielder, and I didn't really understand all that much about mechanics and what-not, but John said that he could tell there was something about Mo's physical makeup that was different.

When John started talking about all this—and to his credit, even though Mo took over his role, John was never bitter about it—I started thinking about the times in spring training when I'd stood behind the mound while the Mets pitchers got their side-work in. When Pedro Martinez released the ball from his hand, it came out with a distinctive sound, a kind of sizzle that you didn't hear from any other guy's delivery. That was true for Mariano as well. Neither of those guys was the biggest physical specimen, but there was something about the looseness in their wrists, the size of their hands and fingers, that imparted spin on a ball in a way that was special. Mo always said that he received a gift from God, and I know he firmly believed it. I don't know if God gave Mo that cutter, but He might have overseen the production of the combination of physical traits Mo has that helped him throw that thing like nobody else.

As I sit here in 2013, I'm kind of blown away thinking about the kids I watched grow up in the game. And now Mariano's done with his career. You know, as much as I tease Mariano about his look of bewilderment, we all had that same look on our faces when things didn't go well for him on the mound. We had a hard time believing what we were seeing because his performance was so consistently outstanding. The thing is, though, as a player and a person, his response to adversity was equally consistent. He'd be down, but he'd answer all the questions the media had for him, and the next day he was the same guy as always. Pitchers, and closers especially, have to turn the page, forget the previous game, the previous hitter, and just focus on the task at hand. I don't think I've ever seen a guy who was better at doing that than Mo.

I'm sure at some point he's thought back to the ALCS in '97, when we lost to the Indians after he blew a save by surrendering a home run to Sandy Alomar in game 4. I know that we all have our share of bad memories about the Red Sox comeback against us in the 2004 ALCS and Mo's blown save in game 4. Calling those things "blown saves" seems really harsh, but Mariano never complained about the term and always took full responsibility for whatever negative results came our way—even those seeing-eye base hits and bloops that can make the difference between winning and losing a World Series, as one in particular did against Arizona.

In baseball you meet all kinds of characters, and we're not all choirboys or saints. People have their good days and their bad days. I can't remember Mariano having a bad day as a person—there was never a time when you just didn't want to be around him. I can't recall anybody saying anything bad about him either.

And like a lot of New Yorkers, and I think a lot of baseball fans around the country, when I was sitting at home watching on TV and saw Derek and Andy go out to the mound to replace Mariano during his final appearance at the Stadium, my eyes welled up with tears in a mixture of pride, sadness, and a desire that the great things in life could just go on and on.

I don't worry about Mo and how he's going to handle retirement. I know that he's going to be okay, that a new era in his life is going to soon start. That new era isn't going to be that much different than the old one. He's still going to perform to the best of his capabilities, he's still going to be someone the people around him can count on, and he's still going to lift up others in a way that gives them hope. I don't think it's any accident that the man specialized in a statistic called the "save." We'd all like to save our best for last, and I've no doubt that Mo will continue saving games in one form or another for a very long time.

I was proud to wear the same uniform as him, and I'm even prouder to call him my friend.

CHAPTER 15

Running Them Down

For guys who have played the Yankee outfield, it has to have been a bit of a mind-blower to be running across the same patch of grass that Babe Ruth, Mickey Mantle, Joe DiMaggio, and Roger Maris once patrolled. Playing center field for the Yankees may not have the same cachet in the minds of some fans as quarterbacking the Dallas Cowboys or the Green Bay Packers, but for a long time that spot in the lineup put you under a more intense scrutiny. The corner outfield positions haven't had the same mythology surrounding them. Playing center field for the Yankees isn't just about offensive numbers, as it often is for right and left fielders, but I don't think anybody will ever spin tales about the time they saw Babe Ruth run a ball down in the gap or throw a runner out trying to go from first to third. I'm sure he did those things, but c'mon, it was all about what the guy did in the batter's box that made him so legendary.

I use the quarterback comparison purposely because the center fielder is the quarterback of the outfield, the last line of defense on the diamond. Center fielders, like middle infielders, particularly short-stops, are often considered the guys with the greatest overall athletic ability on the roster. They have to cover the most territory, so speed is important. Getting a good jump is important, so good instincts, vision, and baseball aptitude matter a lot. Being able to hit for some power helps, though admittedly not so much as it traditionally does for corner outfielders, and being able to hit for a high average and a good on-base percentage is as important there as it is anywhere else in the lineup.

We talk about a guy being a good "five-tool" player, someone who does well at all aspects of the game—fielding, throwing, stealing, hitting for power, and hitting for average. Ideally, you'd like guys at every position to be one of those, and of course, with some exceptions, you can't be a liability on the base paths, in the batter's box, or in the field unless you've got some other skill that makes up for that deficiency. When I think of Joe DiMaggio and Mickey Mantle, I think of outstanding hitters and great all-around players. Two other center fielders I'd consider, given the parameters I've set up, are Bobby Murcer and Bernie Williams. Nothing against Mickey Rivers or Rickey Henderson, but I can't consider them, not only because they played for the Yankees relatively briefly but because they had the same gap in their game: neither had a very strong arm.

Bobby was a versatile guy, playing short, third, second, and all the outfield positions in his major league career. I've already shared the story of Bobby's contributions to the game we won after we lost Thurman Munson. In my mind, that alone is nearly enough to consider him at the top of the list. Bobby's a sentimental favorite for me since I played with him, he had to deal with the unimaginable pressures of replacing Mickey Mantle at the position, and he was involved with the Yankee organization for so long after his playing days were done. Bobby's contributions to the Yankee organization are extensive, and he's a man I've grown to admire greatly.

Bernie Williams and I had a somewhat unusual relationship. As a coach, I didn't spend a whole lot of time with the outfielders. I wasn't the hitting instructor either, so that further limited my direct responsibilities with him. Despite that, I talked with Bernie quite a bit. As a coach, you kind of have to pick and choose your spots when to speak with guys, and you move in a very different sphere from them a lot of the time. I spoke with Bernie because I saw how talented he was and how he sometimes struggled to just let all that talent take over for him.

I thought it was interesting that Bernie had a locker in the same spot that Thurman Munson did. Where the two sides converged, a V was formed, and that was where Bernie set up shop. It was one of the biggest lockers, and it was interesting to me that a catcher and a center fielder, two guys who played in the middle of the diamond, would occupy that spot and be so different in temperament. Bernie was known for his laid-back vibe and his guitar playing and all that, but I sometimes think that image is a bit of a distortion. Not that he isn't a talented jazz guitarist, mind you. He's released a couple of CDs and was nominated for a Latin Grammy. His musicianship endeared him to me.

What I mean is that you can't get to be the full-time center fielder for the Yankees for more than a dozen years and not have some fire in your belly. Some guys' fire burns hot and intense, and other guys have a slow burn like charcoal. The latter was Bernie. And just like a good charcoal fire, if you don't stir it up occasionally, that fire cools.

I saw how talented Bernie was, but I also saw that he wanted to just blend in with the rest of the guys, that he wanted to just sort of go about his business and be anonymous. Once, back in about midseason of 1994, I said to him, "Bernie, you can't be meek or unassuming and play center field for the Yankees. That's one of the most prestigious positions to play in all of sports. You've got the skills. Own the position. Own what goes along with it."

Bernie's a very, very intelligent guy, and he always thinks and assesses before he speaks. He gets an expression on his face similar to Mo's, but his look would transform from surprised to puzzled to thoughtful.

If I was careful in dealing with Bernie, that was because I could see that he could be damaged by too much pressure being put on him too soon. For a while, some of the guys called him Bambi, and he did have that kind of doe-eyed innocence about him. Mel Hall used to get on Bernie mercilessly. Mel wasn't one to shy away from touting his own achievements, but we had to get him to lay off Bernie, even if the kidding was good-natured. We knew that Bernie had a future and that Mel was just there as a kind of place holder until someone better came along. That was one thing about the Yankees: you knew that Mr. Steinbrenner was always going to write that check after going after the next latest and greatest free agent.

Several years later, in 1998, Bernie put together his best season to that point, hitting .339 with 26 home runs and 97 RBI, and I felt like he was finally coming around to really believing in his own ability and expressing it out on the field. He reeled off some sensational regular seasons from '95 to '02 and he was the quintessential five-tool player. Again, his arm wasn't a cannon, but it was above average and he had tremendous range.

What I especially liked was that Bernie stepped up when the post-season rolled around. I don't know what it was about him, but maybe that laid-back nature served him best when the stakes were the highest. In '99 especially, when we beat the Rangers, Red Sox, and Braves, he was on a roll, hitting .364, .250, and .412, respectively. That last number is especially impressive since he did that against Maddux, Millwood, Glavine, and Smoltz. I think that early success in '95 and '96 really helped him, more so than anything I might have said to him. He was selected the ALCS Most Valuable Player in '96, when he hit .474 with 2 homers and 6 RBI against Baltimore. He also hit .467 with 3 home runs and 5 RBI against Texas. He was raking before cooling off against the Braves in that year's World Series. Can you imagine having a couple of weeks of work against the best the AL had to offer and walking away after 9 games with 16 hits in 34 at-bats, with 5 home runs and 11 driven in?

That was something, and with a couple of exceptions, in every postseason run, he seemed to just get on a tear in at least one of the series we played. When a guy is rolling like that, it's fun to just watch him go up to the plate and be locked in.

Bernie's .298 career average puts him thirteenth all-time in Yankee history. He's seventh in home runs with 287, and seventh in RBI with 1,257. He's also third all-time in doubles and sixth in runs scored. That's quite a body of work numerically, but I also loved watching him go after fly balls with those long legs of his.

Paul O'Neill, who played alongside Bernie for eight seasons, was a real fan favorite. Paul was Bernie's opposite in terms of temperament. Paul wore his emotions on his sleeve and on his face, and that, along with his talent, seemed to charm the Yankee faithful. If Bernie was jazz and classical guitar, then Paul was Nirvana or some other grunge rock band baring their angst publicly. Paul demanded so much of himself, brought so much drama and intensity to his at-bats and performance on the field, that the possibility of spontaneous human combustion was always present. Don't get me wrong, I loved Paul's intensity and desire. I was sometimes frustrated by his inability to slide—that was a part of his drama—but I also had to laugh about it. He couldn't seem to get his feet coordinated the proper way, and he'd attack the ground in the same way he took some ferocious hacks at the baseball. I used to tease him that when he was going into a base, we needed to spray down some foam and put a couple of fire trucks and ambulances out there.

But Paul was a very productive hitter and run producer for us during our great run of championships and staying in contention. He averaged .303, 95 RBI, and 20 home runs for us. Compare that to Reggie Jackson's .281, 28 home runs, and 92 RBI, and it's clear that Reggie had more pop, but Paul was a very good RBI guy for us. Compare their OBP and you are in for a bit of a surprise, with Paul topping Reggie by six percentage points, .377 to .371. Well, not so surprising when you consider that Reggie averaged 36 strikeouts a year more than Paul—114 to 78. I'm not trying to diminish my friend Reggie's contributions to the Yankees. His Hall of Fame credentials are obvious, but like a few of the other HOF members I've discussed, a lot of Reggie's best years were with the A's.

Paul wasn't Mr. October, but he had some very strong postseasons. In 85 games, he hit .284 with 11 home runs and 39 RBI. All-time, he ranks twelfth in average, eighteenth in home runs, and fourteenth in RBI among Yankees.

In spite of all that Paul accomplished, I have to give this to Reggie. He had so much pressure on him, and to achieve all that he did while carrying that weight says a lot. The other outfielder I have to give major credit to is Dave Winfield. He was an amazing athlete, and most everybody knows that he was drafted in all three major sports in the United States. In fact, he was drafted by four different teams, since the NBA and the ABA were both in existence back then. He pitched at the University of Minnesota, went 13-1 as a starter with a 2.74 ERA while also hitting .385, earned All-American honors, and led his team to the College World Series, where he was named tournament MVP despite his team's third-place finish. I think he also swapped out the transmission on the team's bus when it broke down somewhere in Iowa.

Dave reminded me of Reggie Jackson a bit. He was his own public relations firm, but he always said things and then smiled that big grin of his. He was really good-natured, and he could afford to be since he didn't have to put up with some of the same stuff that Reggie did.

At six feet six inches tall, Dave towered over me, and with his deep voice and big laugh, he was a huge presence in the locker room. Some guys just radiate confidence and assurance, and in that way Dave was very different from Bernie. Dave was also a great defensive player, and he took that role very seriously. He had one of the most powerful arms in the game, and because of that, though his assists numbers may not dazzle you, few guys tried to run on him.

Dave is charismatic and very well-spoken, and as one of the first really big salary guys in the game, he could have just taken the money and run. He was one of the first athletes to establish a charitable foundation, the David M. Winfield Foundation, and it's still going strong some thirty years later. The foundation branched out into substance abuse prevention, and Dave's been active in sitting on a number of charitable and advisory boards, including the Peace Corps and Major League Baseball. He's also won a number of awards for his work: the YMCA's Brian Piccolo Award for Humanitarian Service, MLB's first-ever Branch Rickey Community Service Award, the American League's Joe Cronin Award, the Josh Gibson Leadership Award, and MLB's Roberto Clemente Award. Most impressive, in my mind, was his coming up with the idea in 2008 of honoring Negro League players on the day of the draft.

And along with all of this, Dave was elected to the Hall of Fame in 2001. I know that he was stung by Mr. Steinbrenner's criticism of him when, after becoming the highest-paid player in the game in 1981 when he left the Padres to join us, he hit only .294 with 13 home runs and 68 RBI. Both Steinbrenner and Winfield were proud men, and the tension between them was fierce. I don't know how you can call a man who is in the Hall of Fame "Mr. May," and anybody would be upset about that unfavorable comparison to Reggie Jackson, but eventually Dave proved Mr. Steinbrenner wrong.

Dave was a great base runner and fielder; in fact, he won the Gold Glove from 1982 to 1985 and then again in 1987 while with us. Those weren't the kinds of accomplishments that would put fans in the seats or, in our owner's mind, justify the kind of money Dave was earning, but we knew that he brought a lot to the table. We only went to the postseason once in Dave's tenure, his first year with the club, but I think it's really unfair to hang too much of the blame for our futility on one guy, no matter how much money he was earning.

Even at the age of forty, in 1992 while playing with the World Series Champion Blue Jays, Dave was still very, very productive, belting 26 home runs, driving in 108, and hitting a very respectable .290.

I can't say that Dave and I were close and became great friends, but he was someone who commanded respect for his accomplishments on and off the field. They say it ain't bragging if it's so, and in Dave's case, he was so talented in so many ways that it's impossible not to include him here.

Afterword

I f you were around during the late 1970s—after 1978 to be a little more precise—and you were a baseball fan and a lover of comedy, you no doubt remember these immortal words: "Besebol been berry, berry good to me."

Those words were uttered by the legendary Dominican player Chico Escuela—a product not of that island nation but of *Saturday Night Live*'s writers and the comedian Garrett Morris. His character might not have passed the test of later political correctness mandates, but he did get a lot of laughs. As you know, I spent a lot of time around Latin people and ballplayers in all my years in the game, and there's no shortage of a sense of humor there.

I don't know if Mr. Escuela could take two and go to right, or go to his right and come up throwing, but he did speak a truth about my life as well. As I mentioned earlier, I probably would never have left my neighborhood, much less my borough, if it hadn't been for sports, and baseball in particular. Baseball gave me opportunities to go places, do things, and meet people in a way that I could not have dreamed of back then. As a kid, my dreams were confined to what I would do out on the field, but as time passed and those on-field dreams were realized, the off-field adventures made themselves known.

One dream I never had was to be on a television situation comedy. But when the offer came, how could I resist? I'll admit to having a bit of the ham in me. I like attention as much as the next guy, but I normally did my acting-out in front of close friends and my teammates. Being in New York for so much of my career, I had the opportunity to meet a lot of people inside and outside the game, and through a series of connections, I got to meet Kelly Ripa and her husband, Mark Consuelos. They're a wonderful couple, and Gretchen and I have become friends with Kelly and Mark.

In 2004 I got a chance to be a guest star on Kelly's TV show, *Hope and Faith.* The plot involved an autographed baseball that went missing and the women's attempt to replace it. Roger Clemens was the one who signed it, and he also appeared in the episode. I admit that putting on makeup—or more correctly, having makeup put on me—and having other people fuss about my hair and "wardrobe" was a bit strange, but we were playing ourselves so it wasn't that big of a deal. The good thing was that the show wasn't live or in front of all the people who would eventually see it on TV. I sometimes wish baseball came with the kinds of do-overs, or takes, as they call them in film and TV, that allow you to make up for mistakes really easily. It was a good experience, and I later did another TV show.

I can't say that I was really shy as a kid, and I do like talking with people, so I can't say that baseball allowed me to get out of my shell, since I didn't really have one. That doesn't apply, though, when it comes to another "baseball has been good to me" moment. Let me clarify a bit here. *Life* has been good to me as well. One of the proudest moments I've experienced was watching my daughter Ciara graduate from Fordham University at Rose Hill on May 19, 2007. What made it even more special was that I'd been asked to deliver the commencement address at the ceremony. When I was first approached, I was like, "Sure, that will be fun." Well, as the time drew nearer for me to get up in front of a group of people and talk about something other than baseball, butterflies the size of baseballs began fluttering in my gut.

I knew that I wanted to say some things about hard work and dedication and all the lessons that my mom and dad had imparted to me, so that's basically what I did. What I didn't know was how much hard work it was going to take not to have my heart jump out of my chest when I looked out at all those people looking back at me. Knowing that Ciara was out there along with Gretchen, my mom, and my dad (who was celebrating his seventy-fifth birthday that day) made things easier and more gratifying. I never went to college, obviously, but the University of Baseball was a pretty good alma mater, I thought. That Fordham was going to confer an honorary degree on me that same day was, well, an honor.

I knew that those pregame jitters were going to ease up once I got into the thing, but standing in the on-deck circle, waiting to be introduced, I felt like I was going to go all rubber-legged and collapse. I was hoping to find some pine tar smeared on the sides of the lectern to help still my shaky hands.

I'm proud to say I got through it, and even prouder of Ciara for persevering through school. She was a great student and had that good old Randolph discipline working for her. Seeing her standing up with the other graduates, all of them in their caps and gowns, was quite a thrill. I had a game to manage later that day, just another reminder that duty calls and takes you away from family too often. It occurred to me that maybe Gretchen was the one who Fordham should have been honoring, the person to whom those graduates should have been paying attention. She'd been mother, father, and coach to the kids and to me for so many years, the too frequently unsung hero of the Randolph family.

I can't say that if it wasn't for baseball I might not have had another great honor bestowed on me. I'm not here to dispense advice on the subject of marriage. (Marry your best friend.) I wouldn't pretend to be equipped to do that. (Marry your best friend.) And besides, this is a book about my life in baseball, not a marital how-to manual. (Marry your best friend.) All I will tell you is that I had the great honor of marrying my best friend on February 1, 1975, in Pilgrim Baptist Church, right next to the Tilden Houses. Gretchen was wearing a cream-colored dress, and I was wearing a cheesy polyester suit. Wedding photographer? No, we just had a couple of aunts and uncles with instamatic cameras, snapping away. Our reception was a big dinner my mom cooked in my parents' apartment. A couple of weeks later, it was off to spring training.

Marrying Gretchen was only the best decision I've ever made. There's no way I'd be where I am today without her. To this day, when I'm on the road, it is not unusual for us to talk six or eight times a day. Some of the calls won't be more than a minute or two, a quick check-in, but that's how we are, how much we like to stay in touch.

We always pulled the kids—Taniesha, Chantre, Andre, and Ciara—out of school during spring training and brought them down to Florida, where we had them tutored, so we could all stay together. We'd make annual treks to Disney World, and years later I started a family tradition called The Conference—wherein we'd all put on our pajamas, gather in one of the kids' bedrooms, turn out the lights, and then talk in the pitch-black about whatever we wanted to talk about.

Some of my fondest memories of fatherhood are from The Conferences and the bonding that went on during them.

Still, there's no denying that I was away a whole lot, and that meant Gretchen spent a ton of time changing diapers, going to the pediatrician, cooking dinners, and supervising homework—alone. She did all of this, and much more, while I was off playing games.

You tell me who deserves honoring.

Gretchen's loyalty and steadfastness know no bounds, then or now. I can still see myself in my dorm room in Bradenton, Florida, after I signed. I had just turned eighteen and was living on my own, trying to fight off homesickness. Most every night some young kid with a Southern drawl would come on the intercom system and say, "Willie Randolph, long distance. Willie Randolph, long distance."

In the pre–cell phone era, the only place to make and receive calls was the pay phone in the lobby. When I heard my name, I would take off running, a full-body rush taking me over, for the caller was almost always Gretchen. By the time our conversations were done, Gretchen was usually in tears and there was a line of ballplayers waiting to use the phone.

"You must be in love," a beefy aspiring Pirate growled at me once. "You're on the freaking phone nonstop."

During the years I was going through all the managerial interviews, Gretchen was a rock for me. She comforted me, advised me, and consoled me and was at least as much of a fighter as I was, sometimes more. After I lost out to Art Howe for the Mets job the first time around, I was really down.

"You're not going to stop now. You can't stop doing this now," Gretchen said. "You can't give in to pessimism. You have to have faith that good things will happen if you keep putting yourself out there. Your chance is going to come. I know it."

More than anyone, Gretchen knew where we came from. She knew the significance of an African American kid from a housing project becoming New York's first manager of color. If my resolve to keep going back out there ever weakened, she was right there to pick me up.

That, to me, is what families do. You are there for each other, no matter what. You don't think about inconvenience or adversity. You are just there. That's how my parents were, and that's how I am.

I was used to being around the civilizing effects of a strong woman. As I've said, my mother took us to church every Sunday and nourished our souls every other day.

It's probably not up to me to decide whether I deserve that Fordham honor or any of the other side benefits I've experienced from having a life in baseball. I'm grateful for them all, and I've tried to give back to the game and the community. I know that's one category in which I'll inevitably fall short, but not for lack of desire.

Baseball, and New York, have been very, very good to me. I plan to continue to be very, very good to the game and to the city I love. That's the Yankee way.

Acknowledgments

My life has been blessed by so many loving and supportive people who helped me along the way and without whom this book would not have been possible. I don't know how I would've made it without my first coaches and mentors. My very first coach, Gallieo "Gally" Gonzalez, pushed me to my limits no matter what and taught me how to love the game even more. Frank Tepedino, the groundskeeper at Tilden Houses, gave me my first shot to play on a real field against tough competition. Gordon Williams Sr., my old basketball coach and mentor, helped orchestrate my first contract with the Pirates. Thank you to my high school coach, Herb Abramowicz, who was always there to protect me and never stopped believing I could make it.

When I joined the Pirates and had to change positions to second baseman, Gene Baker, a former Negro League player and my first coach in rookie ball and pro ball, Eddie Napoleon, and Chuck Cartier were all there to help me make the transition. My early mentors on the Yankees, Chris Chambliss, Roy White, and Elston Howard, took me under their wings and taught me what being a Yankee really means. Thanks to Roy Guirdy, my teammate, my cocaptain, and my close friend. Thank you to all the players and coaches I was lucky enough to work with over the years. I would never have made it this far without your support on and off the field.

George Steinbrenner took a chance on me as an inexperienced

third-base coach. He always treated me with respect and made me feel a part of this great Yankee family. I wouldn't have been a part of the organization if it hadn't been for George. Gene Michael was instrumental in helping me in the Yankee organization as well. Yogi Berra really welcomed me into the family. He taught me so much about the Yankee tradition and connected me to the great legacy of the team. Joe Torre stood up for me and trusted me as the last holdover from Buck's coaching team. I thank them all and the entire Yankee family for their kindness and support throughout my career.

I want to thank Wayne Coffee for helping me get started on this book. To Ray Negrone and Robert Skollar for all their help on this project. To Gary Brozek, my talented writer, for pulling all the pieces together and putting words to my story. I thank Tom Hopke at HarperCollins for getting me started on this project. Thank you to my editor, Matt Harper, for keeping us all on track and helping me craft my story into a book that I am truly proud of. Thanks also to my agents Ron Schapiro and Michael Moss who looked after me for so long.

I thank my parents for helping me follow my dreams, no matter how unlikely they were. From day one, my mother was there packing up my sandwiches for little league and supporting this kid from Brooklyn who just wanted to play ball. Even when I was homesick in Canada and about ready to retire as a minor leaguer, she never let me quit. My brothers were all athletes in their own right, and they always pushed me, helping me compete at the highest level. To my brother Terry, who's always been a levelheaded confidant whenever I needed one. My little brother Timmy has always been my biggest fan. My sister, Debbie, is the smartest of all of us and I'm very proud of the path she's chosen as a schoolteacher. My brother Lamont (Shorty), who supported me in his own way by, among other things, letting me use his head for a whiffle ball batting tee and ended up with seven stitches in the back of his head. Thank you to Gretchen, my beautiful wife, and our four wonderful children, Taniesha, Chantre, Andre, and Ciara, for never giving up on me—all of you have been with me throughout this incredible journey and I couldn't have made it without your love and support.